SCOTTISH BORDER
Carlisle
THE LAKE DISTRICT
THE NORTH WEST
THE PENNINES
BARROW
Morecambe
FLEETWOOD
Burnley
RIVER RIBBLE
ACCRINGTON
Fylde
PRESTON
SOUTHPORT
BOLTON
Salford
Oldham
Liverpool
UBI FIDES IBI LUX ET ROBUR
Tranmere
Manchester
Droylsden
FLETCHER MOSS
STOCKPORT
NORTHWICH

ON THE BRINK

A JOURNEY THROUGH ENGLISH FOOTBALL'S NORTH WEST

SIMON HUGHES

EXCLUSIVE PHOTOGRAPHY:
ALEX BAILLIE

ON THE BRINK

A JOURNEY THROUGH ENGLISH FOOTBALL'S NORTH WEST

SIMON HUGHES

EXCLUSIVE PHOTOGRAPHY:
ALEX BAILLIE

First published as a hardback by deCoubertin Books Ltd in 2017.

First edition.

deCoubertin Books, Studio I, Baltic Creative Campus, Liverpool, L1 OAH.
www.decoubertin.co.uk

ISBN: 978-1909245600

A CIP catalogue record for this book is available from the British Library.

Cover design and typeset by Leslie Priestley.
Photography: Alex Baillie.
Cover image: Offside/Simon Stacpoole.
Endpapers: Phil Galloway

Printed and bound by Jellyfish.

In memory of Richard Bunt

CONTENTS

CONTENTS

INTRODUCTION

'WHAT HAVE THEY SAID, THEN?' COMES THE QUESTION FROM THE desk each Saturday evening around five-thirty just after the managers have filtered out of the football ground press room having either probably, a) delivered anodyne observation if a result was a positive one, appreciating their words are scrutinised so inexorably it is sensible to avoid dishing out superlatives for fear of engendering overstatement, or b) bitterly pointed out a referee's shortcoming for getting a decision wrong, appreciating it will generate the headlines that might masquerade personal failing completely or, at least, bury defining and damning details further down the report.

Outstanding reportage still exists, but it sometimes feels that the coverage of football, sport and world affairs generally has been reduced to 140 characters on Twitter or he said/she said type analysis because the profile of the person saying it somehow makes it more newsworthy, resulting in context, the real stories, the wider shifts – the ones that require digging and, most importantly, time and investigation – being lost amidst the noise.

It is not necessarily the managers' fault that football in particular has gone this way. Sean Dyche told me during the writing of this book that managers are now really spokesmen for the clubs they represent because they are obliged by rules to talk before and after matches, while players – or the faceless accountants answerable to the interests of American groups, Russian oligarchs or Middle Eastern emirs that actually run many clubs – are not.

This in turn brings enormous pressure and in some way explains why nearly half of the managers across England's 92 clubs had been sacked by late April during the 2016/17 season. If it seemed like they were on the brink of insanity, answering questions relating to their own future, it was assumed they were.

I had wanted to write this book fundamentally because I figured it would take serious study to understand the depth of the feelings involved in the game, how it has changed – and where it is heading. Some interviewees, like Dyche, told me they were happier to speak truthfully about the challenges they face because a book allowed room for the necessary context.

The reason many of us become journalists or writers is to understand nuances, to build relationships and break them if necessary, to seek truths, and to disclose what would otherwise remain hidden. It is not to sit at a work station for seven hours a day while being watched, trawling through social media platforms, writing clickbait headlines to catch ridiculous online audience targets. Behind the din, I think of this project as a pause button. Hopefully it reflects what football is like in 2017; what it really does to people at the very top, at the very bottom and everywhere in between.

I started my journalistic career covering non-league football and felt it was under-represented in the media then. By the time I left the Crosby Herald the local football team, Marine, had at least three pages of coverage in the paper each week. Regularly, there was eight pages of sport, with cricket, rugby and bowls all given the space they needed to breathe.

The narrative around what happened next usually starts with the readers, who apparently stopped buying newspapers, prompting advertisers to withdraw. This underplays the significance of basic circulation figures, which though reasonably healthy were ultimately determined not to be healthy enough to satisfy the demands of avaricious shareholders at the organisation that printed the papers.

By the time the Herald closed in 2015, sport had frequently been reduced to just two pages in total. When the cuts began newsrooms shrank, cover prices increased, wages were frozen, offices shut, editorial teams merged. Seasoned journalists with years of experience and bulging contacts books were replaced by keen but inexperienced university graduates – or not at all. Meanwhile, council meetings, court hearings and matters of genuine public interest were not scrutinised as they used to be. It now feels as though social media has replaced the unappreciated art of chatting to the shopper as the primary form of news gathering; the shopper who pops into the office willing to tell you what you need to hear to do your job because the said office is located conveniently and they trust the reporter due to face to face access.

This is not a story exclusive to Crosby and it is one repeated across the country and elsewhere in the world. It has not only meant non-league and lower-league clubs from sizeable towns are not receiving the coverage they need for supporters to be informed nor floating fans to feel urged to get involved and enrich the sport themselves, it explains why people in these areas felt as though they had no one fighting their corner in the media. It felt like to become a story, your team had to be either at the top or the bottom, ignoring the idea there might be much to be told about the clubs, the people, whose struggle is the same season after season – to stay afloat. They manage this through a lot of hard work – but for how long? These clubs and people represent a majority rather than a minority.

Of the twelve teams that contested the first season of the Football League, which ran from autumn 1888 to spring 1889, six of them were from the north-west. Jack Gordon of Preston North End is regarded as scoring the first goal of the new competition – although this is disputed in some quarters due to claims that Preston's game kicked off 45 minutes later than others that day. What is not disputed is the fact that Preston went on to lift the first Football League Championship without losing a game, and won the FA Cup without conceding a goal.

Though southern sides gradually began to find a foothold in the previously northern-dominated league, from its formation until the end of the 2016/17 season, accounting for war years, 119 football seasons had been played in England and in 58 of those seasons a team from the north-west had finished as top-flight champions.

The north-west is a region that has pushed boundaries in football. The first English club to embarked on an overseas tour came from the north-west. When the first purpose-built football stadium was constructed, it was located in the north-west. A north-west club issued the first programme to supporters at a football match. The first shirt numbers were worn by a north-west club; the same club first installed dugouts and, later, undersoil heating. When a footballer was transferred between English clubs for the first time for more than £100,000, that footballer was from the north-west and he transferred between two north-west clubs – reflecting the economic strength of a region where many owners were local industrialists who had grown rich from the land. The footballer on this occasion was Alan Ball and the club responsible for all of these 'firsts' was a single one, Everton.

In this book Everton feature in a section called Independent Land, a title which reflects how Merseyside is almost a separate place from the rest of the north-west, with geography and industry shaping political beliefs. Liverpool as a city has more in common with Naples and Marseille than, say, Blackpool and Burnley and yet is not quite so different from Manchester as it would like to claim.

Manchester, though, is considered here as the core of the region, with an orbit of clubs circling around it almost like satellites. The parts of the book looking at the margins of the very north and, to some extent, the valley, the hills and the marshes of Southport analyse how location can impact upon existence, while the coast looks at how an area once so synonymous with Englishness (because it was the place where many used to holiday if they could afford it) survives and in some parts actually appears to be flourishing even though so much around it has failed.

I hope that On the Brink reflects the modern football landscape of the north-west which remains England's most successful football region, though in the last five years it has lost four Premier League clubs, three of whom were well-established with the other, Blackpool, falling briefly to the bottom tier of English professional football. This had happened at a time where the threat from the south of the country has gathered because of the wealth it now accumulates and the willingness of foreign owners to invest there because of transport links.

There are other books that detail precisely how football became a financial machine but I hope this one helps explain how geography, industry and, indeed, politics detail why certain things are the way they are in certain places; why, wherever you go, this football era is viewed as being either the very best or the very worst of times. I wanted to find out how money has affected the game – or at least how it is perceived by those operating at the coal face: the managers, the owners, the players, the directors, the politicians and the fans. In a season where Real Madrid earned £80million for winning the Champions League, Sunderland received £93.5million for finishing bottom of the Premier League. What happens when rank failure at the top is rewarded so handsomely while success further down is worth so very little economically by comparison?

By June 2017, Kyle Walker was on the brink of signing for Manchester City for £50million, a world record deal for a right-back. While there was no sign of austerity in the Premier League's transfer spending spree, League Two's Morecambe were on the brink of being bought by new owners who claimed the darkest days would not happen again, the days when staff looked at their bank balances at the end of each month only to find they had not been paid. It had happened on three occasions during the 2016/17 season alone. Right at the bottom, one of the proudest names in non-league football, Northwich Victoria, appeared to be heading towards the lowest tier of semi-professional football after yet another demotion. Each club felt like they were on the brink of something.

THE MARGINS

1

CURSED

WHEN THE RIVER EDEN SWEPT THROUGH THE VILLAGE OF LAZONBY, Danny Grainger, the captain of Carlisle United, was playing an FA Cup second-round game against Welling United in south-east London. A friend back in Lazonby, who lived in a low-lying home, filmed the scene beyond his kitchen window, relaying the terror as Grainger – a father, husband and dog owner – sat nervously in a cold changing room hundreds of miles away. As the waters continued to rise the pressure on the glass was audible, scraping at first then creaking like below deck on an old wooden boat. The lights behind flickered. The electrics were out. Then, darkness.

Record volumes of rain had fallen on land already saturated from a soggy autumn. Not far away the picturesque tourist spot at Pooley Bridge had collapsed. The bridge, which had stood since 1764, was one of more than 500 hundred bridges in Cumbria damaged and declared unusable. Meanwhile, on Warwick Road, the thoroughfare that leads past Carlisle United's Brunton Park ground, some houses were so consumed by Storm Desmond that residents decided to attempt an escape through upper floors by jumping from windows and swimming for safety, even though they did not know where safety was exactly.

'The scariest thing was the noise of the water,' Grainger remembers, pulling a mobile phone from his pocket and playing the video sent by his friend. 'If you listen, it sounds so powerful. You always think about water being peaceful but this was the opposite: aggressive, destructive.'

Grainger says he will never forget Saturday, 5 December 2015.

'Leaving the village didn't feel like a departure, it was more of an escape,' he recalls. 'We left for Welling in the morning just as the storm was coming in. There was a huge flood right across the road. I was thinking, how am I going to get out of here? My sister's partner came past in his four-by-four. The solution was for him to drive in front, clear the water, and for me to follow. A few hours later this wouldn't have been possible because the whole place was flooded.

'Driving south through the Lakes, the bus was swaying from side to side in the wind. Wagons were turned over. When we arrived at the hotel in London, the news was everywhere. Neil Dalton's the Carlisle physio and a Cumbrian. I asked him what he thought. "Worse than last time," he told me. "The river didn't get breached this early." He was talking about 2005.

'I woke up and the TV footage made Carlisle look like a disaster area. In the meantime, we had a game to play, which was very difficult. Even though I knew by then my family were safe, other lads had suffered. Mark Gillespie, our goalkeeper, hadn't travelled because of illness and he was left stranded on the top floor of the club digs where he lives. Somehow we beat Welling 5–0 but the bus on the way home was very quiet. Michael Raynes was the vice-captain and we decided that we – as players – had to do something about it.

'On the Tuesday after training the waters had receded and we were able to walk down Warwick Road. It took seventeen of us fifteen minutes to strip a house. After a few hours pulling furniture out we'd helped all the people who'd contacted the club on social media asking for help so we started knocking on doors: "Do you need help with anything – want the house emptied?" It's a horrible way of putting it but we were literally ripping family homes out and chucking their lives on the street. There was no other option. Not one of us did it for positive publicity or anything like that. It's the sort of mentality we have at the club. The supporters have followed us through hard times so we had to give something back. It was as simple as that.'

Fifteen months later, it would appear normality has returned to Warwick Road until you analyse the small details. Before meeting Grainger, the owner of a convenience store had told me his takings were down by two-thirds. All of his stock was lost when the floodwaters rushed through the doors, reaching the top shelf of his magazine rack. Outside his shop, skips remained filled with carpets, mud and grass, while trees were tied with silky blue ribbons to indicate the high-water mark of the storm, which caused the River Petteril to topple the nearby Botcherby Bridge. The cost to Cumbria of Storm Desmond was estimated at £500m or more. But, as a report from the Carlisle Flood Action Group pointed out, the damage was not only financial. 'The human cost of the storm and its aftermath is similarly incalculable,' the report read. 'The effect of evacuation and displacement on physical and mental health, with lives put on hold, was significant and remains so for many.'

Some residents had since decided to live upstairs in case another flood hit while others simply could not face returning to their once handsome Victorian three-beds with their high ceilings and bay windows. There is a story in the local paper about a couple who sold their house for £80,000 rather than £170,000 because they did not want to be around when the next flood hits.

Grainger, who was born and raised in Cumbria, was playing in Scotland the last time it happened back in 2005 and he admits to being as guilty as anyone for not appreciating the impact of the devastation. 'I saw a football pitch where I used to play and the water was up to the crossbar. It's only when you stand on the pitch again you realise, hang on, this is quite high . . .'

He thinks the government could be doing more to help Carlisle.

'Because we're so far out of the way people forget about us,' he says. 'There are news channels which beam footage from anywhere in the world twenty-four/seven. In many ways it has normalised tragedy because it is there all of the time, only a click away on remote control. It's easy to sit behind a TV and go, "Wow, that looks terrible." It's only when you visit somewhere that has suffered badly and see with your own eyes that it begins to really affect you – and you realise how bad a situation is. I do think something has to change drastically for this not to happen to our region again.'

To reach Carlisle from the south you have to cross stark mountain ranges and deep forests. There are isolated farms and close-knit villages. Shap, the highest motorway service station in England, feels like a staging post to a wild interior. It was here, hundreds of years ago, the border reivers operated; raiders of the Anglo-Scottish borderlands, who stole ruthlessly and without consideration of nationality.

In 1525, when the reivers were pillaging deep into Scotland, the Archbishop of Glasgow, Gavin Dunbar, wrought a whopping 1,069-word curse on the invaders. 'I curse their head and all the hairs of their head, I curse their face, their brain, their mouth, their nose, their tongue, their teeth,' he began. 'I curse them going and I curse them riding; I curse them standing and I curse them sitting; I curse them eating and I curse them drinking; I curse them rising, and I curse them lying; I curse them at home, I curse them away from home; I curse them within the house, I curse them outside of the house; I curse their wives, their children, and their servants who participate in their deeds; their crops, their cattle, their wool, their sheep, their horses, their swine, their geese, their hens, and all their livestock; their halls, their chambers, their kitchens, their stanchions, their barns, their cowsheds, their barnyards, their cabbage patches, their ploughs, their harrows, and the goods and houses that are necessary for their sustenance and welfare.'

He was merely halfway through his diatribe when he added, 'May the thunder and lightning which rained down upon Sodom and Gomorrah and all the lands surrounding them, and burned them for their vile sins, rain down upon them and burn them for their open sins.'

The reivers withered and the curse of Dunbar slept, until 2001, when as part of the Millennium celebrations Carlisle City Council asked Gordon Young, a local artist and descendent of the reivers, to carve 383 of the archbishop's words into a stone that was placed on a dank underpass between Carlisle Castle and the Tullie House museum.

There is a whispered belief that the curse has tortured Carlisle ever since, that the city is doomed. One such believer was Jim Tootle, the Liberal Democrat councillor who campaigned for the stone to be removed from his ward and preferably destroyed. The Daily Mail made a big deal of it when Tootle died suddenly in 2011. He did not see the floods of 2015 but he did see those of a decade earlier, around the time there was not only a fire at Rathbone's Bakery, but also devastating redundancies at Cavaghan & Gray, the food manufacturing plant in Carlisle that made coleslaw for Marks & Spencer. Carlisle United had not been immune from hardship either. In 2004 – three years after the stone's installation – the club was relegated out of the Football League for the first time in its 99-year history.

The twenty-first century had not started well for the city of Carlisle at all. It began with the foot-and-mouth outbreak in 2001, back when Danny Grainger was a fourteen-year-old junior footballer living on his parents' farm, having recently been released by the club he now captains. Grainger had retreated to the Kent Valley League when the competition was shut down for eight months to stop the spread of the disease. At the height of the crisis, Danny, his parents Les and Hilary, plus sisters Lisa and Kerry could not leave their land in Eamont Bridge near Penrith. As smoke from the fires burning livestock carcasses filled the air, food was left at the end of the drive, school was cancelled and socialising forbidden while the government attempted to prevent a nationwide epidemic.

'Life froze for what felt like a long time,' Grainger remembers. 'I could see the concern on my parents' faces, though they tried their best to hide it. It felt like everything we ever knew had been wiped out in one day because the animals had to be culled as quickly as possible. Everyone in the area knew everyone and the phone would ring each night. "Have you heard about such and such a farm?" It was heartbreaking to see everyone's dreams shatter like that.'

I had chosen to meet Grainger for a number of reasons. His path as a professional footballer is connected to the land he was brought up on and the tragedy it has suffered. Because of foot-and-mouth, because of the lockdown, the nearest active football competition was just over the border in Scotland, and so he started to play junior games for Queen of the South. From there he went to Gretna, remaining in the Scottish system for more than a decade until he signed for Carlisle in the summer of 2014, his first and only English club at the age of 28. Within fourteen months he was appointed Carlisle's captain – their leader – at a time when Keith Curle was casting his net further to recruit players than any other manager the club has appointed in its recent history. Grainger, indeed, had never played for a club based south of Carlisle and so, whenever Carlisle travel away, team-mates tease him for his provincialism. 'As soon as I get off the bus, the boys start: "Look, it's the farmer in the city," they say. I'll be honest with you, I hate city life. Even when I played for Hearts I lived right on the edge of the city boundaries, as close as possible to the countryside. Edinburgh's a beautiful place but I like being able to jump over the back fence and take my dog for a walk. She's a Patterdale Terrier cross.'

Grainger grew up a long way from the north-west's main football centres, Manchester and Liverpool; Carlisle is, in fact, much closer to Newcastle than either. In his football travelogue, The Far Corner, Harry Pearson writes about Carlisle's special relationship with the north-east. '"Have you been to Carlisle yet?" they'd say when I told people about my book. When I pointed out that the Great Border City as it likes to bill itself was actually in the north-west they'd nod thoughtfully and say, "Aye, I suppose it is, really," as if they'd never noticed before.'

Pearson reasoned that the confusion was easy to understand because of media coverage, with reviews of Carlisle United's matches featuring on local north-east magazine television shows. Not only that, Carlisle United and Workington had both played in the old North Eastern League before gaining Football League status, while Penrith – twenty miles south of Carlisle – had spent half a century competing in the Northern League, travelling over the Pennines every other weekend. 'I felt a million miles away from anywhere when I was younger, to be honest,' Grainger admits, '. . . the end of the bloody world.'

Cumbria is England's third largest county, but its 41st most populated, with Carlisle its only city. Rather than connections between people, Grainger believes Cumbrian identity is based around the earth; what it yields, how it suffers. 'Everyone I know has some link to manual labour, whether it's a farm or a building site, mates – their brothers or cousins. Carlisle is classed a city but it's more of a relatively small market town and not a centre of big business. We know what hard work is up here and we're not afraid to get our hands dirty. It can get unbearably cold in the winter.'

For some, Carlisle's isolation is too much. Brunton Park is a throwback, with more terracing than any other football ground in the country. The main stand still has wooden seats and a large paddock ensures that fans can direct their opinions clearly to visiting coaching staff. When the young player-manager Ivor Broadis signed from Tottenham Hotspur in 1946, he described the move from one of London's fashionable clubs as like 'stepping down from the Savoy Hotel into the Jungle Café'. Three years later Broadis became the first manager in English football to arrange his own move elsewhere by going to Sunderland. Though Bill Shankly replaced Broadis, he only stayed for two years because Carlisle's board reneged on promises to pay players a bonus if the team finished in the top three of Third Division North.

In the 1970s, Cumbria had three Football League clubs: Carlisle, Workington and Barrow. When promotion to the old First Division was earned in 1974, Shankly, who had since become the most influential manager in Liverpool's history, described Carlisle's achievement as 'the greatest feat in the history of the game'. Following victory at Middlesbrough, Carlisle played their first top-flight home match against Tottenham, when a Chris Balderstone penalty sent them top of the English Football League.

The high did not last for long. Although home and away victories over Everton had a decisive say in the title race – effectively handing the League Championship to Derby County – relegation was confirmed at the end of that campaign and by the 1990s Carlisle consistently looked like following Workington and Barrow out of the Football League. The club's vulnerable position explains why Michael Knighton, a businessman who had been close to purchasing Manchester United, bought Carlisle in 1992 when the team was only able to retain its Football League status because Aldershot went bust.

His failure to seize Manchester United had been very public and so Knighton wanted to show sceptics and media that he wasn't just talk – though he could not resist promising to take Carlisle to the Premier League within a decade. Knighton's masterplan had started promisingly but in 1996 doubts about his credibility surfaced when a recently launched local paper ran a story about him, claiming that he had seen a UFO while driving on the motorway. While the story made headlines all over the country, Carlisle's supporters squirmed.

The club's spiral accelerated in 1997 when Knighton sacked manager Mervyn Day, who had just won promotion and the Auto Windscreens Shield at Wembley. With that, Michael Knighton decided that the best person to replace Day was, in fact, himself. After BBC's Football Focus featured Knighton the chairman in conversation with Knighton the manager, the Knightons fled to the Isle of Man to live, faxing instructions to the group of players left behind; a group which did not include Rory Delap, Matt Jansen and Paul Murray, because Carlisle's best local players had already been sold for combined fees of £2million. By the time Knighton decided to step down a year later, none of the profits had been reinvested in the team and Carlisle were the fourth-worst team in the Football League.

With Grainger watching from the Warwick Road terrace, safety was secured that season only in injury time of the final game, thanks to a goal scored against Plymouth Argyle by Jimmy Glass, the on-loan goalkeeper. His manager Nigel Pearson reacted to the famous moment by saying, 'If I could write scripts like that, I wouldn't be in this game. I'd have a very good publishing contract.'

The antipathy towards Knighton in Carlisle remains raw, however. Many believe he considered the club a soft target, a place he could try and live out his fantasies because of its location far away from the main media glare. His legacy lives on because there is an inherent distrust of owners – even if they are local, but especially if they are outsiders making big promises. When I visited Carlisle there had been speculation about a takeover simmering for nearly two years. A Syrian national living in Canada, Yahya Kirdi, was thought to be behind a move. Like Knighton, Kirdi had a past, having been allied to the purchase of Liverpool in 2010 when the club was close to administration under the ownership of Tom Hicks and George Gillett. Nobody was quite sure how Kirdi had accumulated his wealth. His only business links were a pizza parlour in Montreal and a one-man-band agency business for low-level ice hockey players. There were two theories about Kirdi, one of them being that he was connected to Gillett – the owner of the Montreal Canadiens NHL franchise – through the sale of hockey players and that Kirdi's interest was planted in the media to fend off the banks, who were close to recalling their loans with Liverpool inching towards administration. Also supposedly involved in the deal was Celtic left-back-cum-financial-advisor Andy Lynch, who met Kirdi during a spell playing indoor football for Montreal Manic in the early 1980s. Lynch claimed to have strong relationships in the Middle East. The second theory involved Kirdi and Lynch being chancers, who just wanted to see their names associated with one of football's great sporting institutions.

For the time being, Carlisle supporters were having to make do with 82-year-old Andrew Jenkins being in charge, a wealthy benefactor – but not that wealthy. Much of the frustration lay with John Nixon, a co-owner who had stood down from his position as managing director in 2015 because of fan pressure and been replaced by Nigel Clibbens, whose new role as chief executive was considered to be more of a fireguard against criticism. Clibbens gave an interview to the Carlisle News & Star in March 2017 saying the club had an agreement with a 'billionaire' investor after a 650-day saga, insisting, 'Yes, I do know when it ends.'

There was hope that the mystery buyer would be the owner of Edinburgh Woollen Mill, Philip Day, a 51-year-old who grew up on a council estate in Stockport but now lives in a castle near Carlisle. Day sits on Carlisle United's board and, according to the Sunday Times 2016 Rich List, his net worth was £1.05billion. Day, though, was said to be reluctant to buy the club because he did not want his involvement to extend beyond casual sporting pleasure.

It was not as if Carlisle required assistance to get themselves out of financial problems. Their attendances were among the biggest in League Two and their wage bill reflected not only what was coming through the gates but also the remuneration paid to players to convince them that moving to the very north of the country wasn't such a bad thing. Among their squad were players who commuted every couple of days from Manchester and Liverpool, staying in digs provided by the club close to Brunton Park. Like men that work on oil rigs, these players would tell their families they were 'working away'.

Before signing for Carlisle, Grainger spoke to his friend Lewis Guy, a Penrith-born centre-forward who was deemed not tall enough for Newcastle United's first team and spent his career switching between clubs in England and Scotland.

'Lewis said to me, "The travelling – you'll find it difficult".' In the 2015/16 season, Carlisle did more miles than any other season in the club's history having been drawn away in most of their FA Cup and League Cup fixtures to opponents based in the south of the country. 'By the end of the season I was really flagging,' Grainger concedes. 'Anybody who signs for Carlisle has to accept that it's a club that will take up more of your time.'

Grainger says Carlisle's squad cannot complain because the club spends more money than any other in League Two on ensuring the comfort of their players over the long distances involved with away games.

'The coaches are class and the club pays for us to stay in nice hotels,' Grainger adds. 'The location means we're allowed more days off as well. The manager understands that the players who travel in need to spend as much time as they can with their families. There are a dozen or so teams in and around our standard from the central belt around Liverpool and Manchester. For us to go toe-to-toe with a Bury or a Morecambe, we have to pay them £200 or £300 a week extra. For us to attract players, we have to push the boat out a bit more.'

Carlisle's location places an extra pressure on recruitment. It is not just a case of targeting the most talented players, there are also issues around finding those who won't be affected by the travel – finding players who don't suffer from homesickness. Carlisle has a strong tradition in scouting, considering two of the greatest talent-spotters of the 21st century came from the city: Liverpool's Geoff Twentyman and Ipswich Town's John Carruthers. While Twentyman's playing career took him from Carlisle to Liverpool and back again before being appointed by Bill Shankly as Anfield's chief scout, then serving under Bob Paisley and Joe Fagan, it was Carruthers who recommended a sixteen-year-old Kevin Beattie to Twentyman only for the future England defender to find nobody waiting to meet him at Lime Street Station in Liverpool after he travelled south for a trial. Beattie promptly went straight back to Carlisle and upon his return Carruthers mentioned Beattie's extraordinary talent to a local man, Donald Lightfoot, who knew Bobby Robson. After one trial game at Ipswich Town, Beattie was signed. Carruthers, whose remit under Robson included the north-east as well as Cumbria, later suggested he sign a 'podgy lad' playing for Dunston Working Men's Club in Gateshead, but Paul Gascoigne did not impress at Portman Road.

The tales of Beattie and, indeed, Carruthers reveals that historically footballers have been found in Cumbria. Today, Grainger has concerns about the number of children playing football in the region. Northern Cumbria is serviced by just three 3G pitches: one in Penrith and two others in Carlisle. Grainger thinks it would be helpful to have more facilities for organised leagues because the weather is so bad and so many games get called off on grass pitches. 'To get more kids playing there needs to be a cultural shift,' he says. 'There's nothing better than playing with your mates on a field and coming home head to toe in mud but parents are more concerned about their kids' welfare than ever.'

Grainger would like to sit beside more Cumbrians in Carlisle's dressing room. Steve Rigg was the last one, a striker who signed from Penrith having scored 64 goals in 85 games. In the summer of 2016 he moved across the border to sign for Queen of the South, having found the step up of five leagues too big to take at once. 'There is a gap between the levels in terms of individual talent. But I also think that if you look at a club like Workington (who compete in the Northern Premier League, three divisions below Carlisle), the team is almost always competitive despite the huge distances they have to travel. Many of the lads there are Cumbrian so you realise that locality counts for something because there is a natural bond between players and a spirit exists.'

As the only Cumbrian – and as the captain – there is more expectation on Grainger as a Carlisle United player. He says his toughest time was at the beginning – when he first signed – because relegation from League One had been confirmed not long before and they quickly found themselves rooted to the foot of League Two.

'You take it personally when the criticism comes,' he acknowledges. 'You go to the local shop and you hear it all the time, "Didn't play well on Saturday, did you, son." I'm only trying to buy a chocolate bar for my kid! The reminders are everywhere. It's even worse now because of social media. Whereas ten years ago, the players from elsewhere could disappear after matches and the local lads would get it in the neck every week, everyone is a target because each person is reachable through the Internet. It makes me angry when people think it doesn't hurt when we get beat because it really does. We played Cambridge and lost 3–0 recently. My whole family was there including my kids. It felt like I'd let everyone down. A lot of my friends are Carlisle fans. They'll text you, "What was that?" Just leave me alone!'

Grainger loves being a footballer and he is proud of being captain of Carlisle United, where there is a sense of community with the football club central to it – thanks in no small part to his work in the aftermath of the floods. It remains a place, however, where globalisation has left a tangible sense of frustration; 60 per cent of voters in Carlisle opted for Brexit in the EU referendum of 2016. Grainger is not alone in wondering whether the perception of the Premier

League impacted in some way when football supporters went to the ballot box in the smaller cities and towns where clubs have less money. On a personal level, he thinks the wider view of footballers as workers – the money they supposedly all earn – is widely inaccurate, especially at the lower end, because of the Premier League.

'When you look at the Premier League and you see all the money, all the marketing, all the coverage it is given, people compare it to their own experiences and begin to feel bad about football,' he says. 'On a personal level, the impression of what footballers earn and are as human beings affects basic everyday life. Mortgage companies have the retirement ages of footballers down at thirty-five. They look at my earnings and expect to see a lot more when the reality is, League Two players aren't paid a great deal more than the average person. Because our careers are short and because the reality doesn't reflect the impression, it means many of us are judged unfairly even by banks.'

In total more than 2,000 properties were directly affected by Storm Desmond. Brunton Park was submerged under filthy water and Carlisle United were unable to play home games for two months. Danny Grainger and the rest of Carlisle's players were forced to train in the nearest city Newcastle, 58 miles to the east. Home games were played in Blackburn, Preston and Blackpool. That attendances at Ewood Park, Deepdale and Bloomfield Road remained similar to Brunton Park is a testimony to the endurance of Carlisle supporters, considering the domestic pressures many of them were under and the distances they had to travel just to give their team some backing. Carlisle had been at the top of the league before the floods, having suffered only one defeat in eleven games. After, there was just one win in twelve. Perhaps Carlisle United's story – perhaps the club's unique geographical position – reveals that the league table sometimes does lie at the end of the season after all.

2

KING CANUTE

HEAD WEST TOWARDS BARROW-IN-FURNESS FROM THE M6 AND IT feels like you have fallen into a forgotten kingdom. There are signs and dark tracks for mysterious-sounding villages like Witherslack and Ulpha. You pass Cark, Arrad Foot and Greenodd, skirting the deep south of the Lake District; the beautiful mountainous region that inspired among many others William Wordsworth, Samuel Coleridge and Beatrix Potter. The road seems to go on and on and on. An hour later it drops southwards, suddenly crooking around the top of Morecambe Bay. The russet colours of the Lakes are left behind. Ulverston arrives – the birthplace of Stan Laurel – then Loppergarth, Great Urswick and Little Urswick. The mood becomes austere. During winter, day resembles a permanent dusk. There is steel, noise and grime. The grey of the Irish Sea is close. The charcoal clouds are so heavy, the sky is inseparable from land and water. You enter what appears to be an ocean world. That ocean world is called Barrow-in-Furness.

Barrow – or 'Barra' as it is pronounced by locals – hangs down from Cumbria like a nail on the arthritic finger of an old man. At Christmas 1929 the news that winds of 115 miles had shaken the town took a week to spread to the nearest major cities, Newcastle, Liverpool and Manchester. 'The end of the longest cul-de-sac in the world,' many call it. One road in, one road out, where lorries carrying industrial components have place names like Glasgow, Clydebank and Carlisle across their wagons.

Kendal is the closest settlement in terms of population and Kendal is back the other way. When the announcement was made that Kendal's magistrates court would close and move to Barrow, campaigners warned that it would leave people without access to local justice. It would also force victims, witnesses and defendants to embark on an eighty-mile round trip. The hourly bus service from Kendal to Barrow takes around one hour and forty minutes, with a return ticket priced at £10.80. The train journey, meanwhile, would require two changes and a travel time of up to two and a half hours, costing £25.90. It is understandable why Barrow is thought of as far away even within its own region. In remote Carlisle the reaction was a question when I told someone my next stop was Barrow: 'That's far away – why go there?'

In his 2008 travelogue Pies and Prejudice, Stuart Maconie describes the mood of coastal Cumbria, comparing West Cumberland to the natural romance of the soulful Lakes. 'From cottages to boarded-up flats, from Gore-Tex and real ale to Burberry and Smirnoff Ice,' he wrote, concluding, 'Barrow-in-Furness is a bloody long way from anywhere.' The BBC Cumbria website backed him up. 'To get a real understanding of the Barrovian, you should consider its geographical location. One of the most significant things about Barrow-in-Furness is that only the most hapless, dazed orienteer could possibly visit by accident – you have to have a purpose to get there.'

The purpose of my visit was to meet Paul Casson, the chairman and owner of Barrow AFC, who begins his conversation with me by admitting, 'There's a joke that goes round about the fact many who live here have never travelled any further than Kendal. I think it's a little bit true. On one hand people can be narrow-minded and sometimes unforgiving as a consequence, but on the other, they can also be loyal and passionate. The Barrovian is fundamentally a proud person.'

Before you reach Holker Street, the ancient home of Barrow's football team, there are further reminders of the town's detachment. A wooden plaque says Furness Abbey is nearby. Back when powerful theocratic monks ruled the area in the Middle Ages, Barrow was a fishing village and cut off entirely; surrounded on three sides by water and hills on the other. On my departure, when I pass the plaque for a second time, it feels like going ashore. It explains why Barrow is similar to an island community and has a reputation for looking in on itself. Maconie had described it as being like a Stephen King town: the kids who depart for an education tend not to go back. One of those that eventually did was Casson, who grew up in Barrow before studying electrochemistry at the University of Loughborough. From there he moved to Texas where he became a millionaire after starting a company in the early 1990s that specialised in wireless communication. The age of the Internet was just around the corner.

Casson had originally left Barrow in 1971. A year later, Barrow AFC were voted out of the Football League following 51 seasons as a professional club. Casson is not the only person in Barrow who believes rival chairmen had Barrow's historically strong home record, the town's awkward geographical location as well as the cost of getting there in mind when the vote was taken.

Hereford Town, who replaced Barrow, had beaten Newcastle United in the FA Cup a few months before thanks to Ronnie Radford's famous goal. Everybody liked Hereford. '. . . and nobody liked Barrow,' Casson says. 'Holker Street also had a speedway track around the pitch – a pitch you couldn't really play football on without putting plywood down and covering it with turf. The facilities weren't great here but there were other clubs worse than Barrow.'

Casson is sitting in Holker Street's general office, dressed unprepossessingly in a navy fleece, a pair of jeans and white trainers. I see him on the first Friday morning of January and it is busier at Holker Street than usual because Barrow are preparing for a third-round FA Cup tie the following afternoon at home to Rochdale, a club flying the highest it has ever flown in League One. It is an ironic subplot that Barrow's full-time players spend their weekdays training not in Barrow, but at Hopwood Hall College in Rochdale. The location for Barrow's training operations helps the club attract players from all over the country, 'because the idea of living in Manchester is a lot sexier than Barrow', Casson concedes. Paul Cox, Barrow's manager, travels to Manchester from Nottingham where he lives. For each training session, that means spending a rough total of five hours in the car. For home games, Cox's commute time can be as long as eight hours depending on how bad the traffic is.

Casson says Carlisle United pay a premium for their players to live as close as possible to Brunton Park and, ultimately, for the club to breathe from the place it represents. For Barrow's level, one league below Carlisle, and for Barrow's geography – the drive from Manchester to Barrow is longer than Manchester to Carlisle, for example, because getting to Barrow involves A roads and Carlisle involves quiet motorway – the only economical way for Barrow to be based in

Barrow would be to use local talent. Ahead of the Rochdale game, the only Barrovian in Cox's squad was Elliot Newby. Upon the release of Newby's brother Alex in May 2016, along with two other local boys, Cox admitted the decision may well have made him 'the most hated man in Barrow'.

The person photographed on the front of the matchday programme for the Rochdale game proudly clinging on to a football is one Brian Arrowsmith – 'a local hero – hundreds upon hundreds of appearances', someone who will soon have Holker Street's main stand named after him. Casson also tells stories of the great Colin Cowperthwaite – 'hundreds of goals – another local hero'. Casson would like more surnames like Arrowsmith and Cowperthwaite to feature on Barrow's teamsheet but that inevitably would have an impact on their quest to return to the Football League. 'People might point out if I'm serious about the community in Barrow moving the team back from Rochdale is something I should consider, but you have to be realistic even if it's a nice thought.'

Casson's big aim is returning Barrow to the Football League but he needs the town to buy into his vision if the club is to become self-sufficient. When he first started watching games at Holker Street the average attendance in the old Fourth Division was around 6,000; a tenth of Barrow's population. 'Now we are lucky if we get 1,500 if we're winning and as low as 600 when we are losing,' he rues. 'After getting kicked out of the Football League, for a few years, only 200 came here. Essentially the town has gradually disassociated itself from the football club and that is not right.'

Casson still sees busloads of supporters leaving the town at weekends bound for cities like Manchester and Liverpool, where fashionable football clubs exist, and it frustrates him. He understands that Barrow has been mismanaged in the past but hopes the club, now it is financially stable under his leadership, will become more of a 'thing' for townspeople.

'I want this football club to be about more than sport,' he says. 'You see a lot of Liverpool shirts, Manchester City shirts. What's wrong with parents buying them the kit of their home-town team? It's because it's not cool – we're not on the TV.'

'I went to the rugby a few months ago and for the first time away from Holker Street I saw a kid wearing a Barrow football shirt,' he recalls. 'That's what makes my involvement worthwhile here. We've started selling more hats and scarves. I want people to feel a sense of civic pride, for people to have that good old northern spirit – that we can do whatever we want to do if we try. Somewhere, that was lost.'

I had been to Barrow many times as a junior reporter covering Marine, when Barrow were in the Northern Premier League. I realised it was not the goals but the bad fouls, the horrendous refereeing mistakes, the yellow and red cards and the fights that really got the crowd twitching. It prompted me to conclude that Holker Street's pitch might as well have been a scaffold from the Middle Ages; the game a public hanging, with the players and the officials all having nooses around their necks. I sensed local spectators wanted to witness brutality. They wanted to witness gore. They wanted suffering.

*

Emlyn Hughes was the captain of Liverpool and England. The title of the opening chapter in his autobiography, 'Back Home', seemed like recognition that even in the mind of the town's most famous footballer, Barrow was a distant place. 'Wherever you stand in Barrow-in-Furness, there is no escape from the sea and ships and the deeds of men who helped win wars,' Hughes wrote. This was a time when huge cranes soared over Barrow's dock front, when the streets were named after great vessels and admirals: Blake, Hood, Parry, Nelson, Raleigh, Cook, Anson and Keppel representing a sea battle on every corner. 'Barrow folk are proud of the part they played in the days when Britannia ruled the waves,' Hughes concluded.

Barrow had been known as the English Chicago during the nineteenth century because of its steel and shipping boom in the years after the Furness Railway opened. The turquoise-tinted statue of Sir James Ramsden stands in Barrow's Ramsden Square for a reason: the industrialist had been the managing director of the Furness Railway Company for 29 years until a year before his death in 1896. His fingers had been in every significant town pie, for he had the same role with the Barrow Hermatite Steel Company and the Barrow Shipbuilding Company: positions which allowed him to sit unopposed as the mayor for decades.

In 1897, Ramsden's shipbuilding company was bought by Vickers and the shipyard at Barrow became the Naval Construction and Armaments Company. The two world wars that followed brought misery for the cities of the north-west, but for Barrow it signalled growth and prosperity. Docks soon extended on to the spit of Walney Island, where a new settlement was formed and named Vickerstown.

Barrow was soon manufacturing submarines. In 1888 Abdül Hamid, built for the navy of the Ottoman Empire, became the first submarine in the world to fire a live torpedo underwater. Then came a contract with the Royal Navy. Holland 1 was built there in 1901, the Navy's first submarine, and over half a century and many warships later, HMS Dreadnought launched in 1960 – the UK's first nuclear-powered sub. 'In crowded billets and sweaty hammocks, beneath the inky waters of the world's oceans, Barrow built the sleek and deadly nuclear subs that the cold warriors criss-crossed the globe in,' Stuart Maconie wrote, proceeding to explain that the thaw towards the end of the Cold War might have warmed many, 'but it brought a chill to Barrow'.

There had been more than 20,000 workers in the shipyards at the start of the 1980s. By the Millennium, there were just 3,000. The mood slumped further two years later when Barrow suffered Britain's worst outbreak of Legionnaires' disease. A faulty air-conditioning pipe at the town's arts centre led to seven deaths and 172 people falling seriously ill.

Paul Casson had left Barrow when it was still a reasonably prosperous but fundamentally working-class place. He had grown up in a neat semi-detached house on Willow Road, just half a mile from Holker Street. Having helped build the Titanic in Belfast, Casson's great-grandfather, who was born in Glasgow, had moved to Barrow to work in the shipyards. Casson's grandfather did the same thing. And so did his father, Walter. 'My dad was a fitter and turner,' Casson says proudly. 'I was the first one to do something else.'

Casson's imagination as a child reached out across the scudding seas beyond Barrow's harbour walls. It was his ambition to live in the United States and that's where he's been since the summer of 1978, settling in Dallas, Texas. He currently lives in the Fort Worth area, travelling back to Barrow once a month for meetings with his 33-year-old son, Andrew, who runs Barrow AFC when he is not there.

Casson believes the collapse of the shipbuilding industry had a profound effect on the confidence of Barrow's people. 'It killed it,' he says flatly. 'You could do only one of two things living here. You either went to the grammar school, through sixth form and to university. Or you went to the shipyard. That's what my whole family did until my father decided to move jobs, working at the Central College for Further Education. It meant we didn't have access to shipbuilding union places like Vickers Sports Club any more. In many ways, from that point onwards, I felt disadvantaged.

'It was a big choice to follow education and leave the town instead of putting your future in the shipyard and going through an apprenticeship which usually meant you'd be here forever,' Casson continues. 'For many, the decision was made for them when they took the eleven-plus. The shipyards acted as a safety net because it was always there for people who didn't pass them. By 1991, the number of workers in the shipyards had reduced dramatically.'

Casson laments the decline of the shipyards. 'What do you do? What do your kids do? The town is still suffering,' he believes. 'There is a lack of self-confidence. It makes me sad because I want things to be different for everyone. I've always thought you can achieve something if you believe in it profoundly enough. But when the rug is pulled from beneath your feet so dramatically, it's a challenge to rise again.'

Barrow is now a community relying on the prospect of nuclear war for its survival. Employment figures in Barrow's shipyards were up to 7,500 in 2016 because of the contract signed with BAE Systems to build the UK's next fleet of submarines. And yet, Casson describes BAE as a 'fundamental disappointment'.

'This town should be a shining light for what that type of public spending can do,' he says. 'Walk around Barrow and you would think the place is dying. You wouldn't know that BAE have just committed umpteen billion pounds towards developing the latest Trident submarine; that Barrow is going to be a boom town for the next twenty years. Instead you walk around and you see shops closing down, people looking at the floor. BAE should take more of an active role in building the community again.'

Barrow is also confused, and – perhaps – understandably so. It had traditionally been a strong Labour constituency. People do not know what to believe in any more, or who to trust because of the proposed threat of unilateral disarmament under Jeremy Corbyn, the party's leader. Casson knows friends who speak of the fear among fellow workmen the last time this happened under Michael Foot in the 1983 general election campaign. It led to a Conservative MP representing the Barrow and Furness constituency from 1983 to 1992.

John Woodcock, the local Labour MP, had described Barrow as 'a unique working-class town on the edge of the stunning Lakes and Cumbrian coast. There are things we want to make better, but we are deeply proud of Barrow's sense of community that always welcomes newcomers with open arms.' In 2015, with the future of Trident in the minds of many, Woodcock saw his majority plummet from 5,208 to 795. In 2017 it shrank again to a mere 209. Woodcock reminded people, however, that it was under the Tories that the shipyard workforce had plummeted in the space of just a few years. Woodcock insists that 'the big failing' of the Thatcher government was its closure of Barrow's shipyards, not only decimating an industry that provided life for a town, but doing it also too quickly and therefore losing the experience of specialised older workers. Aside from the disastrous social implications, the Tories left a gaping skills gap when it came to the next nuclear defence contract – building the Astute class submarines. 'Once-proud working people, who were trained to do the most advanced manufacturing on the planet, lost that dignity of being able to get to work, and ended up languishing on benefit,' Woodcock said. When the order came through for Astute in 1997, indeed, Barrow simply did not have the depth or skill in its workforce any more and this led to long delays in production.

Once upon a time, a helicopter took off from Squires Gate near Blackpool. 'A Scouser in a shellsuit' had paid £750 in cash for an instructor to take him up and the notes, according to the book Cocky, 'were new and crisp'. The plume of Merseyside was behind them and, having then passed over the red steel of Blackpool Tower, the helicopter veered out into the Irish Sea before heading north towards Barrow-in-Furness. The Scouser had a bodybuilder's neck. This squat, solid figure also had arms like jack-hammers. When one of those arms pointed out a square of mud and grass below, the words followed casually: 'I own that.'

That square of mud and grass were the grounds of Barrow Athletic Football Club. The Scouser's name was Curtis Warren and he was, according to Interpol and Her Majesty's Customs and Excise, the northern European agent for the Cali drugs cartel in Colombia. On the street Warren was known as the Cocky Watchman. To the authorities he was Target One. Warren had become so wealthy through drugs that by the mid-1990s he was the highest mixed-race person on the Sunday Times Rich 500 list. Warren was estimated at being worth somewhere in the region of £80million, though many chasing him consider that figure to be a conservative guess because he was often one, two or even three steps ahead of the authorities.

It was only when the anti-money-laundering units of the Netherlands and Britain got closer to him that Barrow AFC came into their investigations. Police raided the club's offices and arrested Stephen Vaughan, a boxing promoter from Liverpool. Mr Vaughan's company, Northern Improvements, was the Holker Street ground's major shareholder and he wrote the following letter to Boxing News in February 1998:

> *I am sure you will be aware that I was recently arrested by HM Customs and Excise in relation to the investigation into Curtis Warren. You will be aware that the allegations centre on the laundering of millions of pounds of supposed drugs money. This is something I have categorically and strenuously denied and I cannot stress how vehemently any potential prosecution would be defended.*
>
> *Unfortunately, the rumours and stories have reached us through the grapevine and I have heard some fantastic versions of events, most of which are untrue. The investigation surrounds Curtis Warren's 'missing £185m'. Because I'm a past associate of Mr Warren, the HM Customs have deemed it necessary to investigate matters concerning me and some of my assets, such as the acquisition of an office block, a wine bar, Barrow Football Club's Holker Street Stadium, and to look into my land deals and residential building investments over the past six years. That is all.*

Under Vaughan's ownership, which began in 1995, Barrow had risen as champions of the Northern Premier League and into the Conference under the management of Owen Brown, who used his knowledge of the Liverpool scene and the money available to him to convince former professionals like Mark Seagraves and Andy Mutch that the two-and-a-half-hour one-way drive for every home game was a mere skip across the road. Vaughan had built a new grandstand and promised to take Barrow back into the Football League. In November 1998, though – with all the investigations taking place into his business dealings, particularly his acquisition of Holker Street, he resigned claiming that he was owed £269,000, having ploughed between £350,000 and £400,000 into the club. Ultimately, the withdrawal of Vaughan's finances saw Barrow go bust in January 1999 and, on the brink of extinction, the club – by now being run by a members' consortium – was expelled from the Conference before being left in limbo when the Northern Premier League refused to accept them back in, a decision which left Barrow with no option but to apply for the North West Counties League, the lowest level of semi-professional football. Barrow's prospects only became brighter when the FA intervened and ordered the Northern Premier League to accept Barrow or face the prospect of not being recognised by the English game's governing body.

By the time Paul Casson came along in 2014, Barrow was a very paranoid town indeed. Its football club were towards the bottom of the Conference North by then. Winning the FA Trophy at Wembley by improbably beating Stevenage Borough in 2010 had not been the cue for a return to more stable times. A relegation from the Conference National followed and with that went joint-managers Dave Bayliss and Darren Sheridan.

It wasn't even in Casson's plan to buy Barrow. He says that he – as much as the club's board – needed convincing his involvement was a good idea. Casson believes any person wanting to get involved at Barrow would have been met with the same question: will he be another Vaughan?

'They were quite sceptical about me for a long time,' he admits. 'I think ultimately the board realised that the members' model had taken them about as far as they could go: there might be the odd year where an FA Cup run would pay some of the bills but what about the bad years when there's no cup competitions to fall back on? There would always be a struggle.'

Casson's rugby league connections in the town had made him think about getting involved in Barrow's football club.

'Mick Murphy is a famous rugby player who came from Liverpool and left a bit of a mark in Barrow,' Casson explains. 'Mick had taught in the same college as my dad. One of his younger brothers, Cormac, was a guy I knew at university. I've known the family for a long time and they invited me to a big reunion at the Marriott Hotel in Liverpool. You can imagine what that must have been like. When it came to three a.m. and after quite a few drinks one of the Murphy brothers who still lives in Barrow said to me, "Why don't you buy Barrow Football Club?" My response? "Why would I do that?"'

Sport in Barrow had never been lower. Barrow's rugby league side were also in the process of dropping down a division.

'Barrow sport seemed to be heading for a place I don't remember it being,' Casson says. 'When I was growing up here, 14,000 people would show up at the rugby and we'd sign people like Keith Jarrett and Tom Brophy. In football, we climbed to the heights of the top of the old Division Three for what felt like ten minutes. My memories of Barrow sport were of it being both active and vibrant.'

Steve Shaw was the Barrow reporter of the North West Evening Mail. Casson had stopped discussions with Barrow's board by the time he received his phone call. Casson's father Walter had died and he'd originally wanted to help the club for him – to instil some civic pride back. 'Steve said, "By the way, rumour has it that you are the guy trying to invest in Barrow AFC – is that true?" I told him it was but it ended when my dad passed away.' Casson met Shaw at a hotel in

Lancaster. 'When your dad dies, you are mad at everything: mad at the world. Steve was the one that talked me down. "Maybe it's not such a bad idea ..."' Seven months later, Casson was announced as Barrow's new owner. 'I guess it shows you the value of a local paper. Sometimes that's all it needs – a good press man to push you in the right direction. The big national daily newspapers, they don't really care about Barrow. All they care about is the top six in the Premier League.'

*

The floodlights of Holker Street are so tall and powerful-looking, they might be long-legged space machines with gamma-ray eyes. Before satellite navigation systems were available on cars, and when maps were for readers of the National Geographic Society members, these steely beasts must have acted like tractor beams for visiting supporters in the winter, drawn like moths towards a candle. Casson, certainly, is reluctant to change them, not because he cannot afford it but rather, he thinks it gives Holker Street a sense of place and history. 'I'd like the replacements to be similar but finding someone with imagination who doesn't charge something like the equivalent of the national debt to do it is another matter altogether,' he says.

The sight of the floodlights leads him to think about the facilities at Barrow's ground. For anyone used to the trappings that accompany sitting down for matches in the new stadia of the Football League, Holker Street must be like a wormhole to a lost decade. 'But I sort of like the place,' Casson continues. 'On our best day if we are going to only pull two to three thousand, why should we build a shiny new stadium? There's nothing worse than a bunch of empty seats. It looks awful. Slowly we'll improve the infrastructure, with the changing rooms being the start. But in League Two you need a thousand seats and we have that already. Ultimately, we wouldn't be denied promotion because of the ground.'

His conclusion is also based on discussions with the former chairman of Barrow Raiders, Dave Sharpe, about the issue of a stadium-share. Craven Park is less than a mile down Walney Road, and closer to Barrow's town centre. The arenas are almost identical: one blue-seated stand (though the football club's is slightly bigger) accompanied by a mix of covered and uncovered terracing. Casson went to Rochdale as well, who share their Spotland ground with rugby league's Rochdale Hornets. 'They hate it . . .' Then he went to Halifax, who have a similar arrangement with the local rugby league club, to find '. . . they don't love it either.'

'I'm pretty proud of our surface; I wouldn't like the idea of rugby players chewing it up,' he adds. 'I don't think a multi-purpose stadium in Barrow is ever going to happen. We also have to think about our financial interests overlapping with theirs. Rugby league isn't in such a good place. Bradford Bulls is a huge club and they've just gone into administration. What would happen if we built a ground together and one of us went under? It might result in no sport existing at all in Barrow.'

Casson references King Canute when describing the possibilities at Barrow, trying to 'push back the waves', despite the inevitability they will crash into the coastline.

'If you do too much too soon, it will swamp you,' Casson says. 'When we had the draw for the FA Cup third round, the general reaction was: anybody but Rochdale. For about thirteen nanoseconds I felt the same way. But then I realised it was the perfect draw for us, a) because it is at home, b) we haven't had a third-round game at Holker Street in forty-nine years, and c) it's a team we can probably compete with – we're not just going to be showing up as a dressing on some party cake like Manchester United; it will be a proper game against a proper team with whom we have some history, albeit in the distant past. And d) we played Middlesbrough away a few seasons ago. Everybody piled out of the town for the day to see us lose and they've never been back. If we beat Rochdale here tomorrow in front of a sell-out crowd, the fans might see and feel what is happening.'

Casson is softly spoken. He delivers his thoughts slowly. His accent is more Scottish than English and certainly more British than American. He feels strongly that traditions should be maintained and this explains why there is need for reform across football. From here, his thoughts rush. He begins by telling me he has investigated what is happening at other clubs in the Conference National and it concerns him what he sees.

'Tranmere Rovers, for example,' he starts. 'They were pushing for the Premier League twenty-five years ago. They're in our league now and this is what can happen when it all goes wrong. They're desperately trying to get it right. They've had two years of parachute payments from the Football League and next season they won't hold a financial advantage over other clubs. I don't think they're going to make it this season. The competition to go up is fierce. Lincoln City seem to be doing all the right things.'

To get Barrow on a steady financial path, Casson has spent around £2million so far, though he prefers to describe it as a figure that equates to 'ten minutes of

Wayne Rooney's salary'. Thanks to Barrow's FA Cup run, he thinks he will lose 'only' £400,000 in the 2016/17 season, largely because he now knows which mistakes to avoid when dealing with players and other figures who affect decisions.

'Agents . . .' Casson continues with a level of disdain – you know exactly what is coming next – '. . . are a cancer on the game. They get involved with players way too early and make promises they can't keep. We had one player who was well thought of at the Football League club he played for but got released because his career stalled after he became bogged down by personal issues. That resulted in him signing for Barrow and when he showed up last pre-season, he'd put on an incredible amount of weight. I spoke to his agent and said, "This person cannot play football – he's not fit for purpose." I asked him what he was doing to help. "Nothing." He didn't care. All he wanted was his up-front payment for securing the move.'

It is understandable why even Premier League owners like Liverpool's John W. Henry describe the transfer business as the 'Wild West' when you listen to some of Casson's other experiences.

'Only yesterday I received an invoice from some guy purporting to be a representative of one of our players. We checked his contract and it confirmed there was no intermediary involved. We called him up and he tried to explain that it was for what he described as an introduction to one of our scouts. "Get out of here!" I told him. "Stop wasting my time." This happens a lot . . .'

There are plenty of things that annoy Casson about the modern game and some of these issues explain why he'd rather invest his money in Barrow than be seen like many other wealthy businessmen quaffing champagne in the executive suites of Old Trafford or Anfield.

'I don't think the Premier League is relevant to anything that is normal, unless you aspire to feature in the Daily Mail with your girlfriend and want everyone to comment on what you're wearing,' he says. 'The average footballer's salary is too far away from the common working man. When I was growing up the only difference was, a footballer might be able to afford a new car while the common working man would go for a used car. They still lived in the same houses and, in some cases, had another job in the off-season to supplement their wages. Now, they live on another planet.

'Football started as an outlet for the working man because life was so rubbish that he had to go and do something and take his mind off his problems. That something was standing on a miserable terrace somewhere at a ground where there were absolutely no facilities whatsoever; catching the odd glimpse of a ball in the masses of people. That was more than fun in an era where there wasn't wall-to-wall reporting or comment and the local paper's opinion held some sway. That is the very basis from where football's popularity grew. We are so far from that now, where you've got to spend a hundred pounds a month subscription on a stupid TV network to watch game after game after game, most of which you don't care about. Football has become an extension of people's financial concerns and that is immoral and irresponsible.

'They shouldn't call it the Football Association any more, they should call it the Top-Six of the Premier League Association because the interests of the top six are always reflected first,' he continues. 'The rest of us don't matter. They don't bother with clubs like Barrow – I think they consider us a bit of an inconvenience. It's all about making money. I found out only yesterday that our game against Rochdale is being broadcast live in countries around the world. You know how much we get for that? Not a penny. I have no explanation why. I am told it is simply the rules. You get £144,000 per team if you are featured live in Britain. Of course, the teams chosen are Manchester United, Arsenal and Liverpool. That shows great imagination, doesn't it?'

The FA Cup is a competition Casson loves.

'But they've subjected the competition to ignominy,' he says. 'I'd like someone to explain why they've scrapped replays in some rounds and decided not to have the final on its own day like it used to be. The FA Cup used to have parity with the league in terms of importance. Now, a manager wins the cup but finishes halfway down the Premier League and he gets fired. Winning the FA Cup, it used to ensure you a job for life.

'The game is completely out of whack. What happens is, when the pendulum swings too far – before it goes back to the middle – it swings in the opposite direction. You can apply that to politics too. I think that the good old Premier League won't know what's hit them. The TV audiences will become bored of the saturation and switch off so the TV money will start to dry up. The teams which are right there on the regular edge of finances, and Manchester United are one, will all of a sudden start to struggle on the pitch. The hundreds of millions of dollars that are allowed to sit on their balance sheet because of goodwill won't be worth flip any more.

'The Premier League will eat itself if it is not careful,' Casson says. 'The obsession over the top six teams means there is overexposure and unless they are taken out of the Premier League and into some form of Pan-European league, the interest and attendances will eventually start to fall. Maybe that's the grand plan of the people in charge, who knows?

'At that point, I think the people of the UK will react by falling back on the teams in their own league because they simply can't afford to follow a club playing away every other weekend in a galaxy far, far away.

'I hope that rationality prevails instead and that this financial model where you have Manchester United and Arsenal worth billions, Chelsea not quite being worth billions but the owner has billions; Manchester City – I don't know what they even are any more. Eventually I hope it comes back to truer clubs like Burnley. I think what has happened there truly is spectacular, especially when you see how the people within their community feel about the club even if they do bounce between divisions. I'd love to know how they've done it.

'If Barrow could even sniff getting close to League One I think the whole place would rise up,' Casson concludes. 'There really still is nothing that you can physically do that makes you feel like you do when you are in a football ground, when – as you say – a public hanging is taking place, and there's a smell of blood in the air. You don't get that in the pub watching the TV because you are detached from all the true senses of football: the masses, the mob, the desire to chop someone's head off. It's like a fever. That's what I think clubs like Barrow can do, offer an escape from the humdrum of life, an escape from the couch where football is like some reality TV contest, full of wannabes and millionaires.'

THE COAST

3

EVERY DAY IS LIKE SUNDAY

IT IS TOWARDS THE END OF FEBRUARY AND EMPLOYEES AT Morecambe Football Club are worried they might not get paid for the third time already this season. The previous six months had been the most turbulent since the club's rise into the Football League a decade before. Peter McGuigan, the former owner and a former chief executive at Umbro, decided to sell up in the summer of 2016 to foreign businessmen nobody in the town had ever heard of. McGuigan reasoned it would 'secure the long-term financial viability of the club'. Diego Lemos, a 35-year-old Brazilian, installed Qatari Abdulrahman Al Hashemi as co-chairman within days of his purchase being approved by the authorities, having reportedly paid around £400,000 to transfer the club's shares to G50 Holdings Ltd, a business registered in Co Durham.

Lemos came in September and received applause when he took his seat in the Globe Arena's main stand ahead of a game against Carlisle United. 'A lot of supporters were thinking the same thing,' recalls Richard Allan, who by December had helped form Morecambe's first supporters' trust because of what was to follow under Lemos. 'What would a Brazilian and a Qatari want to do with a small football club located on the seafront in the north-west of England?'

Lemos gave interviews to Morecambe's website where he commended the club's 'family atmosphere' having looked 'all over Europe' for two years to find the right place to invest. He met with Jim Bentley, the third-longest-serving manager in the Football League, and his assistant Ken McKenna over dinner and, according to Bentley, came across as genuine. 'A cracking fella,' Bentley thought.

At the end of October, though, neither Bentley, McKenna nor Morecambe's players – nobody at the club, in fact – was paid on time. Though Lemos apologised and the wages eventually came through eleven days late, scepticism began to rise and morale slumped, with Morecambe losing seven in ten league matches.

For Bentley, the campaign had started with grave concerns anyway. His playing budget had been cut under McGuigan's administration and when Morecambe went to Halifax for a friendly they lost 6–2 with more or less a full-strength team. 'Halifax are two leagues below us and had just been relegated so the alarm bells were ringing straight away,' Bentley says. 'I was thinking, we might not have enough to stay up here.'

On the opening day of the season, Morecambe travelled to Grimsby Town, who were playing their first game as a Football League side after six years in the Conference. 'Again, we lost – this time 2–0 – and it could have been a lot more,' Bentley recalls. The following Tuesday, a spectacular 5–4 victory at Championship side Rotherham in the League Cup created confidence. 'We beat Blackpool here in a derby match 1–0 and turned Portsmouth over, 2–0. Suddenly, we were top of the league and I was manager of the month. We had a bit of momentum with the bit of luck you need: no injuries and no suspensions. And then the club was sold to Mr Diego Lemos.'

Lemos had claimed that he had spent ten years working as a football agent in Qatar, where he met Al Hashemi. Supposedly football was in his blood. His father, Luisinho Tombo, had twice been leading scorer in the Rio State League of Brazil. His uncle, Caio Cambalhota, was at Flamengo with Zico and another uncle, César Maluco, was selected in Brazil's 1974 World Cup squad. Through conversations, Bentley was convinced Lemos 'knew football'.

What Bentley did not envisage was Lemos disappearing, as he did on 17 November – and not returning. Al Hashemi left the country eight days later and, though contact with officials at Morecambe had since been made, it was claimed that he had fallen out with Lemos over money and that now Al Hashemi was considering taking Morecambe on by himself. By January, though, Companies House records showed that 99 per cent of the shares in the G50 Holdings, the vehicle Lemos used to acquire Morecambe, had been transferred to a Durham-based tax consultant, Graham Burnard. At the end of January, the payroll did not run for a second time.

'We'd already agreed to sell Tom Barkhuizen, our best striker, to Preston in November, to ensure all of the club's financial commitments were met,' Bentley says. 'If you're not paying wages there's the threat of a points deduction, administration and even liquidation. The community training facility has been locked up for the last six weeks or so which means nobody can use the Astroturf – a pitch we use in the wet months, as well as the youth teams. Instead, we've been training on a school field, which is usually waterlogged at this time of the year because it's clay-based and we don't have the machinery or the manpower to keep on top of it. Overall, it has been really, really hard to manage.'

At the start of February, it had seemed that Morecambe were close to being bought by Joseph Cala, a Sicilian-American businessman, who spent a decade trying to raise funding for a series of underwater resorts and casinos built in glass-bottomed boats, before he tabled and subsequently withdrew a bid to take over at Portsmouth in 2012. Cala, or 'the Man from Atlantis' as he was known after claiming Portsmouth would be his, claimed he had support from a US private equity group to take Morecambe on. 'When Diego left, we know (sic) the club is in financial disaster so we thought it would be helpful to take it over,' Cala said.

In the two weeks Cala spent at Morecambe looking through the club's books from inside one of the Globe Arena's executive suites while getting to know staff, he managed to rub quite a few of the non-playing employees up the wrong way, according to Bentley who somehow had managed to arrest the form of October and November and get Morecambe to within five points of the League Two play-offs. Cala's takeover was stopped by Lemos, who obtained a court order that prevented a sale.

'You couldn't make this season up; it's been an absolute mess off the pitch, everyone has been scarred,' says Bentley who, when we meet towards the end of February, has a team to prepare for a home fixture against Grimsby the following day, though his thoughts are already drifting to Tuesday and what he might find out when he checks his bank balance.

'I walked into the changing room today and heard the tail-end of a conversation – the players were talking about it as well, will we get paid? You have to realise that the players – what everyone earns here – isn't the Premier League. It affects your ability to pay the mortgage.'

'I can understand the negativity and concern,' he says. 'When it happens the first time, you can give it the benefit of the doubt. But for it to happen again in January, which is the next pay day after Christmas – when you've got plenty of bills to sort out – it hit us hard. There's only so much goodwill you can get from people. We've lost office staff over the last few months because they can't take the risk staying on, and so they've sought alternative employment.

'Another problem I've got as a manager is, a lot of our players are out of contract and if I want to tie them up for next year, they'll wait on their decisions – and while they delay, other clubs will come in. This season by some miracle we might end up OK. But next season is another matter.'

*

A decade from now, Barrow might not be considered quite as far away from the rest of humanity as it is at the moment. There are ambitious plans to build a twelve-mile 'green' bridge costing £8.6bn running across Morecambe Bay and the Duddon Estuary, potentially linking Furness and Heysham. It has been described as the difference between life and death, with residents in favour of the project, believing it would mean fewer accidents on the notorious narrow roads that slither west before ending in Barrow.

There is the life-or-death argument for the economies of the largest towns involved as well: proposed wind and tidal turbines would produce enough green energy to power two million homes and in turn create more than ten thousand jobs; it would also cut journey times to Lancashire and beyond, in addition to making south and west Cumbria far more accessible for people wanting to visit. If they live in Manchester or Liverpool, the journey for Barrow's footballers will become a little shorter and maybe Paul Casson might not have to pay so much in expenses.

The arguments against it happening are aesthetical. No longer would you be able to look out across the bay from Morecambe and see nothing but water between the art deco Midland Hotel and the spit of Walney, the next land which shimmers in the distance on mild afternoons. If one building embodies where Morecambe has been and where it is now, indeed, the Midland is that building. It first opened in 1933 but fell into disrepair and ended up closing, as Morecambe went from boom to bust as a workers' seaside holiday town. With the local council helping Urban Splash find the money to refurbish it, Morecambe had aspirations about re-establishing itself as a fashionable middle-class resort and descriptions about it becoming 'the Brighton of the north' were brandished. The hotel's appearance is a reminder of what regeneration can achieve. Yet look elsewhere in Morecambe and you realise what happens when nobody else can afford to catch up.

On Morecambe's promenade, you have crisp Irish Sea air, you have fish and chips, you have all-day breakfasts priced at £2.99 and you have chain pubs serving two meals for the price of one. You have lurid signs with clashing colours advertising slot-machine arcades; you have towering three-storey limestone guesthouses in need of fresh paint; you have pensioners wobbling past on their Zimmer frames with tubes stuffed up their noses. What you don't have is small-scale entrepreneurs with the money to open boutiques and bistros to accommodate visitors. What you don't have is galleries or performance spaces for the next Eric Morecambe or the next Thora Hird to learn their craft. Morecambe's Winter Gardens was originally built as the Victoria Pavilion Theatre in 1897. The theatre has been closed to the public for forty years and a campaign for its restoration has been ongoing since 1986.

Walk from the Midland a couple of minutes and you arrive at Frontierland, an amusement park that once had the biggest big wheel in Europe. Owned by the Thompson family, who still operate Blackpool's Pleasure Beach, Frontierland's demolition in 1999 meant there was no more log flume and no more runaway mine train; today, it truly resembles a Wild West, with old wooden structures set on dusty grounds.

Frontierland's closure means there isn't much for young people to do and so families don't arrive – meaning accommodation like the Midland probably does not flourish as it might otherwise. It feels like Morecambe is at a standstill. It is in the town's west end where you can see the harshest realities. When the tourist trade collapsed and the B&Bs closed, students from nearby Lancaster University moved in. They were succeeded by construction workers building the nuclear power plant at Heysham and when they left, there was an abundance of cheap property used to house the unemployed and the mentally ill. It is by the sea, the Lake District is half an hour's drive away, but here you can purchase a five-bedroomed house for less than £100,000. Morecambe's once-proud west end has become synonymous with social depravation.

And so, how does a football club exist in a place where there has been years of economic decline, where the possibility of regeneration was snuffed out by the blow of recession? How does a manager convince players to sign for the club with the lowest budget in the Football League? Can he convince them to live in Morecambe or does he have to do a Barrow? Like the town itself, to what extent is Morecambe FC left at the mercy of decisions being made far away?

Morecambe's compact stadium, the Globe Arena, is a mile inland from the west end, up Regent Road and past a series of speed cameras and sprawling caravan parks. The move to the Globe had been a delicate operation. Joseph Christie, a Manchester merchant and benefactor of the 1920s, gave the previous ground, Christie Park, on condition that 'it should be used by Morecambe FC for as long as they existed and, if the club was ever disbanded, it should become a playground for the children of Morecambe'. Today, the children can only cause mischief in the aisles of a supermarket: the old site's sale to Sainsbury's funded the new £12million Globe, a facility which, despite serving up the champion of pies at the British pie awards for its £2.50 variation of chicken, ham and leek, has not met everyone's taste.

Richard Allan, the secretary of Morecambe's supporters' trust, set up towards the end of 2016 in reaction to the mess left behind by Diego Lemos, had grown up as a Manchester United fan – 'only in the 1980s when they were crap' – but was priced out of attending games at Old Trafford because he was a student and the cost of watching the best team in the Premier League was rising year after year. He studied at Lancaster University, got blind drunk at his first Morecambe match, was introduced to all the directors and players in the clubhouse afterwards, and from there was hooked.

Allan agreed that Morecambe needed to find a new home because Christie Park was outdated and the club needed to diversify its revenue streams to support being a Football League club after promotion from the Conference in 2005.

'But that did not mean we needed to totally change our mindset as a football club,' he says. 'We used to have a few professionals who ran it day-to-day and the rest involved volunteers, who got free tickets, patted on the head and made to feel special for their work. The selling-point of the club was its sense of community. It won't survive without its non-league mentality. The race for professionalism isn't a bad thing but it should never have been at the expense of the core reason that made the club so brilliant to be involved with in the first place.'

In its first few seasons, Allan believes average attendances increased to just under the 3,000 mark because ground-hoppers keen to claim that they'd been to all 92 Football League stadiums started showing up. Five years later, that figure has dropped to below 2,000, with some long-standing supporters giving up, not only because of the team's performances but also because the Globe Arena has never felt like home.

'Christie Park had a big open terrace behind one of the goals,' Allan remembers. 'We've now got something half its size and, instead, a lot of the investment was piled into the main stand, which is very, very nice: great views and good corporate facilities for hospitality and weddings, but delivered with a few rudimentary errors. They forgot to build a place for the groundsman to keep his mowers. They built a bar without a cellar. The club appointed a building firm from Warrington to rush it all through on the cheap. The phrase "grasping defeat from the jaws of victory" was made for the building of this stadium.'

On the afternoon I met Jim Bentley, Morecambe's manager was wondering whether the game against Grimsby less than 24 hours later would be played because of yet another structural flaw: the main stand's height and north-facing roof means that a quarter of the pitch rarely gets any light, and in winter it becomes rock-hard as a consequence. As he pulls down the blinds and looks out of the window to check, a black sheet over the affected area makes it look as though dead bodies might be beneath.

Bentley had arrived at Morecambe at an exciting time. The club had consolidated as a Conference outfit six years after earning promotion from the Northern Premier League when they finished second but went up because the ground of Merseyside champions Marine was three-sided and did not satisfy grading standards. Bentley had met Morecambe's manager, Jim Harvey, and his assistant Andy Mutch in the Village Hotel in Birkenhead.

'Morecambe had a big Liverpool contingent in the squad,' Bentley recalls. 'It's not a bad stretch of the M6. I used to have the other stretch (south) going in the opposite direction when Telford used to train at RAF Cosford, getting over the Thelwall Viaduct. Coming up this way, apart from on a bank holiday when everyone is going to Blackpool and the Lakes, it's not a bad journey. I was in a driving school with Dave McKearney, Robbie Talbot and Adriano Rigoglioso – a Scouse lad with an Italian background who'd played in the same Liverpool junior teams as Steven Gerrard. His nickname was Celi after the Italian singer [Andrea Bocelli] because his family thought he looked like him.'

Its location high in the north means Morecambe is far away from the main media outlets and the club's status in the lower end of the Football League means few national journalists pursue the story when owners like Lemos suddenly vanish mysteriously. Both factors support the impression that geography might have contributed towards Lemos's interest in the first place. Despite travelling all over the country to play games, Bentley is operating in a small area when it comes to recruitment and one thing that hasn't changed at Morecambe is the migration of Merseysiders and Mancunians that go there for a game of football.

'We can't afford to pay players a relocation fee like other clubs,' Bentley says. 'It's hard to convince lads to uproot a family when they might only be here for a couple of years, which is the maximum contract we can risk giving out. If you're in the Premier League, the financial gain softens the blow of moving around. In League Two, you have to consider the whole position of your family because the wife has got to work as well and the kids are settled in school.

'At the moment we've got a lot of lads who live in Kirkby and Huyton. From the M58 you can be in Morecambe within an hour. I reckon 95 per cent of our players have come from Liverpool and Manchester. They'll travel for an hour and a quarter every day, but professionals won't travel every day much further than that.'

Morecambe had not paid a relocation fee in three years.

'When you're struggling for finances, it's the last thing you want to be spending money on,' Bentley says. 'There is a danger with bringing young lads in from London because they might not settle. How's he going to react to living on his own for the first time? Meanwhile, moving house is one of the most stressful things you can do, especially if you have a family. If the player is single you also have the issue of them wanting to go home all the time. Suddenly they're driving to London straight after a home game, maybe three or four hours depending on the traffic, and having the day there before travelling all the way back up. When you add the travelling that's already required, it gets too much for them quite quickly.'

Bentley has one scout and other freelance contributors. Mostly, he relies on the recommendations of contacts and the opinions of trusted friends, and his success in trading proves that you can have Wyscout, you can have spreadsheets and statistics, but there is no substitute for a manager with an eye for a player and one that appreciates what the standards are because he's played himself. Through his assistant Ken McKenna, Morecambe signed Jack Redshaw from Altrincham before selling him to Blackpool for £175,000. Tom Barkhuizen – a cast-off from Blackpool who Bentley had seen on loan at Hereford – was sold to Preston North End for £150,000 having arrived eighteen months earlier for nothing.

'We've got to be able to do this regularly if we're going to survive as a Football League club,' Bentley warns. 'The problem you have is, selling inevitably disrupts the progress of the team because we don't have the benefit of financially being able to train up a ready-made replacement and have him waiting in the wings. Our aim every year is to stay in the Football League. To do that with the lowest budget, the lowest attendances – to keep selling your best players and keep reacting in the best way, it's a huge challenge.'

Sometimes, Bentley loses players when they are out of contract, and this does not help Morecambe at all financially. He'd signed Shaun Miller following the forward's release from Coventry City, putting him on a season-long contract. With his confidence restored, sixteen goals later Carlisle United offered him an improved deal including a relocation fee. Miller had travelled to Morecambe from Alsager in Cheshire every day and Carlisle is an hour and twenty minutes further up the motorway. Jamie Devitt, an Irish winger, went the same way as Miller later in the summer of 2016.

'We tried to keep both of them having put them back on the path they wanted to be on but the financial gains at Carlisle were much greater than ours. They were offered a bigger wage, bigger appearance money and a goal bonus. Fair play to them, you can't afford to say no to that. Carlisle are looking to get out of this division. Morecambe's aim is to stay in it. Who can blame them when they move?'

The odds therefore, were already stacked against Bentley before Lemos arrived and disappeared, causing the players, the manager and everyone else employed by the club to look anxiously at their bank balances at the end of each month.

Richard Allan from the supporters' trust, like Bentley, recalls a 'natural apprehension' when the takeover happened but, having mobilised the fans since – 'to salvage the wreckage if Morecambe ends up in administration' – he believes the prospect of Joseph Cala taking over had a galvanising effect on mind-sets. 'I have no idea why he'd want to buy us either,' Allan says. 'Because he said so much about what Morecambe were doing wrong, a lot of people reacted by saying, "Hang on, Morecambe have been around for more than a hundred years and we've done very well, thank you very much." We're a non-league football club in the Football League and we're very proud of it.'

Allan recognises 'it is always the supporters left holding the baby' when the very worst happens, but the very worst has not happened yet and it's down to the work of Bentley.

'Jim Bentley is one step away from being given the keys to the town in my eyes,' Allan says. 'If that man leaves, the football club will fall apart. He's had his critics over the last few years because the team hasn't done well and the football hasn't been great. But people forget he's got a low budget and the club has been haemorrhaging money. I can't believe another club hasn't moved for him.

'We've got the lowest attendances behind Accrington Stanley, he's sat through transfer embargo after transfer embargo and we've never really sniffed at relegation. We've always had enough to pull clear and he's also brought young kids in and sold them for big profits. Jim Bentley is Mr Morecambe. At some point someone will come with a bucket of cash to prise him away and we'll be a lot poorer for it. I think that time might be coming.'

*

If there is one story of a football manager which reflects exactly where a club has been, then Jim Bentley is that manager. Bentley, a forty-year-old Liverpudlian, has served Morecambe both as a player and a manager for nearly fifteen years. He is an imposing figure at over six-foot tall, with tank shoulders, a shaven head and hands like paint brushes. That he might appear to make an effective nightclub doorman does not mean he is merely a show of extreme muscle and strength. He is forceful and convincing when delivering opinion, as well as perceptive and persuasive. Listen to him and you quickly begin to realise why he has been able to make Morecambe flourish in the most exceptional of dire circumstances. You realise he should win awards for the job he is doing in a crisis and begin to consider what he might be able to do if another club in a stable position decided to hire him.

Bentley has experienced enough disappointment, misfortune and sadness in his life to be able to rationalise what is happening and remain calm in Morecambe's ominous situation. There had been his release from Manchester City as a 21-year-old. He realised he might not be good enough to play Premier League football but considered himself ready for life as a professional lower down. So when deals with Rotherham and Port Vale collapsed because of Danny Bergara's sacking in 1997 and ITV Digital's collapse in 2002, meaning Vale's manager Brian Horton had his budget cut overnight, it might have been tempting to stop dreaming.

Bentley signed for Morecambe from Telford and there it took five years to achieve promotion out of the Conference, a period that included two campaigns where Morecambe's season finished battered and brusied from defeat in the play-offs. Bentley and Morecambe kept going, though, and by beating Exeter City at Wembley in 2007 it meant they were members of the Football League together for the first time, with Bentley finally getting to where he wanted to be at the grand old football age of 31. Amid the celebrations, however, arrived sadness. A week after Wembley, Bentley's father, Jack, died suddenly and he never got to see his son fulfil his lifelong ambition.

Bentley says he might not be where he is now if it was not for his father. Jack Bentley had been with Everton as a junior, playing one game for the first team.

It was at Telford where he became a legend, scoring a record 431 goals over a fourteen-year period between 1963 and 1977. He nearly signed for Leeds under Don Revie and could have signed for Ron Atkinson at Kettering, but remained loyal to Telford because he was enjoying himself. It meant that Bentley's surname was his way in at Telford some twenty years after his father's departure. That summer, Shrewsbury Town had dithered over whether to offer him a contract. Jack Bentley was running a removals firm in Liverpool and so, after deciding to become a part-time footballer and appreciating he needed to make ends meet, son Jim joined his father in the removals business.

'Hard graft,' Bentley calls it. 'It was the fittest I've ever been: dumping furniture and beds all over Merseyside. I'd work from eight a.m. until five, I'd get home and wolf some dinner down then get in a car and drive an hour and a half to Telford using the A roads before training or playing, driving all the way back; getting my head down and waking up the next morning – going to work again.

'To play part-time football and hold down a job, it's a job and a half. If I had any bumps or bruises or kicks on the ankle, there was no way I could let my dad down. He'd need me lifting three-piece suites and it's impossible for one man to do that. There was many a time, I wobbled around the next day after a game. A lot of furniture now is flat-packed so the job has become easier. In the late 90s, you were using glaziers to take glass out and using all your strength to carry settees through window spaces.'

Bentley is conscious of his path sounding like one of those educations at the school of life. It nevertheless reflects the reality of what he had to do to reach where he is. Arriving at Manchester City as a teenager taught him that chance and fortune has a role in opportunity. He was playing for a Sunday league team in Netherley as a fifteen-year-old alongside Derek Hatton's son, Ben, when Derek – the famous left-wing politician from the 1980s – was asked by his friend Terry Darracott, the former Everton player and then a youth coach at City, whether he knew of a side prepared to play a friendly match at short notice in the first week of January. 'I was a centre-forward back then but our centre-half didn't turn up and so I played there. A gang of scallies from Liverpool rocked up at Platt Lane, City's training ground, and won 1–0. Afterwards, Terry asked about me.'

It was arranged for Bentley to spend work experience the following month at Platt Lane under Darracott's wing. 'All the lads in our school were going off to work in factories and shops, so how lucky was I? Two weeks in a football environment, playing a couple of games for the A and B teams. I travelled in with Steve Redmond, who was City's club captain and a Scouser. When he couldn't take me I had to get the train to Maine Road, which is right in the middle of Moss Side. For a fifteen-year-old kid, it was a bit of an eye-opener.'

Upon leaving school, Bentley signed a two-year YTS contract. It meant a train journey every day starting at West Allerton Station, changing at Warrington Central then again at Manchester Oxford Road or Piccadilly, before finding the bus that would take him through the traffic to Maine Road.

'I was the only Liverpool lad in the youth set-up,' he remembers. 'I found the discipline hard at the beginning.' It was a turbulent time to be a City player. Bentley signed when Peter Reid was the manager. After him there was Brian Horton and Alan Ball following a takeover by Francis Lee, the club legend. Steve Coppell lasted forty days as Ball's replacement before Frank Clark was appointed. Bentley captained the reserves and though he was included in match-day squads he never played a first-team game for City. Aside from the move to Rotherham falling through, he later experienced rejection following trials at Burnley, Grimsby and Walsall.

He says he'd have remained longer at Telford had the club not suffered a financial crisis of its own. Two years into his stay, the chairman Andy Shaw decided to go full-time and Telford finished as high as fourth in the Conference. This was before the play-off system was introduced, however, so the achievement was not marked by a chance at promotion. When Shaw moved Telford back to a part-time operation, Bentley had a decision to make. His father had become a taxi driver by then and, having enjoyed being a professional footballer and at the age of 25, he did not want to return to the balancing act of before. Chester made him an offer. Morecambe did too. Chester were run by Stephen Vaughan, the former Barrow owner. Morecambe's manager was Jim Harvey and his assistant was Andy Mutch, old players with the ability to make more persuasive football arguments: Morecambe was becoming a full-time football club for the first time and it excited him that history was being made. He had opportunities to leave, going to places that would have earned him better wages. 'But I was enjoying myself and, like my dad, the routine of being somewhere brought the best out of me,' Bentley says. 'I've never had an agent touting my name around, I always did my own deals going in with a figure that I thought I was worth. There'd be a little battle with the vice chairman who was in charge of the contract negotiations. But we'd settle on a handshake and that would mean something.'

I'd also overheard a conversation between players at another club having lunch together when they thought nobody was listening. Players tend to speak most honestly about the people they encounter in such relaxed settings.

It involved a story about Bentley, who 'everyone loved' because of his spectacular party trick on the back of buses returning from away games, where he proved his ability to eat 'seven or eight' Cadbury Creme Eggs one after another without a break, and without being sick.

Bentley admits he needed to change when he became manager in 2011, succeeding Sammy McIlroy, who had lifted Morecambe out of the Conference. Bentley is not embarrassed to admit that he had fantasised about becoming a football manager since he was a child when he entered a play-by-mail football game where contestants would receive fortnightly updates of their team's fortunes through the post having decided on training sessions, tactics and players.

'I'm more a manager than a coach,' he says. 'It was always something I wanted to get into. As a kid, my dad managed the team I played for, Mossley Hill. He played for the veteran side and he'd drink in the clubhouse with my mum. I'd seen him operate; setting up the team on a Friday night; phoning up the parents of the other kids, making sure everyone knew the arrangements. I'm very hands-on too. As a captain, I enjoyed organising on the pitch as well as off, making sure the lads knew where to be for social events, setting up a fine system for indiscipline and collecting the money; arranging the end-of-season holidays. As a manager, I'm happy to delegate but I like to have an input on as much as possible.'

He thinks being a captain helped develop the communication skills that have underpinned his management, because both roles involve listening to the thoughts of others while maintaining the ability to act decisively. He was used to walking into dressing rooms and the noise levels cranking up a few levels because of his considerable presence, but within a month of becoming a manager his new role would mean the room would go much quieter rather than louder.

In his Morecambe team, 38-year-old Kevin Ellison and 34-year-old Michael Rose are the leaders. He believes there are fewer leaders in football, 'but there are fewer leaders in society – especially when you look at the state of politics', reasoning that social media has had a negative impact on human interaction.

'As much as leadership is about making decisions, it's also defined by the ability to interpret a situation and appreciate how much time is needed before you understand which way is the right route to take,' he says. He realises football managers are considered in black and white terms too, the old school and the new age, and when you're thought of as being in one camp, it can be damaging to reputations. Bentley considers himself 'a bit of both'.

'Lads used to grow up a lot earlier,' Bentley says. 'There was no holding your hand. You had to find your own way. This contributed towards social understandings and leadership qualities. I had a player here. He didn't say a word for years. He was a very, very quiet person. He left the club, went to college, and ended up playing non-league football. I knew someone who went to college with him and they were saying, "God, he's so funny – you want to see the stuff he puts on social media!" I said, "I knew him for two years, he never said a word to anyone!" I couldn't understand why anyone would think someone else is a character based on what he says over the Internet when face to face he's the total opposite. He didn't have any interactive qualities whatsoever. Social media isn't a true reflection of the way things really are.'

Bentley became a football manager just as platforms like Twitter and Facebook became applications on mobile phones, meaning users could pass comment on anything they wanted at any moment of the day or night. He believes this has made the career prospects of managers a lot bleaker than before. Because of his loyalty to Morecambe and his improbable achievements during the 2016/17 season, he's considered a messiah now, but it has been difficult for him to prove his ability as a manager because social media has been empowering for the average fan who wants a say on everything.

'Football crowds have changed a lot,' he says. 'I'm not a sensitive person whatsoever and I've deserved criticism during my time here because everyone is entitled to an opinion, but I'd much rather someone came and knocked on my door and had a pop at me face to face rather than hiding behind a computer screen, caning you when you can't defend yourself. You'll get some championing it as freedom of speech but where is the freedom for the person on the receiving end when they haven't got a clue who's saying it, even if it's nasty? For all the claims social media brings people into contact with one another, the reality is it's driving people apart.'

Simultaneously, another form of media has had an effect on attendances. Morecambe built a brand-new stadium with more space and corporate facilities at considerable cost but in the years since, more games than ever have featured on TV.

'BT Sport are pushing the Champions League. Sky have the Premier League, the League Cup and the Football League. BBC have the FA Cup. It means that people don't have to leave their living room to watch football. A lot decide to stay in. It's cheaper to drink at home, so if you want a couple of pints you don't have to go out. Meanwhile, the cost of living is going up all the time, isn't it? Electricity, water, gas; the weekly food shop has become expensive. I'm a dad and I know what it's like trying to satisfy kids. Years ago you were happy receiving a football for Christmas or a birthday. They want PlayStations and top-of-the-range bikes. I've got a ten-year-old who wants to be seen wearing North Face gear, Berghaus, Canada Goose or Moncler jackets. A lot of parents will do it. There's even more money going out of a household than there was before, even though wages have stayed the same after the financial crisis of 2008. Something has got to give and unfortunately it means live football takes a hit.'

His words lead you towards a conclusion that the work of a football manager is increasingly being judged by a more voracious yet frequently absent supporter base, which means they don't always have direct contact to appreciate fully what is happening. Despite these conditions, Bentley stresses how much he loves his job: 'I consider myself very fortunate to be one of ninety-two professional managers in England.' His approach is practical and unspoiled by the dogma you see in career coaches who speak like they have swallowed coaching manuals. Bentley says things because he believes them, not because he wants to affect the way you think about him. Listening to how he deals with the twin threats of victory and defeat is a free lesson about the reality of management.

'Honest hard work is a basic requirement in my teams,' he says. 'There will be games when we try our best and it won't be good enough. But I can't stand players who go missing when the going gets tough. They are privileged to be professional footballers. The least they can do is battle, scrap and work hard. After that, you're looking for a goalscorer and a bit of experience at centre-half because it's a key position.

'When you're a player and you win, you go out on a Saturday night, everything is buzzing and you feel like you're on top of the world for the next twenty-four hours until your eyes turn to the next game,' he continues. 'As a manager, the stress is enormous. You win the game and you might be happy for a minute. Then the relief takes over and it totally drains you. By the time you get home on a Saturday night, you're done in. You're already looking to the next game. You don't celebrate as much. As soon as the game is finished, you're looking at the other results. "How did they get on? We're playing them Tuesday . . ." You're planning and doing homework straight away. The focus goes from one game to another quickly.

'I've played under managers that come in on a Monday morning and they are down because we've been beaten. They drag it on to Tuesday and they end up having a go at you later in the week about something that has happened on the Saturday. I try not to say too much at the end of a game because emotions are running high and it's never as good or bad when you look at the DVD. Instead, we'll have a meeting before the next training session and identify what messages we need to get across to the players either as a group or individually. The key is never being too high and never being too low. If you're too low, it creates a negative atmosphere amongst the players but if you're too high players can lose their focus.

'At the moment, people tell me I should be looking up because we're only five points off the play-offs,' he says. 'But the first results I look for are the bottom two because that's where we should probably be as a club. At the start of the season, I'd have taken that: lowest budget in the league, nineteen players, transfer embargo, ownership uncertainty, training facility problems. Everything was stacked against us.'

4

FEAR AND LOATHING IN FYLDE

DAVID HAYTHORNTHWAITE IS PARTWAY THROUGH A PACKET OF salted kettle crisps, when he pauses to think about a rival non-league chairman, someone whose fate he learned a great deal from. Like Haythornthwaite, this particular chairman – who ran a club that was pushing for promotion into the Conference North until his health deteriorated – was putting lots of his own money into his local team. The chairman was rushed to hospital and, as Haythornthwaite describes him, 'on death's step' when his wife burst through the doors of the private ward demanding to know precisely where £10,000 a month was going.

'The club was his own thing,' he says, reaching into the packet, holding one of the crisps between two fingers like a prop for emphasis pointing in my direction, as if this was a lesson I should be learning from. 'You know; a football club can be a gentleman's private pleasure.'

The big problem, Haythornthwaite proceeds to explain, was the ailing chairman came from the 'old school', where it was his responsibility to underwrite all the cheques that needed paying at the end of each month, including the players' wages, the water, the gas and the electric.

'His wife was furious when she found out,' Haythornthwaite tells me, grinning

– indicating he might have faced similar wrath. 'Apparently she screamed at him, "If you don't stop with this, I'm going to divorce you!" As I say, he might have died that day. His condition was really serious . . .'

Haythornthwaite is nearly 62 and seemingly in peak physical condition. He has cropped silver hair, he wears a tailored suit, bluey-purple in colour, his cufflinks sparkle and his dark shoes are polished. He speaks with his left leg crossed over the right one and his leather chair squeaks as he leans back into it and finally crunches his way through the last of the crisps, staring out across Mill Farm, the modern 6,000-capacity home of AFC Fylde; the club he has built from a former farmer's field.

What makes Haythornthwaite really interesting are the motives for his involvement at Fylde. The son of a farmer made his millions in animal feed, through his company Vetplus. He was a season-ticket holder at Blackpool for five decades and he tried to buy the club twice from Owen Oyston and his son, Karl. By the way he speaks, you can sense the whiplash of those failures still sting.

'The main reason why I got involved here was because I was a massive Blackpool fan, I'd always gone to Bloomfield Road, and I was fed up,' he doesn't mind saying. 'I didn't think the Oystons had the best interests of the club at heart so I made them a good offer to leave. I suppose now you could say I was prophetic because you can see what's happening. Under [Ian] Holloway, they got lucky – everything happened right for them: they went on to the Premier League and stayed there one season. Look where they are now, though: back where they started.

'I have a saying and that saying is, "I want to 'cos I can. I can 'cos I want to. I want to 'cos he said I couldn't." That's my motivation, because the Oystons mocked me when I tried to take that football club over. "He's got no money, he doesn't know what he's doing," or something like that. I wouldn't describe them as nice people. A lot of the time, that's all the motivation you need, to prove people wrong.'

Haythornthwaite could have got involved in the club he owns now earlier than he did. His friend Dai Davis, the current president, is a wealthy man who had put his own money in before realising Haythornthwaite's deeper pockets could take Fylde much further.

'After my last attempt to buy Blackpool failed my wife, Sharon, said, "You're not even enjoying it any more. Why do you go? All you do is get annoyed." She was right. I was annoyed at the players. I was annoyed at the team. I was annoyed at the manager. I was annoyed at the chairman. They did everything on the cheap. The service in the box I had was poor. I said to Sharon, "You know what, you're right."

That night, Haythornthwaite went for a pint in his local pub and he thought about all of the things that had happened at Blackpool. Owen Oyston had warned in 1988 when he took full control that his running of the club 'had to be done my way', and in 1990 his £60million Soccer City was announced. The arena would be a part of a twelve-acre leisure and commercial complex. Six years later, though – and with Bloomfield Road remaining as it had always been – Oyston was sentenced to six years' imprisonment for raping a sixteen-year-old girl. In 1998, the season Haythornthwaite intervened when Blackpool were so short of cash players had been told they had to buy their own boots, plans for a new stadium at Whyndyke Farm finally fell through and over the next six months there was the first anti-Oyston pitch invasion and sit-down protest, followed by two funeral marches in the town. Karl Oyston was soon to assume control and, though Blackpool would later reach the Premier League, their survival was undermined by what fans view as examples of penny-pinching. In 2011, when the home dressing-room boiler broke down before a game with Liverpool, it had still not been fixed twelve days later when Manchester United came to town. Though chairman Karl Oyston objected to the 'mad world' of 'arms race' salary payments and criticised players for chasing money – saying, 'Sometimes, I think ambition goes out of the window in favour of personal financial gain' – Blackpool's financial accounts for 2010/11 revealed that one of Blackpool's six directors was paid a staggering £11million in remuneration for the season that ended with the club's relegation back to the Championship. The Daily Mail later exposed that director as Owen Oyston, Karl's father. So much else has happened in between that a book is bound to be written about the fall of Blackpool eventually; but by 2017, with fans boycotting matches, Bloomfield Road was almost as ghostly as the town's promenade on a freezing winter's night.

When Blackpool lost in the Championship play-off final to West Ham United in 2012, Haythornthwaite – despite long being Fylde's owner by then – was there at Wembley, wearing his tangerine Blackpool scarf. He'd paid for a corporate hospitality suite.

'Lo and behold, Andy Pilley was in the next box along with all his family and friends,' Haythornthwaite remembers. 'Andy's a massive Blackpool fan too but he bought Fleetwood instead and they're now in League One – in the division above Blackpool.

'If you go on to any of the fans' Internet forums they will say: "Andy Pilley and David Haythornthwaite are the dream ticket. Will Pilley bail on Fleetwood? Will [Haythornthwaite] leave Fylde?" I still look out for Blackpool's results but I've lost the love. That's what the Blackpool fans don't understand: the ones who think I'll return if the chance is there. I won't. Two reasons: I love this club now, AFC Fylde. I also have a responsibility to all the people who've helped me. I could have built all of this with the money I have. But if you don't have fans you don't have a club. You don't have anything. It would be good if the people in charge at Blackpool recognised that too.'

It is not unrealistic to think that within a few years of the publication of this book not only Fleetwood but Fylde too will be above mighty old Blackpool in the English football league structure. Halfway through the 2016/17 season, Fylde were six points clear at the top of the Nationwide North, two leagues below. That eight divisions separated the clubs when Haythornthwaite first got involved at Fylde makes you believe him when he says he will deliver on his promise made in 2007 that by 2022, Fylde will be in the Football League.

The greatest threat to that happening, Haythornthwaite believes, is sustainability. Fylde's first game in the North West Counties First Division in 2007 against Darwen attracted 101 paying spectators to their old ground, Kellamergh Park. Although 2016 has seen the old attendance record of 1,110 being broken five times since moving to Mill Farm (the highest gate being 3,858 for the visit of Lancastrian rivals Chorley on Boxing Day), Haythornthwaite knows that in order for the club's upward trajectory to continue as far as he hopes, it will need more than just his money and vision.

'We don't have a generation of supporters that have been born into following Fylde,' Haythornthwaite admits. And so, while the club's community foundation would be the envy of many a Football League club (on match days free buses run to Mill Farm from Freckleton and Lytham and during the week, cars emblazoned with the club's crest zip between primary schools and junior football teams to undertake coaching sessions), the real short-to-medium-term opportunity in terms of fan recruitment is capitalising on the disenfranchisement felt nearby by presenting something fresh and ambitious.

Haythornthwaite says Fylde can profit from the mismanagement at Blackpool. He was quick to act when he found out Brett Ormerod, a Blackpool icon with goals in every tier of league football, decided he did not want his testimonial to take place at Bloomfield Road because the atmosphere at a ground where he not so long ago scored in a 3–1 victory over Tottenham Hotspur in the Premier League had become 'too toxic' following relegation to English football's bottom tier. The venue for Ormerod's big game? Mill Farm. The Blackpool Gazette described the decision to relocate the game as 'a new low in the seemingly ceaseless saga'.

'Once AFC Fylde came forward and offered their fantastic new stadium as a venue, it was an easy decision,' Ormerod reasoned. 'With [some] fans banned from Bloomfield Road and others refusing to step foot inside, I couldn't have held it there.'

Right outside the door of the boardroom at Mill Farm, under the word 'Inspiration', there is an oil painting of Bloomfield Road as it used to be, with a bank of concrete open terracing behind one goal and a tangerine sun setting over the Irish Sea. On the plaque underneath it there is a message from Haythornthwaite. "I spent many happy years with my father supporting the club at this dilapidated ground," he has written. "Fond memories . . . but it also was a massive lesson to me on how not to run a football club."

There are other images further down the hallway which reveal quite a bit about Haythornthwaite's way of thinking. There are giant photographs of great sporting achievers: Muhammad Ali, Pelé, Ian Botham, Steve Redgrave, Daley Thompson and Nick Faldo; all men who at some point in their lives were considered second to none in their field. On another plaque, there are more words, this time from Vince Lombardi, the legendary NFL coach, who says, 'You've got to pay the price; running a football team is no different from running any other kind of organisation – an army, a political party, a business. The principles are the same. The object is to win – to beat the other guy.'

Brian London stands next to Stan Mortensen under "Fylde Legends". The former Commonwealth heavyweight champion wears a heavy coat, a full moustache and a nose like a squashed potato, standing there on Blackpool's beach in front of the famous Tower, the casinos and grand hotels back when the town was considered a place to be seen. Confusingly, perhaps, London was born in Hartlepool but had earned himself the nickname of 'Blackpool Rock' because he used to work at the factory that made them.

Then you have the three board members who backed Haythornthwaite's involvement at Fylde from the beginning, when many others walked away, 'because they were scared of the progression we might make', as Haythornthwaite sees it.

There is Queen Elizabeth, with her half-smile. There is Winston Churchill

– who one of Mill Farm's three restaurants is named after. There is Margaret Thatcher, with her royal-blue double-breasted Aquascutum skirt suit, her gold buttons and her sense of superiority. 'All of them are people I respect,' Haythornthwaite says, breezily. 'I'm obviously one side of the political spectrum. When it's your own club, you can put who you want up on the wall.'

It is not unreasonable to think that a few years from now, Nigel Farage will be up there as well, the person Haythornthwaite was photographed shaking hands with by the Blackpool Gazette in June 2016, just before Britain went to the polling stations to decide whether it wanted to remain in the European Union. Haythornthwaite grew up as the son of a well-respected farmer and, like many of the working-class Conservatives in Fylde, he has turned to UKIP because he feels the area has been forgotten about by Westminster – even though leaving Europe might cost him lots of money due to his business connections across Germany.

Like Farage, Haythornthwaite has a taste for upsetting the establishment. If Farage went for the traditional elites, Haythornthwaite makes it absolutely clear he is desperate to make Fylde a success to show the Oystons they were wrong to turn him down.

One of Haythornthwaite's central beliefs – something he thinks will help the rise of Fylde – is that what happens in society is replicated in football. Like with Brexit, 'which exposed the chasm between the establishment and the rest of us', as he puts it, he thinks football supporters will abandon Blackpool and Preston North End because they have been taken for granted and many are becoming fed up with the lack of progress in front of them.

'We won't take them for granted here,' Haythornthwaite insists. 'We'll cater for everyone: the bloke that wants to come and have a pint with his mates on the terraces; the companies that want to come and invest. We've got the facilities. We're building the football team.' And then he looks across the pitch from the window of his boardroom, over towards the banner which evokes his promise to deliver league football, one that warns, '2022: Stop Us If You Can'.

'This whole area has been starved, starved of a proper team,' he continues. 'Blackpool languished. They played in a horrible stadium and did not invest. People want to be attached to success. I know people round here go to watch United, City, Liverpool and Everton. For quite a long time, they went to see [Blackburn] Rovers when [Alan] Shearer was there. Preston and Blackpool lost massive support and they haven't been able to get it back because Jack Walker went for it. Things change. They go the other way from where it came.

Many have now walked away from Blackburn because of poor ownership. I want those people from our area who went to Blackburn to come here. Blackpool fans? They are always welcome at Mill Farm. Preston North End? We're on your doorstep too, you know!'

Motorists that travel regularly between Preston and Blackpool should know about the existence of AFC Fylde because the Mill Farm Sports Complex – to offer its full title – is visible from junction three on the M55. You can see Fylde's club crest at night because Haythornthwaite pays the bills for it to be lit up. 'We need to let people know who we are and where we are,' he says. 'We have restaurants and want them filled in the evening.'

Mill Farm not only means AFC Fylde are not hidden from view like they were before, it has brought the club across the fields and back towards Wesham. Until 2016 Fylde were based at Kellamergh Park, which is a few miles south and closer to Warton, the village where BAE Systems have a site and Eurofighter Typhoons are built. It explains why Fylde's badge – the one that lights up for all to see – includes a fighter jet.

Kellamergh Park was a typical semi-professional football ground, surrounded by remote farming land with the Birley Arms public house at the bottom of its car park. At Mill Farm, the fittings and furnishings are of Premier League standard. When Haythornthwaite tells his full-time press officer (hired from Blackburn Rovers) to assist with a guided tour, it begins in the swanky Bradley's Bar – named after Sir Bradley Wiggins, another British champion Haythornthwaite admires. Upstairs (by lift or spiral staircase) there is Milano's, a Mediterranean restaurant that has pumpkin and ricotta tortellini on the menu, along with venison and dauphinoise potatoes. Just over the hallway you have Churchill's, a venue which serves dinners on Christmas day. While plans exist to build a cocktail bar on the roof of the 2,000-seater main stand, six corporate boxes offer what Haythornthwaite describes as 'the sustainable future of this club'. Each one had been sold for the 2016/17 season at prices that rise from £16,000 a year to £20,000. For £65 a game, up to ten guests receive a three-course meal, a well-stocked refrigerator of chilled beer and white wine, as well as access to the cellar where the red is kept.

'The food is as good as anything you get at Arsenal, I swear by that,' Haythornthwaite maintains. 'I want people from here to realise they don't have to drive down the motorway to spend their money. OK, the football is not the same quality as it is at United, City or Liverpool. But I'm a sports guy and I think I understand what makes supporters tick. I love football, cricket and rugby. One sport I don't have any interest in is horse racing. But if someone says to me, though, "Hey, do you fancy Haydock Park for the day?" I'm first on the bus because I know it's going to be a great day out – and that's what everyone will get here too.

'At United they have ten to fifteen thousand people in corporate. You're just a bloody number there, aren't you?' he continues. 'They outsource all the catering and they can do that because they are United. That's my advantage: the top clubs don't treat fans – or corporates – with the attention they should. It's certainly happened at Blackpool. I can capitalise on the wider disenfranchisement. Lots of people deep down want to support the local team. But you've got to give them facilities to go with success. Otherwise, you'll get found out over time.'

Haythornthwaite's aims are high. Though they might prove to be unreachable, he's been involved at Fylde for nearly a decade now. He knows how to run a football club. He understands the non-league scene by the way he speaks authoritatively about the game's governance, other clubs, managers and players. Fylde's growth has been gradual so his optimism is convincing, even if you happen to disagree with his politics or his visions for the area.

For someone who appreciates that perception is everything there are some inconsistencies, indeed, and these might lead to doubts about the potential of Fylde's development. Like Haythornthwaite, Fylde as a region is rabidly Conservative. In the general election of 2015 almost 50 per cent of the vote went to the Scottish-born Tory candidate, Mark Menzies (this increased to over 58 per cent in 2017). Meanwhile, Haythornthwaite's views on Brexit are also in keeping with the majority of people living in his region. Blackpool was revealed as one of the big council victories for Leave campaigners in the country (and Fylde wasn't far behind), with more than two in three voters choosing to back separation from the EU. When the result was confirmed, Peter Greenhalgh, a local agent for Leave, declared, 'The result is not really a surprise.'

And yet, there is one rather controversial issue in particular which might separate Haythornthwaite from others in Fylde, leading me to wonder whether his football club's popularity might eventually suffer as a consequence. Like Boris Johnson – Farage's Brexit accomplice – Haythornthwaite is a supporter of fracking, describing the possibility of it being widespread in Fylde as a 'once-in-a-lifetime opportunity which we must not miss', despite Cuadrilla, the energy company behind the operation, admitting in 2011 that drilling near the Preston New Road had caused two earthquakes.

The morning I visit Mill Farm, Cuadrilla had held a meeting there –

in Churchill's restaurant. Haythornthwaite recognises there will be costs to the natural beauty in surrounding flatlands – 'to some extent' – if he and Cuadrilla get their way, but with Blackpool struggling nearby, he believes this is the region's big chance to rediscover itself.

'I'm a big shale gas fan,' he says. 'We're sitting on the epicentre right here. I have spoken a lot about pride – and I don't think pride is a bad word. I spoke about creating jobs – good jobs. Blackpool is a deprived area. We have pot washers working in hotels on six quid an hour. It's no good, that. How can any person live on six quid an hour? I'd like visitors to come to this area of the country and say, "You won't believe what the little old people of Kirkham have got . . ." rather than look at a place nobody has looked after with no investment.'

It is fair to say that Haythornthwaite's view is not shared by everybody. In 2013, the Defend Lytham group reacted to his pro-fracking stance by posting on their website. Haythornthwaite, they said, had been the group's vice chairman before and had campaigned against a move to deliver social housing on exactly the same Greenlands Farm site where Cuadrilla wanted to move in.

'It does seem peculiar that somebody can spend two years complaining about the impact of a housing development on the town and then ignore the incalculably greater negative impact that fracking will have,' the group pointed out. 'It's like complaining about a wasps' nest and ignoring the articulated lorry which is about to run you over from behind. We do hope he wakes up before it's too late! IT'S BEHIND YOU, DAVID!'

In late 2014, the argument was still rumbling. A letter from John Hobson in the Blackpool Gazette reflected some people's impression of Haythornthwaite.

'It seems like only yesterday that Mr Haythornthwaite, who is himself one of those "wealthy individuals living in big houses" he now complains about, was busy campaigning about a single housing development that he felt would alter the character of leafy Lytham to his own detriment,' Hobson wrote. 'Now he is scathing of people, just like himself, who simply want to defend the local area against an entirely inappropriate level of development, and he claims to be quite happy to accept the wholesale industrialisation. That's really quite a turnaround.'

Maybe it is not a coincidence that a new 'Lancashire for Shale' initiative was launched less than a month after the EU referendum went the way of Leave. Haythornthwaite was there at the group's inauguration in Blackpool's White Tower restaurant. Where he fits in should Cuadrilla prevail and the really big money is made remains to be seen. He describes the subject as 'thorny' but then presses home the idea that the Fylde region cannot ignore the economic reality of the present – relating it too to his political beliefs and the fortune of the football team he runs.

'Ambition is a strange thing: show it when you have nothing and people are frightened – maybe envious,' he says. 'Show it, make progression and, slowly, I believe people will join you.'

*

Old photographs of Dave Challinor usually look a bit like this: his focus is centred on the penalty area somewhere way out of shot; he is leaning on the advertising hoardings at Prenton Park, arching his back; there is a dry towel being applied to a greasy football; his arms are long and fingers even longer. They are the limbs and digits that provide unparalleled trajectory and purchase.

In 1998, the former Tranmere Rovers defender broke the world record for taking the longest throw-in. The distance of 46.35 meters meant he was able to clear more than half of an average-sized pitch and John Aldridge, Tranmere's manager, described his ability as the equivalent of having an 'Exocet missile' available to him.

It unsettled opponents – certainly from a higher level, so much so that it contributed greatly towards Tranmere becoming an excellent cup team. They reached the final of the League Cup in 2000, losing narrowly to Leicester City, and the FA Cup quarter-finals in successive seasons.

Challinor is now the manager of AFC Fylde and attempting to create a very different image for himself. His chairman, Challinor says, works very hard during the week running his animal-feed business, getting up at 5.30 a.m. every day. When Saturday comes around he likes to be entertained by his football team.

'You could argue that the best way to promotion is by going [with] two big lads up front and bypassing the midfield altogether; taking huge throw-ins like mine for Tranmere,' Challinor says. 'Lots of teams go that way but do I think we can progress through the leagues by being a team that tries to pass the ball? Absolutely.'

Challinor has been in charge of Fylde for more than five years. In non-league terms, that's a spectacular length of time considering, as he puts it, 'so many players – and managers – will move upwards at the first sniff, or for an extra twenty pounds a week'.

It is remarkable too because Haythornthwaite is a millionaire chairman who wants to see success delivered in a certain way. For many non-league managers, the challenge is survival; causing the odd upset will do because it offers hope that somehow things might change. Challinor is under a different pressure. Their move to Mill Farm in the summer of 2016 saw the club turn full-time and that means Fylde have an advantage over all the other teams in the Conference North. It is early winter when we meet and Challinor is buzzing because Fylde are top of the league. I believe him when he claims he does not worry about the sack should results turn and his team gets sucked into the play-offs as they have done for the previous two years. Considering Haythornthwaite has planned for three seasons in the Conference North (and then five in the Conference National), Challinor appreciates what might happen if he doesn't take Fylde up this time around.

'You have to enter this job with your eyes open,' he says. 'Football is really cut-throat. I want to manage in the Football League. But I realise too there are 92 teams in the Football League and I am one of thousands upon thousands of people with exactly the same ambition. So it's going to be difficult. It's going well here at the moment and I'd like to take Fylde into the league. But I realise too that dynamics and feelings can change quickly. When things go really wrong, it's the manager that goes first, not necessarily the players – because it's easier to sack one person attached to a contract rather than eleven. You've got to be thick-skinned in this job. I realise that at some point in my management career, I'll probably get that dreaded phone call, whether it's here or elsewhere.'

Challinor achieved unexpected success at Colwyn Bay with two promotions before dropping back to the level he started at in management to take over at Fylde, when they were part-time and in the first division of the Northern Premier League. His application letter to Haythornthwaite was written by hand, something the chairman thought was unusual. 'It was coherent and legible,' Haythornthwaite said at the time, 'very odd for a football manager.' He could have appointed the experienced Graham Heathcote, who'd spent most of his adult life playing for, coaching and managing Altrincham, but ultimately chose Challinor because 'I go with my gut even if it might be viewed as a risk.'

Challinor has since harnessed a reputation for developing young players. Haythornthwaite says he has also taken Fylde forward while working within a strict budget, despite what outsiders might think. Rough spells have been short.

'Only once has the owner come to me on the bus and said, "Chally, I wasn't happy with the application today." That happened at Tamworth when we lost last season 3–1. He wants the players to wear the badge with pride. If we work our socks off but are unsuccessful, he'll take it – he's old school in that way. It would be fair to say that some people are a bit scared of him because he's so confident and ambitious. But he's not unreasonable. There's not a necessity to win here but an ambition to win, to improve and be successful.'

Many will visit Mill Farm and be envious of what they see. Look around the changing rooms, for example, and you could be at Manchester City. Challinor and Haythornthwaite visited City's spectacular Etihad Campus before the final designs for their new stadium were drawn up. There were also research trips to Wembley, Bristol City, MK Dons and rugby union's Saracens. Haythornthwaite is proud that he has been able to replicate all of the small details made possible by Abu Dhabi money at Fylde. 'The toilets are exactly the same. So is the hand moisturiser.' Haythornthwaite recognises other non-league clubs see Mill Farm and are jealous of the facilities but it is the players he thinks about the most. 'I want them to come here and think, you know what – I'll play for Fylde.'

'We've gone from being one of the most attractive part-time propositions to one of the least attractive full-time propositions,' Challinor continues. 'Being able to show players the bricks and mortar of the stadium helps because in the past we've had to show them pictures and designs and some mightn't have believed us.'

Because Fylde are full-time and because their owner is a millionaire, a natural perception exists that Fylde are able to outspend all of their rivals in the division. Challinor is adamant this is a misunderstanding, especially with the emergence of Salford City under the guidance of former Manchester United players, the Neville brothers, Ryan Giggs, Nicky Butt and Paul Scholes.

'This season our highest-paid player is on £750 a week,' Challinor reveals. 'When I go to meet potential new signings, I see the disappointment on the faces of the players and the agents when it comes to sorting out finances. The expression says: "I was expecting double that . . ."'

Although Haythornthwaite is not against selling because 'success in football – like in business – can amount to how well you trade', the club's wealthy reputation explains why Fylde have been able to keep hold of many of their best players. Halfway through the 2016/17 season Danny Rowe was the club's leading scorer with 31 goals in just 21 league games. That run included six hat-tricks and two games where he scored four times. He was well on his way to passing the previous campaign's record of 37 goals by the time I met him (he'd scored 31 times the year before that). And yet, Challinor believes Football League clubs have been put off trying to sign him because they think his wages are much higher than other non-league targets.

Rowe has blond hair and looks a bit like Roger Hunt. At the age of twelve, he made national headlines after leaving Preston for Manchester United in a deal worth £136,000. To many media outlets, none of whom had seen him play, he became a superkid. Listening to him now, there is a sense that he is just about beginning to love the game again after the disappointments that followed.

'I didn't really see the fee United paid for me as pressure at the time as a kid, but as I became a teenager, I lost a lot of interest in football because I probably overdid football,' Rowe admits. 'The demand from the club was enormous in terms of the travel and the time. My performances weren't as good. After being let go at sixteen, I was very close to quitting the game because my enjoyment had gone completely.'

Rowe dreaded bumping into familiar faces on the street in those early weeks after leaving United. 'They'd say, "How's it going at United?" Then you'd tell them what'd happened.' He went on trial to Blackpool and is not afraid to describe that process as 'embarrassing because I went from being the kid from Blackpool at United to the one who's being assessed whether he's good enough to play in the same team as lads he was thought of as being a million times better than a few years earlier.'

Rowe played parks football for nearly four years before being asked to sign for Kendal Town. From there he moved to Fleetwood, where he played a few games in the same team as Jamie Vardy, a future Premier League winner and England international. Then there were loan spells at Stockport County and Barrow. He wonders, at 26, whether what he describes as 'the business of football' rules against a move to a club in League One or the Championship because he might not have so much of a sell-on value in a few years.

There are other players in Fylde's team with more time on their hands. One of them is James Hardy, a nineteen-year-old winger who was released by Manchester City despite Patrick Vieira's recommendations that he should remain at the club. Hardy had been let go from Rochdale at sixteen because coaches believed he was too small and slight to play league football. While Rowe did not grow up with any self-worth issues and rejection therefore stunned him, Hardy has always been driven by the pursuit of proving those people wrong who had doubts about his physical capacity. It says much about his state of mind that he was able to leave City and flourish at Fylde – five leagues below – almost straight away.

'There used to be an attitude towards non-league football: players are there for a reason,' Challinor says. 'Now, because of Jamie Vardy, everyone is looking: can we find the next one? Non-league clubs have become wiser. They are starting to protect themselves financially. Clubs higher up might want the next Vardy but it will cost them. James Hardy falls into that bracket. Ideally we'd like him to carry on his journey with us for a few years. I think it would be better for him. If a Premier League club were to come and take him now, he'd play under-23 football and it would be a backward step in his development. Here, he's playing against real men. He gets to understand what three points really means to a football club.'

Challinor says Fylde's full-time status has undoubtedly helped performances and results, with many outcomes being settled in favour of his side towards the end of games, when true levels of fitness are revealed. Promotion would mean the challenge continues in the Conference National, 'a different beast'. Challinor says he has learned great lessons from the experiences of his close friend, Neil Young. Challinor played under Young at Colwyn Bay before he took over at Chester, a club he led to three successive promotions. 'Suddenly they hit mid-table in the Conference. Suddenly, people started questioning him: "He's taken the club as far as he can."'

In the 2016/17 Conference National season, all but six of the clubs involved were professional. Challinor takes confidence from the idea Fylde are ahead of schedule in their development because they will already have had a year as a full-time club behind them if they do go up, and therefore their first year in non-league's top flight will not be transitional, as it has been for others – who have since been relegated without being able to return.

'We're building a club from nothing, really, so the foundations have to be right first,' he believes. 'Of all the clubs that have made the step we want to make in the last fifteen years, only two clubs are league clubs now and that's what our ultimate aim is. A few have gone out of existence and others, like Droylsden and Hyde, have plummeted back to where they came from. Promotion without planning can finish a club. We don't want that to happen here.'

In England, you have the FA Cup, the FA Trophy, the FA Vase and the FA Sunday Cup in order of profile. At the end of Haythornthwaite's first season as owner of Kirkham and Wesham FC, his team reached the final of the FA Vase, a national competition for clubs at step four of the non-league pyramid (i.e. the ninth tier and below). The final was played at Wembley against Lowestoft Town. His team won, 2–1.

That summer, however, Kirkham and Wesham were no more. Enter AFC

Fylde. Haythornthwaite had been frustrated by the lack of support in London. Among the 19,537 spectators in London, only 3,500 were from Kirkham and Wesham, the merged club founded only in 1988, initially competing in the Lancashire League.

Before the game Haythornthwaite had called a friend from the nearby village of Freckleton whose name did not appear on the list of people that had bought tickets. 'He said to me, "I'm not going to support that Kirkham and Wesham shit . . ." It suddenly made me realise how parochial football is. We were at Wembley but Freckleton was the next village where people had long memories related to the successes of their football, cricket and rugby teams. If I was going to build this club, I had to get the whole of Fylde behind me.'

Historically, indeed, the Fylde region is synonymous with rugby union. Bill Beaumont, he of the cabbaged ears, captained England to the Grand Slam during his thirteen seasons at Fylde Rugby Club, whom he had joined as a seventeen-year-old. Their home in the village of Ansdell is just a few miles away from Mill Farm.

'I haven't told anyone this before, but eventually I want to drop the AFC in our name because it sounds a bit old-fashioned,' Haythornthwaite says, leaning towards me – somewhat secretively. 'A lot of the re-formed clubs call themselves AFC: like Wimbledon, Liverpool and Blackpool. One day, we'll just be Fylde. At the beginning AFC was used to distinguish ourselves from the rugby club. But we're much bigger than them now.'

Since Fylde's rugby club currently plays at a higher level than the football team, Haythornthwaite's opinion might be viewed as an exaggeration, although in terms of facilities and trajectory, you can see what he's getting at. He feels the need to tell a story about his first committee meeting, which was held at the Conservative Club in Kirkham. He remembers arriving at 7 p.m. and by 11 o'clock the hot topic of the day was still being discussed: they were still arguing about why someone hadn't taken the bin out from the far corner of the ground. 'I said to Dai afterwards, "That's the last time I sit through four hours of nonsense."'

Within a couple of months, Haythornthwaite had outlined his 2022 project and Kirkham and Wesham were permitted entry into the North West Counties Division Two, six promotions away from their target.

Ten million pounds later, AFC Fylde are here: a professional club that is able to hire a chief executive in Neil Joy who has traded dealing with ruinous PR wars at Oldham Athletic like the one involving the potential signing of Ched Evans when he was released from prison, for rather more progressive responsibilities, which involve setting up a commercial infrastructure in preparation for what might happen in 2022 or perhaps even before. 'At Oldham, I was fighting fires and trying to keep the ship afloat,' Joy admits. 'Here, it's different. We are only at the end of the beginning.'

Joy prefers to use Burton Albion's rise from the Northern Premier League to the Championship as an example for Fylde to follow rather than nearby Fleetwood Town – the club who, under the guidance of their Blackpool supporting owner, upset Haythornthwaite in the summer of 2016 when they signed Dion Charles, the promising twenty-year-old Fylde winger, for nothing after a mix-up with his registration. It prompted Haythornthwaite to leave a statement on Fylde's website.

'I have made my feelings known in no uncertain terms to their chief executive Steve Curwood and their chairman Andy Pilley,' Haythornthwaite wrote. 'This episode unfortunately shows the really bad side of football and some people's total lack of ethics.'

He concluded: 'The fact that no one from Fleetwood has even had the decency to call us sums it up. It is dog eat dog and nothing else.'

5

COD WARS

DAVID HAYTHORNTHWAITE MIGHT NOT ADMIT IT PUBLICLY BUT THE blueprint for what he is trying to achieve at Fylde has been set by another club located just fourteen and a half miles north of Mill Farm. Fleetwood Town's owner, as Haythornthwaite says, is Andy Pilley, the multimillionaire who decided to invest in football at the suggestion of his bank manager in 2004. Like Fylde, Fleetwood's journey began in the North West Counties League, albeit the first division rather than the second. Unlike Fylde, it took Fleetwood just seven years to reach the promised land of the Football League.

'I never dreamed that I'd get the chance to be involved at a level as high as this,' admits Pilley, who made his fortune quickly by going into business with his sister Michelle, building the energy supplier BES Utilities from his spare room after being left unemployed by the collapse of energy company Enron. A season-ticket holder at Bloomfield Road, he had watched Blackpool for a quarter of a century. He also used to run FC Anchorsholme, a Sunday league team which 'probably had more going for it than Fleetwood when I came here'.

'A very different animal,' is the way Pilley describes Fleetwood at the beginning. 'I think there was eighty people at my first game. The whole place was pretty rotten, in a real state of disrepair. The pitch was terrible; the club house was awful – there's no wonder it was taking something like twenty quid on a match day because nobody wanted to be there.

'It became a project that grew arms and legs. We were fortunate to get out of the North West Counties League straight away because there were twenty-four teams and only one promotion spot without any play-offs. It became somewhat addictive from that point because there's no better feeling than achieving promotion; some palpable success.

'We went on a magical journey through the non-league,' Pilley proceeds to explain, 'six promotions in the last ten years, which was an incredible feat. They were all different and unbelievably enjoyable for different reasons. From the Northern Premier League first division, we went up thanks to a penalty in the last minute when we needed a four-goal swing at Brigg Town in Lincolnshire. Steve Macauley put that one away.

'The next year Witton Albion were fourteen points clear of us at Easter. We were in second place when we went to Witton and turned them over and reeled them in to win the title on the last day.

'The year after that was even more controversial. We amassed more points than Southport but Farsley Celtic went bust in March and the points we earned against Farsley were expunged. Farsley had beaten Southport and it meant that Southport won the league on a technicality. We appealed to the FA. Ultimately, the destiny of the season was decided in an executive box at Wembley following a short enquiry – a huge disappointment.

'From there we found ourselves in the play-offs and were pretty fed up with that. We lost 2–0 in the first leg against Droylsden but recovered to reach the final on penalties. Promotion into the Conference came because of a goal five minutes from time against Alfreton.

'First year in the Conference we got to the play-offs, which was a great achievement even though we got smashed by Wimbledon 8–1 on aggregate. They had a great team that year: Danny Kedwell and Kaid Mohamed up front, players like that.

'The next year we invested five million pounds into the stadium with a new stand. That's where I decided to base my business and it has been a really good fit because I've been able to bounce from one meeting where I'm talking about utilities into another where I'm discussing a new centre-half or a striker. I'm the ideal tenant because I always pay the rent!

'We also made it our business then to go out and get what we considered to be the best players in the Conference. We took a punt on a certain Jamie Vardy from Halifax. That move paid off incredibly well . . .'

After promotion to League Two, Vardy was signed by Leicester City. Three years later, he became a Premier League winner and an England international.

'If anything we sold him on the cheap,' Pilley reflects. 'The record for a non-league player was £250,000. We got a million. Somebody asked me, "How much will you take for him?" I only said a million because I thought no one would pay it. In the end, six clubs made offers and he chose Leicester. I remember saying to him half-jokingly, "I look forward to seeing you on Match of the Day and playing for England one day, Vards . . ." His story has been incredible. A real Roy of the Rovers tale.'

Vardy's success coupled with Fleetwood's promotions has forced Pilley into a rethink, sharpening his business model. Whereas before Fleetwood powered through the divisions by taking the best players from other teams, Pilley realised this approach would be unsustainable in the Football League. In the 2016/17 League One season Fleetwood were competing against Bolton Wanderers, Sheffield United and Charlton Athletic: clubs with significantly bigger stadiums, higher budgets and longer histories – all factors footballers consider when choosing who to sign for.

The competition and Fleetwood's minnow status explains why Pilley's latest investment is the £9million Poolfoot Farm complex, Fleetwood's new training centre in Thornton, a few miles south of Fleetwood. Having been opened by Sir Alex Ferguson, it is just seven months old when I visit Pilley on a wet Monday morning in January. Ferguson recommended to Pilley that he considered siting the facility's main gym in front of the training pitches, knowing the views of team-mates running about in the fresh air would give injured players an incentive to get fit again as quickly as possible. Ferguson had taken the idea home with him following a field trip to Barcelona. So what is Barcelona's is now Fleetwood's as well.

Pilley is a confident talker, taking you through his thoughts at speed and with authority from behind a desk inside his office where the title of 'Chairman' is stretched imposingly across the door.

'Poolfoot Farm is fundamental to our identity in terms of who we are and what we want to be,' he says. 'We're fully aware that we have to develop players and give a chance to lads that haven't made it in the Premier League; we have to give a chance to the lads who are ripping it up in the non-league: we've got to be that rung on the ladder – the stepping stone to the top. But we can only develop players if we have the facility to develop players. We've got to be able to attract raw talent to this part of the world and polish rough diamonds, moulding them into what we want them to be in order to flip them and sell them. In any business, you have to trade well, and the commodity we deal in is football players. We want to repeat the trick again and again: scout well, recruit well, buy sensibly, develop, give opportunity, watch them flourish and then sell them on.

'Football is a food chain and there's nearly always someone who is bigger than you,' he says. 'If your players do well, unless you are Barcelona or Real Madrid, another club will offer bigger wages. Of course, we now have China on the horizon and that puts an entirely different light on what's happening.

'It has been a huge investment but for a club like Fleetwood it is the way forward because otherwise, forever and a day, I will be putting my hand in my pocket and signing big cheques. Sustainability at the highest level possible is the ultimate goal.'

When making a decision about who to sign for, footballers also think about geography. Bolton blurs into Greater Manchester, England's third-largest urban area, with shops, restaurants and wealthy areas to live in close by; Sheffield is a big city in its own right; and then you have Charlton – in London. To get to the finger of land that is Fleetwood you have to miss out Blackpool and follow the murk of the River Wyre until it spills out into the Irish Sea like an infant's bile. Fleetwood, Pilley reminds me, is the smallest town to have a club in the Football League. The aim is to get as many of the 26,000 inhabitants interested in the welfare of the team because, unlike AFC Fylde, Fleetwood's location means the only other direction they can attract supporters from is the south. 'We're on a peninsula,' Pilley says, ruefully. 'We can't get any more fans from the north, the east or the west because we are surrounded by water: river and sea.'

Fleetwood, indeed, is the only place in Britain to have three lighthouses and this reflects where it used to look for salvation. From the Esplanade, which runs parallel to the town's shoreline, two tributes recognise Fleetwood's fishing history. The first, entitled Welcome Home, is a statue of a mother holding a baby beside a young child, gazing out across the ocean with hope and concern. The second is a sculpture called Out to Sea. On a plaque below, the inscription reads: 'Past this place, the fishermen of Fleetwood have sailed for generations while their families have watched from the shore. Their courage and comradeship under hardship is a living legend.'

In the first half of the twentieth century Fleetwood had been a deep-sea fishing port – the third biggest in England. Money was plentiful in those days; the fishermen returning to land after three weeks out at sea would collect bulging wage packets and have their egos massaged as 'three-day millionaires' because of the way their shore leave was relished. One story tells of a strong deckhand heading straight to the nearest British Legion club, sinking one too many pints of bitter and missing the birth of his child as a consequence.

The trawlermen had worked in hostile Arctic conditions, with a number of boats reporting back to the Admiralty during the Cold War, having agreed to carry surveillance equipment in order to spy on the Soviet Union.

Following a two-year stand-off involving Royal Navy frigates, rival fleets and Icelandic gunboats, the fishing grounds crucial to Fleetwood's trawlers were, however, claimed by Iceland due to the European Community's decision to endorse the country's declaration of a 200-mile fishing limit around its coastline.

Though the decline of the fishing industry had started before 1976, Europe's intervention was remembered and it goes some way to explaining why Fleetwood, under the district of Wyre – like Fylde – backed the Leave campaign during the referendum of 2016. At its height, Fleetwood had 120 trawlers and figures were similar in places like Hull, Grimsby and Aberdeen. Considering fishing had directly employed 11,000 people in Fleetwood – a third of the town's population – there were very few people left unaffected by the Cod War with Iceland.

The outlook in Fleetwood became bleaker. A government decommissioning in the 1990s aimed at preserving fish stocks led to many fishermen selling off their vessels. Though 1,300 trawlermen across Britain were given a share of £190million from the government in 2001 for losing their livelihoods in the aftermath of the Cod War, the issue had run sore for twenty years by then because of discrimination between payments to employers and workers. Trawler owners were entitled to reparations in the 1970s but the fishermen who worked on the boats were not. It was argued that many of the workers were 'casuals' and not entitled to financial assistance, even through social security payments. By then, many of those affected by the decision had died – along with any optimism in communities like Fleetwood, where in 2016 the last remaining trawlerman put his boat up for sale because he could not afford to make it pay.

Though the weather is terrible when I visit, a horizon once dotted with masts and funnels is now empty. The nets have disappeared from the dockside and so has the whiff of fishy gold.

*

The seafood isn't caught locally now, but a processing centre in Fleetwood still provides 600 jobs. From another factory the famous lozenge Fisherman's Friend is produced and exported around the world.

In recent times the real energy, pride and ambition in Fleetwood has been displayed through the emergence of its football club, one that had folded twice before Pilley's arrival. Its previous high point was an appearance in the FA Vase final of 1985, losing to Halesowen Town at Wembley in front of 16,000. Between 1997 and 2002, it had been known as Fleetwood Wanderers and Fleetwood Freeport and when Pilley first became interested, the average crowd at a crumbling Highbury stadium was 134. Though Highbury is the smallest of all the stadiums in League One, during the 2016/17 season it was the one closest in the lower leagues to being filled every week.

Pilley recognises the performance of the team is usually reflected in attendances. He recognises too that unless Fleetwood establishes itself as a part of the town's fabric, it will end up dying.

That is why, eventually, he wants to see some local players in Fleetwood's team. It is a contributing factor to the building of Poolfoot Farm – what he describes as 'a community facility with a sensible business plan'. There are five-a-side, seven-a-side and eleven-a-side 4G pitches for hire from £15 per hour. All of Fleetwood's first-team training sessions are open to the public with a bar and a viewing platform provided to watch them.

'My challenge has been to keep the tills ringing and help us get into the black rather than the red. Fleetwood Town is a restaurant and a bar but this facility will also develop footballers,' Pilley states. 'Who knows, there could be England players amongst the kids playing down there.'

It annoys him that he did not receive a single penny in central funding.

'There should be, in my opinion, some of the huge amounts of money from the Premier League finding its way back into grass roots. It shouldn't be for wealthy businessmen to do it.

'The facilities in this country are shocking,' he continues. 'This comes from someone who used to run a Sunday league team. I know the good that can do: the spirit and character building; you make friends for life. I don't think it's too big an ask for the FA to provide funding at least to make sure the pitch is cut and marked.

'There's far too much focus on the very big clubs. On Fleetwood's journey, I've met chairmen who make the cups of tea at half-time. They mop the dressing rooms on Thursday nights. Clubs like that, if they've got a leak in the ceiling, there should be some financial assistance to help them out. There's so much money washing around at the top end, a fairer distribution of the wealth – I think – would be appropriate.'

Fleetwood's first-team squad has Scousers, Mancunians, Brummies and some international players, Northern Ireland's first-choice right-back Conor

McLaughlin being the highest-profile of them. Pilley decided to invite all of the football agents based in the north of England to see Poolfoot Farm because he realises their influence is crucial when it comes to a player making a decision. For those non-leaguers with raw potential from other areas of the country – all of whom are given the minimum of a two-year contract to first prove themselves in the club's under-23 development team – he has bought a house on Blackpool's promenade where they all live together. Pilley seems to appreciate that if he rolls a dice enough times, he'll probably get lucky eventually – like he did with Vardy.

'I like working with people who are on an upward curve,' Pilley says. 'It's sometimes harder when you get players from the Premier League giants and try to sell them Fleetwood. It's not the case with all of them but there are delusions of grandeur. In their eyes, they are still a Liverpool or Man United player. The reality is, they've never played! We have to try and convince those players that it's worth taking a step backwards to take a step forwards. Not all of them get it. They don't see themselves running out at Fleetwood and it being a sign of progression. They think, what the hell's this? A huge amount of success in sport is down to mind-set. If your mind-set is right, your productivity will be right. The good thing about these lads from non-league is, they come to Fleetwood and they're excited.

'I've got a lot of respect for non-league football. I think there are some excellent players out there. We've got several: our captain is Nathan Pond and he's played more than 650 games for Fleetwood. He's been with the club even longer than me and was involved in the team for my first game. The Guinness Book of Records have recognised him as the only player to earn promotions from six divisions, which is an astonishing achievement. His story shows there are exceptional talents if people are prepared to work with them. Pondy's career is one we want to recreate in others. At the moment we have a striker called Ashley Hunter who came from Ilkeston in the Evo-Stik Premier League, a club in Derbyshire that has a great record with young players in recent seasons. We believe that with full-time training, and with the benefit of sports science and analysis, we can turn non-league footballers into established Football League players.'

Pilley's appointment of the heavily bearded former Bolton Wanderers defender Grétar Steinsson as technical director in 2015 reflects that Fleetwood is looking out to sea again for inspiration – even to Iceland, where Steinsson is from. His remit is a broad and significant one; his presence meaning that whenever a manager leaves Fleetwood, a revolution does not have to follow.

'I've been through four managers in thirteen years and I don't think that's too bad,' Pilley says. 'Sometimes there has been a necessity for change, especially with the trajectory we've been on. I'd liken our journey to climbing Everest. You reach certain checkpoints along the way with guides who are familiar with the level. When they move up they're sometimes unfamiliar and in any business you need a change of leadership sometimes. At the moment, we have Uwe Rösler and he's doing a fine job. He understands League One.

'Grétar's involvement is about continuity. You cannot ignore what other clubs are doing and lots of chairmen are quick to press the button and terminate contracts. Though it's not something we like to do, we have to prepare ourselves for the prospect of another club higher up taking our manager – like one of our players. We don't want to be in a situation where the manager leaves and all the backroom staff goes with him and I'm left with a kitman.

'Grétar takes care of our scouting but we arrive at joint decisions. There's a misconception that all technical directors sign the players and the manager doesn't get a say. That would be a stupid approach – we'd never do that. What it really means is, the manager – in this case Uwe – can focus on what he's good at and that's being out on the grass, coaching and making the players better.

'The amount of networking required in football is immense. Grétar spends a lot of time building relations with the big boys in the Premier League, meeting with the scouts, the first-team coaches and the development coaches. There simply aren't enough minutes in the day for a modern manager to do all of that. As and when Uwe moves on, which I guess will happen one day, we can shake his hand and continue in the direction we – as a club – are going in without too many twists and turns in different directions.'

For a provincial club, Fleetwood's model is outward-looking. Pilley does not mind calling it 'European'.

'A lot of the media have been too quick to dismiss the idea this approach can work,' he recognises. 'But when you look at the lack of success the English national football team has had – and really, the lack of success by English clubs competing in European competition, despite the huge wages we pay from the enormous sums of money that comes in from Sky TV – we haven't been hugely successful compared to the Europeans. So there must be some merits to this system. When you study it, it makes perfect sense. I'm quite pleased that we're at the forefront of adopting it. When you look at the other clubs that have gone the same way, they've done really well – they're punching above their weight: Southampton, Huddersfield Town.'

If there is a ceiling for Fleetwood, Pilley concedes it might be in the Championship. He reminds me that during his first few years of involvement, nearly all of the calls to the club went through his office with the conversations that followed going something a little like this: 'Yeah, the kick-off is at three p.m. on Saturday as usual.' Fleetwood's next step – the Championship – would pit them potentially against Newcastle United, who had traded almost £150million worth of players the summer before.

Now, Fleetwood Town employs more than 400 people. Pilley describes the change from non-league to Football League being 'night and day' financially. 'You get around £35,000 in central funding from the Conference and £800,000 in the Football League. That doesn't take into consideration all of the extra travelling supporters you get and the advertising opportunities. In total it is probably a seven-figure swing.'

He insists he takes no pleasure in seeing the demise of the club he supported as a boy, Blackpool. You wonder whether he would give all of this up to bail them out, but he is more cautious when asked questions related to the shenanigans at Bloomfield Road. When Fleetwood first met Blackpool in a competitive fixture, it was an FA Cup meeting between Conference and Championship sides. Karl Oyston reacted to the draw by saying, 'I don't think it is a big fixture at all – I think it is just one that has caught people's imaginations. If we had drawn Manchester United, that would have been exciting, but a Conference club isn't wonderful. I can understand why people are getting excited, but if we had drawn any other Conference side, then a word would hardly have been said.'

Andy Mangan, a former Blackpool striker who had moved to Fleetwood, reacted on social media, writing: 'I find the comments disrespectful and a bit embarrassing. Everyone has to start from somewhere.' He proceeded to claim that Blackpool fans would prefer to have Pilley as chairman rather than Oyston, describing Pilley as a 'proper fan with a passion for football', before adding: 'Let's see what happens Saturday.'

If Oyston was speaking the truth, then he wouldn't have cared that Blackpool's victory was by five goals to one that day in 2012. If that result were to be replicated now, it would be regarded as something of a shock.

'Blackpool's always going to be a club that is close to my heart,' Pilley says. 'It's such a shame they are where they are because it was fantastic for the town when they reached the Premier League. The feel-good factor was evident for the entire Fylde coast. Football is a story of ups and downs. They'll be back – perhaps not in the Premier League – but this current chapter will surely end before too long.'

Pilley thinks it unlikely that Blackpool will soon have a second club from the area overtaking them. He believes there is one key difference between Fleetwood and Fylde: Fleetwood is wedded to a town, therefore commanding a degree of loyalty. AFC Fylde, meanwhile, takes the name of a region – and there are no other professional clubs in England named after regions.

'Fair play to David – he's really gone for it,' Pilley says, presenting a rival's smile. 'I suppose he has the draft for what needs to be done from us just up the coast, though personally, I'm not sure whether I'd fancy doing it all over again because it is so, so difficult to get right.

'You can get through the lower divisions of the non-league if you invest but it gets really difficult in the Conference because there are so many full-time clubs with the same idea and, ultimately, there are only two promotion places – one of them through the play-offs. The best of luck to David, though. The next season it looks as though he will be in the Conference. That will be the real test to see how well set-up and capable AFC Fylde really are. But do I think Fylde can get out of the Conference without investing heavily, though? No.'

What links Fleetwood Town and AFC Fylde is the ambition of their chairmen as well as question marks about their business activities. While Haythornthwaite supports Cuadrilla and many in the area many don't, the offices of Pilley's energy firm were raided by Trading Standards in the summer of 2016 as part of an investigation into allegations of mis-sold energy to customers. Although no charges were brought on that occasion, the company Pilley owns agreed the previous November to pay out £980,000 after Ofgem discovered breaches to its licence.

There is an underlying feeling from speaking to Pilley and Haythornthwaite that in a sporting sense both are motivated by the challenge of shredding accepted norms as well as the thrill of going their own way.

'Critics say, "These clubs – they have no history." Well, I say to them: "So what – we're making history",' Pilley concludes. 'Football over the last 150 years has been full of stories where smaller clubs have risen, replacing more established ones. I don't think it's a bad thing. You live today, the past has gone. Football would be boring if those who say that Stockport County should be in the Football League because they've always been in the League simply as a matter of entitlement. When that happens, you are taking away hope and opportunity. Hope and opportunity is the reason people go through the turnstiles. And if you knew what the score was going to be, you wouldn't even go, would you?'

VALLEY, HILLS AND MARSHES

6

PUBLICITY PETE

PETER RIDSDALE WAS ONCE CONSIDERED AMONG FOOTBALL'S FINEST administrative communicators, the chairman that may have made running the club he supported sound like a timeshare operation by describing it as 'living the dream'; though certainly, everything about Leeds United did smell of glorious potential back then.

Years later, he is inviting me into his confidence, leaning forward and perhaps taking more time to consider his thoughts than he used to from inside one of Preston North End's unprepossessing business offices a few feet away from Deepdale's main stand. Preston are doing well in the Championship and have an outside chance at promotion to the top flight, a level they have not competed at during the Premier League era. Ridsdale has been an adviser to Preston's owner Trevor Hemmings for nearly five years and in that time, Preston's on-field and off-field performances have improved each season. Every person I speak to, whether it's an employee at Preston or a supporter, speaks very highly of Ridsdale. They say he has transformed the mood not only because fundamentally he is a reasonable person who treats colleagues the right way but also because he has helped Preston switch from being a Championship club with a League One mentality to one that is dreaming of achievements above its recent historical station.

It does not take much for conversations about Ridsdale or with Ridsdale to creep back towards Leeds, however. I had travelled to Preston with the aim of speaking mainly about his relationship with Hemmings, the enigmatic and reclusive almost-billionaire who rarely says anything publicly. What happened at Leeds is always there, though – looming over his shoulder like a grim spectre.

The charge sheet against Ridsdale is extensive, it follows him wherever he goes; even if he succeeds there is always that reminder: Remember what he did at Leeds? In the consciousness of the football world Ridsdale is to Leeds what Nick Leeson became to Barings Bank. Unlike Leeson and Barings, Ridsdale did not bring Leeds down because they still exist, and he had long departed when the club reached its lowest point. Yet he is considered responsible for signing the contracts that supposedly relied on revenue from Champions League football, sanctioning agreements with outside sources to pay for players which meant that Leeds did not really own them at all. Critics say that his decisions started a decline, which ultimately meant that six years after appearing in the semi-final of Europe's elite competition, Leeds began the 2007–08 season rooted to the bottom of English football's third tier with a fifteen-point deduction. It has not been forgotten either that after Leeds United Ridsdale ran a sports consultancy firm which failed with debts of £475,000. Subsequently, he was disqualified from being a director of any company until 2020 after an inquiry by the Insolvency Service found that he'd diverted payments into his own personal bank account.

None of this deterred Trevor Hemmings from recruiting him, though. Hemmings, the richest north-west football club owner raised in the region, spoke to people at the other clubs he'd represented. The word back from Barnsley, Plymouth Argyle and Cardiff City was overwhelmingly positive. Each had suffered financial difficulties and each had risen again under Ridsdale. Hemmings needed help making football-related decisions and, though Ridsdale was banned from signing contracts or committing the club towards financial liabilities, the role of chairman and adviser to the owner on his investment was within the law.

Today, Ridsdale seldom grants interviews. 'This is very rare,' he tells me. 'The reason I don't do them any more is because I think a lot has been thrown back in my face. Henry Winter was here at Deepdale before the Arsenal FA Cup tie and he wrote a very balanced piece in The Times. I've known Henry since my Leeds days. I think anyone who knows me appreciates that I always try to tell it like it is. I can be blunt but I always tried to accommodate the media. But now, I try very hard not to do anything. My view is, what's the point? Very few people try to be even-handed. The number of journalists who understand football finance are relatively few so when they start talking about the debt at Leeds, there is little context in the reporting.'

It's quite a retreat from someone who gained a reputation as Publicity Pete.

'Before the fallout at Leeds, I was on the FA board; people were talking about me as a potential FA chairman,' he reminds me. 'It was a role I never wanted or sought because I preferred working for a club – the club I loved, Leeds United. I think it was a classic case of building somebody up and knocking them down. I was certainly built up beyond anything I deserved. So the minute something went wrong, I got a good kicking. It was probably my own fault to some degree for allowing myself to receive the positive publicity. People called me Publicity Pete, they thought that I sought interviews, but genuinely I didn't have try very hard to court publicity. When you are in a leadership position and the club you are representing is a public company, you have no option. With the benefit of hindsight, I'd have done a lot differently in terms of the coverage of the football club. I was naive; if someone called me asking for an interview I'd do it, when I should have said no. To this day, I feel a lot of the criticism about what went wrong at Leeds was totally unreasonable because it didn't happen while I was there. Since Leeds I have worked at four clubs and while I've had the ability to influence, we haven't gone backwards. I brought Barnsley out of administration. I had an outstanding five years at Cardiff – a club that was bust when I walked in. When I went there, the papers said it was a disaster for the football club. When I left Cardiff the journalist who wrote the article was big enough to tell me in private that it was my departure that in the long term was, in fact, a disaster for the football club. Then at Plymouth, the club had run out of cash and nobody was paid for eight months. I agreed to work with an administrator and keep it alive. We kept it alive then found the new owner, James Brent, and it's thriving again. If you talk to Plymouth fans they will confirm I played a major part, though nobody gives me any credit. Not that I want it, but what I don't like is receiving criticism for everything when it goes wrong.'

'I was on the board for ten years at Leeds before I became chairman,' he continues. 'In that time, we won the old Second Division in 1990 and then the last First Division title before it became the Premier League in 1992. For five years after that, the club returned to the wilderness. The year before I became chairman we were mid-table and going nowhere. Quietly, we built a team – initially under George Graham and then David O'Leary. The day I resigned we had a debt of £78.9million. Sixty million of that was on a 25-year mortgage. The issue was, none of the players had relegation clauses but, with all due respect, the club had not been outside the top five during my time as chairman. Whilst you might say, "Well, you should have done . . ." when you're signing Mark Viduka, Robbie Fowler and Rio Ferdinand, you are trying to explain to them that you are aiming to get from fifth to first not from fifth to twentieth. I didn't envisage a relegation. So the debt and the wage bill caused a problem, though that happened after I'd left – eighteen months later.

'Leeds had twenty-two full internationals when they got relegated but many of the players were players I'd never heard of,' he adds. 'I believe – I honestly believe – that the actions taken after I'd gone actually got the club relegated and the relegation caused the problem. Unless a club has a sugar daddy, there are always going to be issues to overcome because you are going from a Premier League TV deal to a Football League TV deal. Was it surprising what happened to Leeds? Not once it had been relegated. Do I believe Leeds would have been relegated had I stayed? No, I don't. Do I believe the debt was a problem? Not if it was a Premier League club. People write that the debt was dependent on Champions League football. Not at all! The club had only been in the Champions League once. But people don't want to know that because it doesn't make a good story. Nobody analyses what happened after I left. The week after I left, the team went to Charlton Athletic and won 6–1. Three weeks later it went to Highbury and won 3–2 against Arsenal, handing the title to Manchester United. That's the team I left behind.'

Ridsdale's departure from Elland Road came soon after a press conference where he sat with O'Leary's replacement, Terry Venables, the former England boss staring into the arc lights and television cameras, not attempting to pretend there was a basic friendship between them. Ridsdale had told Venables upon his appointment that Jonathan Woodgate would remain a Leeds player. Suddenly, Woodgate was being sold and Venables was furious. 'To get to fourth in the Premier League you have to have an excellent squad, not just a team,' he said with Ridsdale shuffling awkwardly beside him. 'You have got to cover all eventualities and we haven't got that. Money is more important than players here. We have lost players I don't think any club could have lost without suffering in the league.'

'From there, the Leeds fans turned,' Ridsdale remembers. 'I had to have security guards at my home and I couldn't walk through the streets on my own. I think Terry did it to mask the fact we weren't doing quite as well under him as we should have been. The reality was, Jonathan had never been the same player since his trial with Lee Bowyer [Woodgate and Bowyer were charged with assaulting an Asian student in 1999]. Jonathan had lost weight, he wasn't fit –

Newcastle were offering good business. So he had to go. Obviously you can't disclose those things when you sell a player because you are trying to get the maximum value.

'Two months before selling Jonathan we had the AGM at Leeds and I received the highest percentage vote to re-elect me that any director has ever had. The shareholders trusted that I was able to run the club. But after six weeks of security guards I went to the board and told them I was leaving. It was a big mistake because from there, I was not able to control the narrative – I was on the outside. I should have brazened it out. I honestly believe Leeds wouldn't have been relegated had I stayed. Easy for me to say, but I think my track record since suggests that might be more than just bravado.'

Though he retained the trust of some shareholders, the same could not be said of the fans. He takes a deep breath before beginning to explain why the blame for what happened is viewed to be his, why that supposed trust eroded so quickly. Ridsdale had two executive colleagues: finance director Stephen Harrison, who had previously held the same position at the spectacles firm Dollond and Aitchison, and fifty-year-old operations director David Spencer, who joined Leeds in 1994 after running a catering company. With them sat two men still described by Ridsdale as 'among the top non-executive directors in the country': the high-flying Asda boss Allan Leighton, who was later to move to Royal Mail, and Richard North, then finance boss of the old Bass brewing firm and later chief executive of Intercontinental Hotels. Ridsdale describes the group as harmonious, though beneath them tensions festered among non-executive members of the board.

'Some people were jealous,' he says. 'We had a number of incidents where I chose to be high-profile, rightly or wrongly. The first of which was Galatasaray; I felt as though I had to show some leadership because two of our supporters had been murdered. We then had the Bowyer–Woodgate issue, which took two years between the incident and the end of the trial [in December 2001 Bowyer was acquitted while Woodgate was convicted of affray but avoided a prison sentence]. I think the world believed that the [verdict] was difficult to fathom. Leeds suddenly went from being a club that everyone seemed to like because of the brand of football we were producing with young players, to a club that everyone seemed to hate. We sold Bowyer and we sold Woodgate because it was something we had to do. The fans didn't understand and there was a backlash. The trial had affected his fitness and form. The biggest mistake I made wasn't the debt, it was the decision to resign and walk away. Having resigned and walked away, two things happened. The first of which was an interview by Professor McKenzie, who took over from me as chairman, where he absolutely lambasted me for overspending and that stuck even though the club was relegated under him and his successors. It might have been an attempt to deflect attention from the fact there were other high-profile figures on the board with power limitations before and some of those were still involved after I left. Mud sticks. I read stuff about my time at Leeds and most of it is nonsense.'

Professor John McKenzie had described Leeds as 'like an oil tanker that was heading straight for the rocks', adding, 'The trouble with oil tankers is they're two miles long and they don't turn around in two minutes.' Tucked away among the invoices in his new office, was one that astounded him – £240 for goldfish to adorn Ridsdale's office. Ridsdale was known by football agents as 'Father Christmas' because of the way he would accede to the most outrageous of their demands, and McKenzie, a professor of economics, confessed he was shocked by the way Leeds spent vast sums on frivolities or, as he put it, 'indulgent spending'. The chairman's goldfish, indeed, ended up becoming as much a symbol of a failed regime as Imelda Marcos's shoe collection.

'Nobody ever bothered to ask, "Who is Professor McKenzie?"' Ridsdale says, frustrated. 'He joined the board. He was recommended to me by one of the non-executives, though I won't say who it was. He became chairman within a few weeks of my departure and a few months after that resigned, never to be heard of again. It feels to me that it was an attempt by the people running the club to divert away from their own shortcomings. Where is Professor McKenzie now? Why did he only stay for six months? Why was his first interview about me? Did he have the necessary experience to run a football club in the first place? Was that six months crucial in sending Leeds in a direction they did not want to go in? Talking about the two hundred quid a year we spend on goldfish in the boardroom, it was pathetic. That stuck with me. To some extent, I'm glad it has. Because if the only thing they can have a go at me about is goldfish, well, I'm happy. The club was turning over eighty to ninety million pounds a year. What they forget is the team that was left behind: Mark Viduka, Alan Smith, Aaron Lennon, James Milner, Nigel Martyn, Paul Robinson, Scott Carson, Gary Kelly, Danny Mills and Ian Harte. If you go through the team it was phenomenal. How did they let that team slip away?

'Very few have ever written the absolute truth,' he believes. 'When I was chairman at Leeds we were fifth, fourth, third, fourth and fifth in the Premier League while reaching two European semi-finals. After I left, it unravelled. In my opinion that happened because the people who succeeded me didn't know what they were doing. People also forget that I was chairman of a club that was a fully listed PLC, with some heavyweight non-executive directors. It wasn't the Peter Ridsdale Show, it was Leeds United PLC. The club had not been outside the top five during my time as chairman.'

I ask him whether he would take more responsibility if others came forward from the shadows to admit their role.

'Am I sitting here saying no mistakes were made? Of course I'm not,' he says. 'Everyone makes mistakes. But do I believe the meltdown at Leeds was anything to do with me personally? No, I don't. Do I think it was to do with the board? I think it was to do with the board in place when they got relegated, not the board that was there when I was chairman. If you look at the decisions that were taken, the summer after I left they appointed Peter Reid – their decision, not mine. They brought in players I'd never heard of . . .

'People inside football are not a problem. People in football know what actually happened. They understand what success I brought to Leeds, they understand the success achieved at Cardiff, they understand what is happening here. I have since proven that I am able to stay within wage budgets and run prudent businesses.

'The major issue is outside of football. I can get on a train and people will use words that shouldn't be allowed anywhere near the English language to me and I've never met them before. They're saying it because they think I did something at Leeds. You think, what's it got to do with you? I had a situation at my daughter's school a couple of years ago where a lad came up and started insulting me about what happened at Leeds. I asked him how old he was. He told me. "How old were you when I was at Leeds – three, four? What gives you the right to say to me what you've just said when you don't know what you're talking about?" This is at a fairly expensive private school where you'd think they'd be able to think things through. That's what I have to put up with. I'm not complaining. It comes with the territory. When you have success it can be very enjoyable.

'Because Leeds was my club, do I get upset? Yeah. I think it's better to run a club that is not yours because it's easier to be balanced. But that doesn't mean I'm not as passionate here today at Preston North End as I was at Leeds. I'm particularly pleased that Preston North End isn't all about me, or at least, it isn't perceived as being about me. This is about Preston North End and Mr Hemmings. A fantastic owner.'

*

Travel east from Blackpool and the signs say you are travelling on Preston New Road. Drive away from Preston and the same tarmac claims to be Blackpool's. It makes it difficult to tell whether responsibility is being stated or relinquished for the A583, the old single-lane highway that used to be the main link between places where proper rivalry once existed way before AFC Fylde were born, when Preston and Blackpool played in the top division and boasted players of superior calibre like Bill Shankly, Sir Tom Finney, Jimmy Armfield and Stanley Matthews.

According to Armfield the rivalry between the clubs had been reasonably friendly before, but things started to change in the 1950s when a key debate emerged between supporters: who was better, Blackpool's Matthews or Preston's Finney? In 1970, the enmity gathered momentum after Blackpool went to Preston and won 3–0 thanks to Fred Pickering's hat-trick. In a crowd of 34,000, 15,000 were visiting supporters. The victory not only meant Blackpool were promoted from the old Second Division into the First but it also contributed towards Preston's relegation to the third tier for the first time in the club's history. 'The real rivalry started that night,' Armfield said. 'It was such a significant result for both teams. Many fans walked back to Blackpool and our bus passed them on the way home, dancing and singing by the road.'

By 1994 Gary Peters had become Preston's manager. He remained until 1998 and throughout that time he would not say the name 'Blackpool' in public, consistently referring to the club 'from down the road', as 'that lot with the tower' (note he uses the word down rather than up).

In 2008 Karl Oyston was still giving interviews and Blackpool's chairman described himself as 'probably the person with the fiercest tribal views you can get', as the sides prepared to face each other. 'I feel like telling the manager to feed the players on raw meat all week,' he said. Preston's 3–1 win at Deepdale, however, meant his declaration that 'it is not to be underestimated how strongly I feel about this game' ended up seeming like it went unheard by Blackpool's players.

There are other, more sinister stories. In 1978, a Blackpool supporter was stabbed to death at a Vibrators concert in Preston. Seventeen years later, 76 arrests were made following several pitch invasions during a Friday night game broadcast live on Sky television. It was a night which proved that at least there was something some people from the area could agree on: both the Lancashire Evening Post and the Blackpool Gazette dubbed it the 'Night of Shame'.

Preston and Blackpool have spent most of their recent history seemingly trying to avoid each other, with Preston's highest league placings correlating with

Blackpool's lows and the other way around. While Preston have not featured in the English top flight since 1961, Blackpool last reached the Premier League in 2010 and were relegated straight away before falling and falling – and so, for the time being, it is Preston in the ascendancy. When you think that Blackpool missed out on David Haythornthwaite's money, and Andy Pilley ploughed money into Fleetwood instead – consider too that a large chunk of Blackpool's town centre, including the Tower and the Winter Gardens, is just one of the many investments made by Preston's owner Trevor Hemmings, along with thousands of pubs, millions of square feet of industrial property, hotels, racecourses, Littlewoods Pools, betting companies and dozens of horses – including three Grand National winners. Hemmings was also behind the proposal to fit Blackpool with Britain's only supercasino, potentially allowing the depressed seaside town to reassert its position as the country's most popular tourist destination; but instead it went to Manchester before plans were scrapped. At the time, Hemmings was only a minority shareholder at Preston. Perhaps business success further up the Fylde coast would have switched his sporting allegiances.

Hemmings, after all, grew up in Leyland, Lancashire – not Preston – and spent his holidays in Blackpool. The son of a munitions operative, he left his secondary modern at fifteen and started working life wiping grease off diesel trains, attending a business studies course at night. Having taken a job as an apprentice brickie, his first fortune was amassed through a housebuilding business. Now worth close to £1billion, Mr Hemmings, as he is known to Ridsdale, is one of Britain's wealthiest – and least known – tycoons; someone who rarely grants interviews and never discusses his work when he does so. Those close to him give little away – as if sworn to protective secrecy.

Ridsdale is prepared to offer some insight into the reasons for his boss's involvement in football. I suggest to him that the majority of owners with Hemmings's wealth would have thrown vast sums in an attempt to reach the Premier League. In 2016 – a summer where Newcastle bought players for £60million, selling for nearly £90million – Preston bought at £650,000 and sold at £2.2million – the kind of transactions Andy Pilley at Fleetwood would be proud of.

'You've got to go back to how he made his money,' Ridsdale says of Hemmings. 'Of all the businessmen I've worked with in football, he is the best. All of the money he's put into this club has been his own. But what he doesn't do is misspend it. He wants to pay fifty pence for every pound. He wants value for money. We're debt-free because he keeps things on a tight rein. Yes, it would be easy to squander lots of cash at it, but that's not him and it's the right way to be. He appreciates that money has allowed a laziness to creep in. There are players being bought and sold in the Championship for nearly £15million when the reality is, they're only worth £2million. There are players on £3million a year when really, they should be on £15,000 a week. The Premier League's income has enabled a shift in thinking and a lot of owners are being very adventurous and unrealistic with it. I think we've got players at this club who are as good as the high earners at the top of our league or even the bottom of the Premier League.'

Perhaps Hemmings appointed Ridsdale because he saw value where others did not, like his approach to signing players. Perhaps he appointed him because he appreciated Ridsdale's interesting background meant questions would get directed one way during points of contact at a club where the trajectory has not been rapid but nevertheless upward. Hemmings knows more than most that empires are not built in one day. He lives between bases in Jersey, the Isle of Man, Ireland and Chorley in Lancashire. I was told there is a black-and-white photograph in one of his studies where a young man in bricklaying attire is ready to go to work. Hemmings has not forgotten where he came from; the old days of firing engines on the railway, from Preston to Ormskirk and Southport, cleaning those engines down with oil rags when he was finished. Rivet-carrying, boiler-making and lathe-milling in a motor vehicle factory were among his other responsibilities.

In an interview with the Daily Telegraph in 2008, where he spoke mainly about his passion for horseracing, Hemmings explained that his perspective is born out of a childhood which involved relocation from Woolwich in London during the Second World War after his father, Monty, was offered a job at the Royal Ordnance Factory in Chorley as a means of escaping the Blitz. He was only four years old then but he could still name the streets on the estate to which they moved. 'Linton, Balmoral and Conway.'

'Nothing was easy,' he admitted. 'I always remember, as you do, my parents not being able to meet the bills and having to ask people to wait another week. They didn't like being in debt.'

From the beginning of their relationship, Hemmings's instruction to Ridsdale was very simple – a message born out of childhood experience.

'First of all, we operate in the black,' Ridsdale explains. 'The challenge I had with the management was to help the team get back to the Championship within three years and we did that in year three. From there, the plan was to establish ourselves in the Championship and do what we could do to reach the Premier

League for the first time in the club's history. I believe we are on that path. Every year since I've started working with Mr Hemmings, we've finished in a higher position than the year before. Our whole strategy is to do better the next year. If you do that, at some point you'll get promoted.'

Preston North End had been the original Invincibles, becoming the only club before Arsenal in 2003/04 to go an entire campaign unbeaten, after finishing the inaugural Football League season as champions. Despite Preston doing the double a year later, despite winning the FA Cup again in 1938, despite greats like Shankly and Finney later playing at Deepdale – as well as David Beckham on loan before he became a superstar – the second half of the century and the beginning of the next witnessed a flat-line, regression and then slight improvements in between, which fell in line with the fate of the area where Deepdale exists. Hemmings bought North End outright in 2010 and since then, Lancashire Council's central government grant has been almost halved from £30m to £18m, leading to cuts in everything from community engagement to parks and leisure centres. Though Preston became the first northern city to implement the living wage and has since been named as the best place to live and work in the UK, it has also been described as architecturally 'hideous', largely due to the presence of one of the ugliest buildings in the country, its bus station – or, the 'concrete lasagne'.

'This is a football club with a fine history,' Ridsdale says. 'Why it has never been in the Premier League, I cannot answer. You'll see from the infrastructure it has the stadium to be in the Premier League. Geographically, if we were in the Premier League we'd be able to attract more players – Manchester isn't far away and players want to live there because of its fashion, its restaurants and its property. Yet it's very important to remember who we are. Because of Sir Tom Finney we've always been able to have the image of being a gentlemanly club because Tom was a gentleman. I only knew him briefly but he was everything you'd want a person to be and an ambassador [Finney died in 2014]. But I think we still benefit from his reputation – in an era where there aren't many gentlemen left.

'I've been asked on a number of occasions, "Would you take X player?" Now, X player might be very talented but if we think there's a certain part of his personality that doesn't fit with this football club, because it's proud Preston, because it's Sir Tom's club, we won't take them. This might be to the detriment of the short-term success but we have spent a long time becoming who we are and I certainly don't want to destroy that and neither does the owner. It means we take our recruitment very seriously and there are certain personalities we wouldn't take come hell or high water. Any corporation would do this: ask themselves what makes the company tick, whether it's IBM, Shell or Apple. Then they hire people that fits their culture. That's what we do and what a lot of other football clubs don't.

'Everything here is professionally done,' he continues. 'Preston has stability in terms of ownership. It's a debt-free business and we don't overspend on wages or transfer fees. It is prudently run. We are the club that wants to demonstrate that prudence can still bring success – much like Burnley, who have smaller resources than us and are flourishing in the Premier League under a fantastic young manager in Sean Dyche and a board that does not get carried away.'

A reflection of the way Ridsdale approaches key decisions came in early 2017 when two Preston team-mates, Jermaine Beckford and Eoin Doyle, started fighting each other on the pitch at Hillsborough against Sheffield Wednesday. It was not another Woodgate–Bowyer moment but Ridsdale needed to help Hemmings decide on how to react, especially in an era of instant media coverage. What followed quickly were bans and big fines – soon enough, Doyle was sold. 'My only thought was, this is our business – this is our reputation – they are our employees. It didn't cross our mind how they would react. If they'd have railed against it, we'd have put them on the transfer list immediately.

'A friend of mine is Stuart Rose, who was the chairman at M&S. He used to joke with me that he was running a multibillion-pound organisation and yet, he could never get the column inches we have in football. I open the Lancashire Evening Post and every day there's three pages about Preston North End and nothing about Marks & Spencer. So football gets a disproportionate amount of publicity for the size of the business. Why does that happen? Because if you've won at the weekend, people go to work with a smile on their face. Our influence on the locality is therefore disproportionate to the size of the business. But that's the unique environment of football. It is more than a business. We can't just be seen to be doing the right thing because fans are smart enough to see straight through it. We simply have to do the right thing.'

'The only advice I ever give to a new owner is to go out and get the best manager he can afford,' he continues. 'That doesn't mean the most expensive, either. If I had a list of all the current active managers and I had to choose one for Preston, the list would be pretty short. Many managers are recycled failures. Many only fit certain situations. Simon Grayson came here because he'd got three other clubs promoted out of League One and he'd done it each time without huge sums of money being thrown at him. He's a very good coach. But we also looked at his personality and how he fits us.

'A lot of owners get suckered into superstar players – wanting them as managers. There aren't many superstar players who have proven themselves. A lot of the best managers have been OK players, but certainly not superstars. Football is filled with people who throw traditional recruitment processes out of the window. If you're in a normal business and you need an IT specialist, you put a job spec together and go and recruit the best person you can afford in that field. Football doesn't do that so much. But the clubs that do are successful.'

Sympathisers of Ridsdale, those who might read his words here and think he is not to blame for everything that happened at Leeds - might afford shades of grey: acknowledging he made mistakes – high-profile ones – before concluding this does not make him the worst football administrator that has ever been. Maybe his role at Preston suits him because his responsibilities are not definitive and it is not his job to sign bills. Comments from Ridsdale in his 2007 autobiography prompted David O'Leary to call his former chairman a 'deranged man'. Ridsdale admitted then to being 'naively intoxicated' by the early success achieved at Elland Road. I wondered whether his passion for Leeds and his ambition to give West Yorkshire some pride back as Manchester United's achievements propelled them into a new financial stratosphere had overcome standard working sensibilities he discovered at Top Man. At Preston, he is a more experienced operator and the club's stable position is a reminder that just because someone might have got something wrong before, it does not necessarily mean that person should be lost to football forever, providing the right position is there to let them back in.

'In football, when you are in a leadership position, the majority of people don't know the basis of your decisions,' Ridsdale says. 'Fans always want to know all of the facts but you can't tell them everything, no matter how much you want to. What you do is, you don't lie to them. You only tell them what you really can. I learned in retail you only really learn when things are going wrong, and when I left Leeds the criticism was a jolt to the system because I still think I did a good job there.

'Loads of people in the States say you're not really a success unless you've already failed, because failure is a part of life and dealing with it is what defines you. In Britain if you fail they'll try and grind you to dust.'

7

LITTLE OLD BURNLEY

AT FIRST AND SECOND GLANCE SEAN DYCHE DOES NOT APPEAR TO be the most sympathetic of characters. He is judged to be the toughest-looking manager in the Premier League. He is six-foot tall with shaven ginger hair, a ginger goatee beard and ginger sideburns that are sharpened at the ends. He is the manager with the voice that sounds like it has passed through a cheese grater, a voice that nevertheless commands authority. He is the manager with the presence of a warden at a maximum-security prison who possesses the sort of tough humour that can deal with dangerous inmates. He is the manager of a football club from a struggling Lancashire town where there are blizzards in late April.

Dyche could be the Lord of Winterfell. With his arms folded and his sensors activated, he is looking out of the sliding windows in his office and scanning the treacherous terrain of Burnley's Barnfield Training Centre, as youth-team players try to control passes in the wind. The snow has turned into bullets of hail and this has been the pattern for a few days. It explains why, on Dyche's desk, there are tissues and a bottle of cough medicine. In Burnley the frosts are longer than they are elsewhere in the north-west due to its meteorological position high beside the Pennines. You have to be prepared to play for Burnley; to play, indeed, for Dyche. This cold is not defeating him, though. He is wearing his Burnley training kit: short-sleeved shirt and shorts short enough to reveal the enormous thighs of a central defender, the sort forwards would bounce off during an eighteen-year career in the Football League. Beneath his flip-flops, there are mud stains on his socks. The marks point to the probability that training sessions earlier in the day had taken place with the help of Benilyn.

Dyche is the longest-serving manager at a Premier League club in the north-west. That three of his five seasons were spent in the Championship is a testament to both the vision and understanding of Mike Garlick, the chairman that appointed him, and his own resilience; to rise, to fall and to be able to rise again. Under Dyche, Burnley were promoted into the Premier League, relegated and then promoted – this time returning as champions. When I meet him, he is on course to becoming the first Burnley manager to survive relegation from the top flight since 1975. In terms of what clubs spend in relation to their league position, Burnley were the third-highest achieving team in the 2016/17 Premier League season. Despite breaking their own transfer records the summer before, Burnley had still spent the lowest amount on players in the division by some distance. Their fourteenth position in the table represented a gap of six above expectation, if money counted for everything.

Despite his achievements, Dyche had become a categorised manager at Burnley, a manager who favours 4–4–2, a manager who favours hard-working, direct and physical football over technique and flair, a manager who prefers British players over foreign. While his supporters admire him for speaking in plain facts and commend his ability to cut through all surrounding hyperbole, critics say that simply answering questions about why British managers get overlooked for top jobs, makes Dyche a Little Englander; that considering Burnley voted overwhelmingly to leave the EU, Dyche is in the ideal place – where people will truly believe him, working for a club that might as well rename itself Little Old Burnley because he mentions it so often when discussing the challenges that face him.

I wanted to know from Dyche what it was like being the Premier League manager with the lowest budget while working in an industry where everyone thinks you have everything. I wanted to know to what extent Burnley's geography dictated the club's fortune. I wanted to know as well what he was really like, whether preconceptions about who he is and what he thinks were true and how he manages them; can he shift them?

There was a simple question to start with and it related to endurance: how he'd remained as Burnley's manager for nearly five years when so many of his contemporaries had been sacked – especially those that had faced relegation or been sucked down the Championship plughole.

Dyche jumps straight in, quoting Howard Wilkinson – Leeds United's old manager, not known for his charisma. '"Win, survive, succeed," Howard used to say. Football is very different to other industries, though it is often compared regardless. If I was planning a financial strategy for, say, HSBC, you wouldn't plan for success in three weeks. You'd look ahead to six months, lay a mark in the sand, and then have a recap on progress. Six months later you'd have another recap. After eighteen months you'd be able to assess whether a plan was working – a year maybe. In football, after three weeks people are already making decisions about you. You are thrown into a pot and you have to swim immediately. You feel like you are floating on a melting icecap. He's right, Howard: "Win, survive, succeed." Win meaning literally: can you win your next game? Survive meaning: can you win enough games for people to trust you? That then gives you the chance at succeeding, whatever that might constitute.

'My definition of success isn't just about results – it's the general state you leave a club compared to when you join it,' he continues. 'I don't like the term "project" because it sounds so transient, like you flip from one project to the next – and some managers do, by the way. It's not just about the eleven on the pitch. Are you affecting the welfare of a club positively? It's a dangerous term to use, caretaker, but that's what I am, a caretaker. The keys are with me for a while. It's my duty to take care of the place.

'Now, recruitment is very, very, very important when you talk about first-team football and winning. Whether you get it right or wrong it can have a massive affect because of the short-termism that I've just been talking about. Whereas if you are in charge of the academy and you are recruiting sixteen-year-olds each player – usually no matter what – you've got a two-year window to try and make that sixteen-year-old become a player. As a first-team manager, there's no way you're getting two years to see if that teenager can become a player. He needs to be ready and settled within six months max.'

The themes of man-management, coaching techniques and recruitment appear regularly throughout this book. I ask Dyche what he thinks are the most important.

'I must say, man-management is not a new thing. It's been around a long, long time. It started, I think, with Brian Clough – or Bill Shankly before him. I was at Forest as a player when Clough was there. It's more vital now just because of the higher standards players set in terms of the way they live their lives and what they have experienced having come through the academy systems. Players are more educated in the mechanics of football than they were: they have certain expectations from managers in terms of the information they receive and the quality of that information.

'I think analysis of off the pitch wellbeing is the future of football personally, that's where the breakthroughs will be because the demands are getting so, so high. The information circulated by your camp (the media) can be so brutal and social media can be so acidic, I think players need help to deal with the intrusion and be in a prime state to perform at the highest level. As players get older they gain an understanding of modern life but they still need aid – no matter what they earn – because dealing with the fact that everyone has an opinion on you is not a thing the overwhelming majority of teenagers and young adults have to deal with.

'Coaching is still important,' he says. 'We've been through an era where coaches have become the managers but I think it will return to the way it was before where the managers manage and the coaches coach because at the top level, the demands are so high – that includes the Championship where the pressure on managers is becoming similar to the Premier League in terms of lifespans because owners are so determined to earn promotion.

'There is a difference between stretching and panicking. Stretching is good: testing yourself, the players, the staff – seeing whether you can deal with a target that usually would not be a target. But when you are stretched to the point where there is so much going on, how are you meant to see the wood from the trees?

'Years ago, I did a football course with the LMA [League Managers Association]. A fella whose name I can't remember came in and did a presentation. It was about politics in football, about managing upwards. It was also about leadership. He spoke about definitions of leadership, about knowing what to do when you don't know what the answer is. That, for me, sums up the pressure of football management because everyone is looking at you to lead. You know what you are doing but you do not always have every answer immediately because there is so much going on. You're often thinking, there's that much to do here – where do you want me to start?

'I remember speaking to managers in the past who were devo'ed when they lost their job – I mean, really devo'ed. They cared, they had big plans and all that. Now, they're almost like, "Oh well!" The change has happened because they are being measured on such an unrealistic landscape, there's not that kind of broken biscuits thing. "Oh well, that happens!"

'The cult of the manager thing? It's gone too far in my opinion,' he concludes. 'I'm amazed at the media attention that's on managers. It used to be about the players and the teams. Games used to be about Keane versus Vieira. Now it's Wenger versus Mourinho. Now they mention the teams and automatically it becomes a war between the managers. Pep coming to the Premier League and managing City at the same time Mourinho's in charge of United has taken it even further.

'I appreciate this is because managers are the first point of contact for the media now – before and after matches. We act as spokesmen for the clubs we represent because we are accessible through contractual obligations and the players aren't quite as much. That means what we say becomes newsworthy and because the cycle of news relies on the most up-to-date thing that has happened and because press conferences follow matches, hey presto.

'In press conferences I go to facts. Where does it leave us immediately? How was the performance? Did they do what I wanted them to do? Did I make good decisions? I try not to get too carried away with the highs or too low with the lows. I always try and find positive realities, appreciating the reality of where we are but reflecting on the positive side of the situation. That's my internal measure.

'I like having conversations like these because you can see authentically how I'm conducting myself. But after a game, there is little room for context in news reporting about clubs the size of Burnley. Nigel Pearson came for me after we played Leicester out of the blue a few seasons ago for no reason at all. When I was asked about his comments, I told the media that my only concerns were Burnley and what we did. The reaction? Headlines: "DYCHE GOES ON MORAL HIGH GROUND". You can't win! I meant it genuinely. This job is so fraught with pressure, stress, emotion, outside influences and inside influences that I understand why Nigel may have said what he said. But I also appreciate that by fanning the flames, you usually bring even more focus on yourself.'

Two days before meeting Dyche, Burnley had lost 2–0 at home to Manchester United. They were not safe from relegation but Dyche was satisfied with the performance, insisting, 'You can't always get above where you are.' Burnley's season had been reported as a season of two halves: the first good and the second . . . not so good at best – largely due to a run of away matches against the best sides where they had lost each time. Burnley had not won an away game in the league all season and their survival was hinging on home form. Dyche says that management becomes more difficult when perception gets in the way of facts. In fact, in Burnley's first seventeen games, they had earned seventeen points. In the second seventeen, they had earned nineteen points.

'I don't read the papers, not because I don't value the art of the industry, but because I don't need the extra noise – there's enough already,' he says. 'I don't want distractions. When we became a Premier League club [in 2014] one of the pundits on Sky said, "The only way Burnley will win a game is when they go back down to the Championship." I was told about this. Saw him later on in the season, didn't I? We were third bottom but making a fair fist of it. I went over, all smiles, shaking his hand – getting him sucked in. "How are you doing – family well?" all that type of thing. And then I said, "It was interesting what you said earlier in the season. That's funny, isn't it, especially now we've got something like seven wins . . ." He denied that he'd said it and started flapping. "This is what I was told, maybe they'd misheard your name and the name of the TV show . . ." If you're going to say something acidic, I think as managers we should be allowed to challenge it. I didn't abuse him, by the way. I was just playing with him. Part of my job is to try and bring balance to a discussion and say, "Hang on a minute . . ."

'At the start of this season every single pundit, columnist, newspaper – every single one – tipped us to go down, hands down. No chance! We would go down! You start well and then they are saying, "Here we go, a wobbly run-in." In an odd way, I'm quite proud they're speaking about us wobbling because it means we've changed perceptions about our abilities. If it's a shock that Burnley are on a tough run in the Premier League, each person at the club can be very pleased with the work they've done.

'I go into businesses and talk to workers,' he adds. 'At the beginning I'd ask them why they wanted me to do it. "Because you're constantly in a form of crisis management – the next thing is always the biggest thing." In the business world, a crisis might come around every blue moon. Football management is not a crisis in the truest sense. If I said that in the media, for example, it would be dressed up as: "DYCHE IN CRISIS". But you are constantly able to see the edge of the cliff. You're not there but you know it's there. You're constantly looking over and behind you, checking: am I tied to the tree? On the horizon you can see the knives being sharpened. You know, Wile E. Coyote always trying to catch the Road Runner, trimming the fibres of the warm tarmac below? It feels a bit like that.'

*

In his book The Football Man, Arthur Hopcraft described Bob Lord, the chairman of Burnley Football Club, as 'The Khrushchev of Burnley'. Presiding over his football affairs and butchery business from the office at his Lowerhouse meat factory, he coordinated feuds with the governing bodies, newspapers, supporters' clubs, television companies, other teams and even Burnley's greatest player, Jimmy McIlroy – sold to Stoke City because Lord found out he was friends with Reg Cooke, who was the club's former vice president, and someone Lord had previously warred with.

Lord ran Burnley in such a belligerent manner that he became the first football club owner to have a national profile. Having had his attempts to take control of Burnley denied by other directors for the best part of nine years, Lord became chairman in 1959. In the following nine seasons, Burnley were competitive in the First Division and were crowned champions of England in 1960 before coming runners-up in both the league and FA Cup two years later. It was not sporting achievements that brought him into the wider public's consciousness, however.

His first controversial move came when he suppressed Burnley fans in their attempts to form an official supporters' club. 'We're not having an official supporters' club at Burnley,' he decreed. 'They cause a lot of problems because the people who run them eventually want the football club power.'

Between 1964 and 1969, Lord banned television cameras from covering matches at Turf Moor, citing they would 'damage and undermine attendances'. When he ruled that the BBC would not be allowed into a home game, there came a warning. 'If the BBC don't shift their cameras from Turf Moor, I'll be down there myself and will personally burn them. They are on our ground without consent and I don't care if even Harold Wilson has given them permission.'

Lord tried to justify his concerns by saying at a Variety Club function in 1974, 'We have to stand up against a move to get soccer on the cheap by the Jews who run television.' He then took great offence at the reaction of Manny Cussins, the Jewish chairman of Leeds United, who said he would leave the Elland Road boardroom if Lord attended a match there. Lord was furious that Cussins had been critical of him and ordered his own board to stay away from the game; with that, the offender turned into the offended because, somehow, he got away with it.

If Lord thought his boycott of television access would be followed by other club chairmen he was wrong, however. While Burnley decided to forego the television exposure and the money on offer, other clubs cashed in during a period where football was adjusting to a new world which did not include a maximum wage cap, as it had done before Jimmy Hill's campaign to have it lifted in 1961. It meant richer clubs could now outmanoeuvre Burnley financially.

Brian Miller had been a wing-half in Burnley's 1960 league championship winning side, having signed his first contract as a fifteen-year-old when his responsibilities included the sweeping of the famous Longside terrace at Turf Moor. By 1987, he was Burnley's manager and the club was the bottom-placed team in the Football League, a 2–1 win against play-off chasing Leyton Orient on the final day just about keeping them up. Fifteen thousand supporters were inside Turf Moor that day – five times the average home gate. During the 1960s, when Blackburn Rovers, Blackpool or Preston North End travelled over the hills on bank holidays, Turf Moor's attendance could be as high as 54,000. For a club that had been champions of England just 27 years earlier, it had taken only nine seasons to slip from the First Division to the Fourth.

Burnley's existence was being threatened by a new order in east Lancashire. In the late 1980s, Colne Dynamoes, bankrolled by millionaire chairman-manager Graham White, who had business interests in property and the timber industry, charged through the non-league pyramid on a budget to make Burnley jealous. In the summer of 1989, White took the club full-time, even though the Fourth Division was still two promotions away. As White's team raced towards the Northern Premier League title in the season that followed, playing in front of crowds averaging 1,300, their Holt House ground was graded unfit for the Conference, prompting White to offer a reported £500,000 over two years to share Turf Moor with Burnley – the club he had previously tried to buy. Burnley's board were panicking about Colne's rising popularity but remained firm enough in their decision-making to reject both of White's offers. When Colne were denied promotion to the Conference because of their ground, White walked away from football and the club folded overnight.

The Premier League era and Sky were a few years away and this was still a time when football clubs were the fiefdoms of the local mercantile class made good. You cannot mention Burnley without mentioning Blackburn, who, like Burnley, were champions of England having won the Premier League in 1995 after huge investment by Jack Walker, an industrialist from the town, only to slip into the third tier 22 years later. Under Indian ownership group Venky's, Blackburn were £100million in debt and paying wages they could not afford when relegation to a level they had not played at in 37 years was sealed. A month before, the Blackburn Rovers supporters' trust met sports minister Tracey Crouch to discuss ownership reform and push Supporters Direct's idea of club licences to protect professional clubs from incompetent owners. 'The whole thing is a shambles,' said trust chairman John Murray. 'We all wanted Blackburn to survive but even if they did stay up this miserable existence would have continued.' It might be suggested that this area has a history of boom and bust, that Blackburn will have the opportunity to rise again – just like Burnley did – but it is difficult to see who might have the means and motive to save this deeply indebted club from an economically challenged former mill town struggling to attract gates of 10,000 in League One.

Burnley might have followed the same path as Blackburn before promotion to the Premier League was earned on three separate occasions. Mike Garlick, the current chairman – someone who made his relative wealth through IT consultancy and was born 200 metres from Turf Moor – had joined the board as a director in 2007 in the aftermath of ITV Digital's collapse, which forced Football League clubs into drastic decisions. Burnley sold Turf Moor and its Gawthorpe Hall training facility and Garlick was dispatched to Rome to discuss a deal that would have seen Burnley link up with an unnamed Serie A giant, resulting in a string of young Italian players heading to east Lancashire for loan spells. Thus Burnley might have become a foreign club's junior side rather than a local priority.

Considering one of the biggest critics of televised football had been Bob Lord, there is an irony, indeed, that Sky's television money has since changed Burnley's financial landscape. Although Burnley is the smallest town to host Premier League football, although Turf Moor's main stand (a stand that still carries Lord's name) is one of the smallest structures in the Premier League with 4,000 wooden seats, although the club has lowest wage bill and although it has the lowest gate receipts, Sky's money accounted for 90 per cent of Burnley's revenue during the 2016/17 season.

Sean Dyche was keen to stress that Burnley had used Sky's money sensibly. It had not only cleared all of Burnley's debts but ensured too that Turf Moor and Gawthorpe Hall were assets again. Burnley had since spent nearly £11m transforming their training ground, which under Bob Lord's instructions had become the first purpose-built training facility in England after he stressed the economic importance of Burnley producing its own players. Gawthorpe had since fallen into disrepair and the new Barnfield Training Centre next door became one of Dyche's pet projects, the manager joking that his rugged appearance made him look like one of the builders rather than a Premier League manager. With so much money washing about in the Premier League era, Dyche says the biggest challenge is managing perceptions, 'the realities and non-realities', as he calls them.

'When I came here, the club was completely out of sync – and it will go there again, just by the nature of football and human beings,' he believes. 'The club had forgotten what it really is. It had been in the Premier League two years earlier. Why are we languishing in the bottom half of the Championship when we should be in the Premier League? I got here and we quickly rose from sixteenth-ish to seventh and everybody thought, "Right, here we go!" But the team was nowhere near good enough. We were lucky to get seventh. The reality was out of the window by then and so we had to remodel the thinking and, of course, people don't like to be told they need to think differently. Slowly but surely you have to nibble away at it. Results don't go so well – which they didn't for me, but there was a lot of good work going on behind the results, things that I was aligning differently to make sure the club was stronger. The majority of people can't see these things and you're only measured on the pitch. Finding a chairman or an owner that can see the bigger picture, one who doesn't panic when the pressure comes, is getting harder. The misalignment of where clubs are at is rife and it never used to be.

'When I was at Nottingham Forest from 1987 to 1990 it was a given that young players would play. The crowd knew it, the board knew it, the manager knew it, the team knew it. All stakeholders were in the loop. So if a young player played and the result didn't go your way the crowd weren't necessarily lenient but they'd understand it. They realised that it was improbable that you get instant success with young players. Therefore, it was accepted as part of the club's identity at that time. All of that is out of the window now. People want, bang – win, win, win. There's no reality or thinking behind it. "Why aren't they winning?" Some say, "Give young lads a chance!" Then when they don't win, the same people say, "The young lads aren't good enough!" There is only a small amount of players in this world that can enter a first team and be good enough straight away – that has always been the case with football. The overwhelming majority need a bit of time. But they don't get the time because everybody wants to win the league.

'To get balance here, I'm not crying this in. I'm stating facts. If this was a post-match press conference the reaction would be "DYCHE LAMENTS FOOTBALL". My words would be spun all over the place. I'm not moaning about it at all. I'm just saying this is how the game is changed and if I fail to appreciate the environment I'm working in, I'm one step behind already. I buy into the working environment. That's why you don't see me upset. These are the realities. I love the challenge.'

In the summer after Dyche arrived at Turf Moor (having been sacked by

Watford after the Pozzo family from Italy bought the club), expectation levelled out because he had to sell leading scorer Charlie Austin to Queens Park Rangers. Dyche replaced him with three free transfers and 'overnight, it was us back to being little old Burnley'. The bonus of this was, there arrived a reality. 'If you have a common reality, you've got a chance.' Then, in the summer of 2016, Dyche spent £30million for the first time in Burnley's history. Though it was nowhere near what other clubs with relegation concerns were spending, the unprecedented transfer deals at Turf Moor inevitably raised expectations at a local level.

'Relegation should be an invaluable experience to a club the size of Burnley and not mean the end of the world, because survival in the Premier League is already a massive challenge,' Dyche says. 'No benefactors, no one who is going to write massive cheques; the club has to be run properly by absorbing the money and redistributing it appropriately. The club has to survive over the next five years – not just in year one, covering all the contracts. At the end of that we still need to be in a healthy shape. Relegation doesn't mean you're necessarily moving backwards providing you learn from your mistakes and stick together. The problems come at clubs who bet the ranch and, oh-oh, it doesn't work. Then you have heaven and hell – a club in bits. I witnessed this at Watford. I left the club as a player the season they got promoted into the Premier League. Then Aidy Boothroyd brought me back as a youth coach three years later. By the end of that season we were nearly out of business: twenty-four hours away from the administrators coming in. If mismanaged, relegation can mean real chaos for a club – and I don't mean football managed. That helps, of course. I mean as a club, reality – the perception of reality, facts within the perception; remodelling it again. It becomes hard because there are a lot of business people now involved in football and they are not used to so many voices in their world saying, "Why are you not doing that?"'

'I'm forty-six so I've seen the change in front of my own eyes, in my lifetime. There is a demand for everything now – the throwaway lifestyle: throwaway fashion, throwaway goods. Growing up I remember watching my dad trying to fix the washing machine when it was broken. He was a consultant for British Steel but he'd try his hand at fixing anything off his own back. When that didn't work he'd ring the geezer that knew how to fix washing machines. Only then, if all else had failed, he'd decide to buy a new one. Now, people are on the Internet straight away buying the cheapest washing machine they can get. They don't worry about paying the bloke that can fix it.

'This attitude has fed into football. A few bad results? Sack the manager. "He ain't good enough!" Bad season? Sell all the players! "What about the owners?" Soon enough the new generation of fan will only know Twitter, Instagram and Facebook. I never cry it in, as I say. But this is how it has factually changed. If we live in a throwaway society, why should football be any different? Opinions are made instantly. There is less of a desire to look at the situation and try and fix things. Instead it's bang, change now. The downside or the upside, whichever way you want to look at it is, the managers get thicker skin. They think, look, I'm going to work really hard, give everything I can to be successful. If it doesn't work out, c'est la vie. They walk off into the distance, not broken like I used to see managers. You'd see them and you'd say, "Sorry it didn't work out," and months later you'd see them again and they'd still have a face on them. Not now. I don't think I'll be like that [not caring as much] – though that isn't me saying I'm better or stronger than other managers. I've never been as black and white and I've learned with time to let things go quickly because this is a constant industry. Win one? "Hurrah! – everything is rosy!" Lose one? "Rubbish! – get rid of everyone." You have to wear a coat of armour. When I signed for Bristol City as a player a lot was expected of me and it didn't work out. There were lots of cliques in the dressing room and I didn't fit in. I'd had great times at Chesterfield before and this disappointment taught me that you have to maintain your independence. The fans might think you've been a waste of money but they don't always know the off-the-pitch circumstances.'

On perfect spring days at Turf Moor, from the top of the main stand the sunlight shimmers off slate roofs; beyond the old mills, the terraced houses and the chimney smoke, the Pennines – when smeared with frost – makes it one of football's most picturesque settings. The football under Dyche, though practical, has seldom threatened to match the beauty of the backdrop. A lot is made about Dyche's preference for certain types of player, specifically British workhorses over foreign flair. The perception about what Burnley are doing is reinforced by Dyche's willingness to talk about the lack of opportunities for British managers in the Premier League.

'Think about it, what business would you be in if you didn't want good people working around you – to at least work hard and care about what they do?' he says of players. 'I don't think I'm the only manager who thinks along those lines. Surely, if I'm the only one that does then the world is in trouble. It's basic values in life – work hard and I'll do everything I can to help the individual succeed within a collective. I'll help try and rub off any edges, I'll try and guide you towards being the best you can be and, at the very least, give us a bit of respect and honesty.

'We signed Steven Defour from Anderlecht. He's played for Porto and he's played in the Champions League. A lot was made of it because he was a big-money signing and because he wasn't British. We've made other non-British signings and they haven't really got a mention in the press. Freddie Ulvestad was one and Rouwen Hennings another. Then there was Johann Gudmundsson, who came from Charlton. We signed Defour and everyone was, like, "Oooh, Burnley have signed a foreign player for once." We've had foreign players here before. I've said this many times but I couldn't care less whether players are green, blue or brown. They can come from anywhere on the planet as long as they can play football. You have to think logically when signing someone, though – the business thinking. Do you know anything about them? Do you know the agent? Does the agent want to play ball? Does the player want to play ball? Do they fit your finance? Do they fit the club? Are they willing to move to the north-west of England where, as you've seen today, it can be minus-six at the end of April and we've just been hit by a hail storm during a training session? Do they want the challenge of being at a smallest club in the Premier League? Well, if they tick all of those boxes why wouldn't you sign them? People speak about recruitment as if everyone is equal, not appreciating that this club is in its infancy with regards to recruitment. We're still hand to mouth. Which division are we going to be in? How much money do we have?

'Admittedly, the geography has changed. A lot of players now live in south-west Manchester, no matter which club in the north-west they play for. It could be Liverpool, Everton, Man City, Man United or Burnley. Players also travel from that area to Stoke. When you try and sign a player he is more likely than ever to know another player from one of those clubs who will say, "south-west Manchester is lovely". I don't think geography is the major issue it might have been before for Burnley. The major issues concern whether we will be in the Premier League because there are no guarantees – certainly at the beginning of the season where most analysts are saying, "You've got no chance." Can we pay as well as the other teams? No. Can we advance your career? Yes, I believe we can – our record suggests that we can help careers move forward, that's a big one for us. Will the player be in a good working environment? Certainly, as you can see now the training ground has changed significantly over the last two years compared to what we were using before. It's the balance of yin and yang: the good things balanced against the not-so-good things and then the buy-in from all parties: does the player really want the challenge – because we don't sugarcoat it. Does the agent want the challenge – and they are ever-more important. It's not just one element. It used to be way easier when I was playing. You either wanted to play for the team or you didn't.'

Dyche says his proudest moment as a manager was sealing promotion to the Premier League for the first time in 2014 when Wigan Athletic were beaten at Turf Moor, 'because the team performed exactly how you'd want your team to perform on a big day after a year's work'. Up, down and up again Burnley went, though Dyche insists he has never asked to be interviewed for jobs at clubs where the ambitions exceeded Burnley's.

'Ownership has changed massively in my lifetime,' he reasons. 'You'll have to check the stats but I think fifteen out of the twenty Premier League clubs are foreign-owned. In the Championship, there's thirteen from twenty-four. That's a start point. So if you've got foreign owners there's an increased chance you'll get foreign managers. Within that, I think sixty per cent of first-team Premier League squads are made up of foreign players. To manage those players, it might seem an easier option to appoint a foreign manager. These are considerations before you analyse who has been successful and which clubs want to achieve that level of success. If you are Chelsea, Arsenal, Tottenham, Man City, Man United, Liverpool and, to a degree, Everton, who are climbing now because of their new backer, do they want a young British up-and-comer or do they want someone who has probably been successful in their own right already? Chances are they're going to go for the second option.

'The demands of being successful are huge. If you look at the careers of those managers, Klopp has been very successful in Germany with Dortmund, Pep's record speaks for itself, Conte and Wenger the same, and then Pochettino who is one of the newcomers. He did a great job in difficult circumstances abroad with Espanyol then established himself here with Southampton. He's since built it steadily at Tottenham and he's my favourite, if you like. There's more to come from him, I think. But the point is, these guys are not novice hurdlers. I've done a bit but not in relation to their achievements. We do need someone to break the mould. I'm a big backer of Eddie Howe because if it goes right for him it goes well for me and all the other British coaches. The media might misconstrue that as some form of patriotism when the reality is, it would be good for the health of our national system – for the good of coaches that would filter through the system and down into the grass roots.'

Dyche has sacrificed family time to become Burnley's manager. He travels back to his home in Kettering usually on a Tuesday or a Wednesday to see his wife and children. As this has been his life for the last four years, I wonder how long he can go on for, whether he'd jump at the chance if an opportunity came to manage a club closer to home. He compares his job to 'working away', like a businessman from Kettering going to London or a builder to Birmingham.

'Football management is a wonderful industry but the challenge to succeed is enormous because there's so few jobs and so many people wanting to do it,' he says. 'I tell loads of young coaches they should be prepared for what is to come if they really want to succeed. "Make sure you're ready to deal with the knockers," I say. If you can handle that, compartmentalise criticism and put it in a box while still moving forward, then that's no problem. If that's not your bag then don't do it because the job is fraught with people picking on what you do constantly. There will be a thousand managers who have done it better than you and they'll still be deemed to have done it wrong. Look at Arsène Wenger . . .

'You wouldn't want a stadium full of people sitting on their hands, though, because it would be boring,' he concludes. 'Football is driven by passion and opinions and people should always feel free to express them. But there's got to be a moment where you can reason with people who disagree with you and you part by shaking hands. Social media means everyone is so desperate to have their voice heard and to be proven right. Sometimes the line is overstepped and it's becoming more of a regular thing.

'When we got promoted the first time, which was an amazing achievement considering the budget – I don't think any team assembled for such a small sum will ever reach the Premier League again – there was still a fan who came up to me at the players' awards. "What an amazing season," he said. "But I still think you should have played this guy more than this guy."

'What did I say back? I said, "OK, nice to meet you, sir . . ."'

8

THICK AS THIEVES

OMAR BECKLES HAS FINISHED TRAINING AND IS DEVOURING leftover chicken chow mein out of a disposable box using a plastic fork. He is having his lunch, sitting alone in the Eric Whalley Founder Members Lounge of the Wham Stadium, the home of Accrington Stanley.

Beckles is 25 years old and from Leytonstone, north London. After suffering rejection from Millwall as a teenager, he signed for Jerez Industrial in Spain before moving on to Boreham Wood, Kettering Town, Boreham Wood again, Billericay, Histon, Margate, Hornchurch, St Albans and Aldershot Town. From Aldershot, Beckles decided to play in the north of England for the first time because he saw it as his last chance to make it as a Football League player. 'Strategic,' he calls it. 'A big call to make.'

Beckles stays for a chat, telling me about his hopes and dreams. Accrington had sold Josh Windass and Matt Crooks to Glasgow Rangers the summer before. A good season here and the strapping six-foot three-inch central defender might earn himself a similar opportunity.

Beckles had taken himself out of his comfort zone. The Wham Stadium is the smallest ground in the Football League. From the low-rise main stand, which hasn't changed much since Accrington were a Northern Premier League club fifteen years ago, snow-capped hills are visible on winter mornings such as this one. To get there, from Burnley you follow signs for Oswaldtwistle and turn off before reaching Blackburn; you have to climb Manor Lane, turn right passing the Crown Pub and then left into Livingstone Road, a dead end of tiny bungalows. From there, a rocky narrow path takes you to a small car park – the smallest in the Football League – where players, many of whom travel from Liverpool in convoys of four or five, disembark for training sessions because there is no actual training ground – Accrington insist they rather than Morecambe have the smallest budget in the Football League.

Though the financial position is steady under owner Andy Holt – whose company What More UK (Wham) make plastic boxes and bins – Accrington's budget on players, wages and staff is set at just £670k per year compared to Portsmouth's £3 million. This is a club that is wary about overspending.

The sign outside the Wham welcomes visitors by identifying Accrington Stanley as 'The Club That Wouldn't Die', but Accrington Stanley did die in the spring of 1966, having been forced to resign its Football League place in the most public way possible four years earlier with debts of £60,000. Bob Lord, the infamous Burnley chairman from just down the road, was criticised for his role in events. He had grown into an influential figure on the Football League's management committee by then and had been asked to assist the situation by Stanley's chairman, Sam Pilkington. Yet at the creditors' meeting that followed, Lord stood up and effectively declared the club a lost cause.

Though Stanley were reborn six years later, it started the 1980s in the second division of the Cheshire County League and because of an advert for milk during that decade they became arguably the most famous minnow club in the world.

It was not until 2006 – some 44 years after resignation from the Football League – that a return was engineered under John Coleman and Jimmy Bell, the manager and assistant talked about within the town as 'John and Jimmy', as if they are one person. I had arranged to meet them because very few management teams class themselves genuinely as friends and I was intrigued how the dynamic worked – especially in the cut-throat world of the Football League.

While Beckles finishes his lunch (every Accrington player has to bring his own lunch), Coleman and Bell bound through the door one after the other and each of them apologise for being late. It is January and Coleman explains that he's had to spend the early part of the afternoon releasing players who were on short-term contracts. For the next few hours, I listen to their story. I begin by asking about Omar Beckles and the risks attached to signing a young Londoner who'd never lived in the north of England before.

Jimmy: We took a punt on him, to be perfectly honest. We needed a centre-half. We'd just had a few lads pinched off us by Portsmouth. He came into our office, we sat him down. And we could see the hunger in his eyes straight away. It was unreal. He told us exactly what we wanted to hear. We'd spoken to people about him and watched videos. He said, 'I want to be a top footballer and I won't let you down.' He was always making eye contact. We walked out of the room and nodded at each other – we had to take him. He's been excellent for us.

John: We can't pay riches here. But we always tell the players that it doesn't mean they can't earn millions themselves. They're not going to earn it with us. But they can use Accrington as a platform. If we get a good two years out of them where they perform to the best of their ability – and they do everything they can to help us – when it comes to the end of those two years, we'll do everything we can to help them. I've never stood in the way of any player who wants to move on and better themselves. Sometimes players think they are better than they are, of course. The first thing I look for in a player is hunger – are they hungry to play? Do they want to play in the top flight? With the best will in the world, Accrington aren't going to play in the top flight. We get players who have been released by Liverpool, Everton, United and Blackburn. They've got to buy into the idea that they can use Accrington as a trampoline to get past their former peers.

Jimmy: We've got the lowest budget in the Football League. It means that we have to nurture young and hungry lads that have been released, lads at eighteen that probably wouldn't get anywhere near the first teams of other clubs in our league. If they sign for a Doncaster or a Portsmouth, the clubs can afford to sit on the player for a couple of years and see how he develops. In their first team they'll use 26-year-old lads and pay them top dollar.

John: Recruitment is what defines the success or failure of any football club. The biggest clubs like to make it as scientific as possible. Sometimes, you have to take a punt – go on what your gut tells you. We know a lot of people in the game and you try and do your homework through Wyscout and watching as many games as you can. But it's impossible to get every single one right. That's why I'm having to release players in January. I think you have to develop a sixth sense – knowing when things feel right and when they don't feel right. The year we won the Conference we were struggling for a goalkeeper. Two games into the season, our number one decided to pack in – he retired. He said his ankle was hurting but I think it was because I threw a Jaffa Cake at him in the changing rooms against Altrincham. We'd won the game 1–0 but we limped over the line. Our goalkeeping coach Andy Dibble was on the bench. He's a good friend of mine but his legs couldn't move and he certainly couldn't be our number one in his mid-forties, so we were panicking. The first two replacements we signed were poor and then I took a call asking me to have a look at Ireland's Under-21 keeper. I spoke to people about him and the messages were positive but they were only second- or third-hand opinions. He'd played for Ireland on the Thursday night, we signed him by fax on the Friday and he wasn't landing at Liverpool Airport until Saturday morning. I didn't even know what he looked like. All I had was a grainy picture of him. I was sitting in the waiting lounge thinking, 'If he turns out to be a dwarf, I'm going to leave him in the arrivals lounge.' Thankfully, he walked off the plane and he was six foot three. His name was Darren Randolph. He's West Ham's first-choice keeper now.

Jimmy: It was a six-month loan and we were distraught when Charlton called him back because we were pushing for the league. Fortunately, they told us: 'We've got one who is just as good – you can have him.' That was Rob Elliot. He's at Newcastle now. The two of them were instrumental in taking Accrington back into the Football League. They were absolutely fantastic. But ultimately they were both punts. They could have been bad signings.

John: Every week we take at least a few lads on trial. You're on your phone constantly. At this time of year and during the summer you get calls from five or six agents a day. You have to sort through a lot of deadwood. We've got a lad here now, Rommy Boco, who's a legend at the club after three spells. He scored our first goal back in the Football League. An agent brought him over from France and we signed him after the first training session. We've looked at hundreds of players like Rommy and they've been hopeless. It's like hunting for gold. To get that one nugget, you've got to sift lots of shite.

Jimmy: We argue about all sorts of things but when we see a good player, we both know straight away. We were both brought up in the same area of Kirkby, Southdene. John's a couple of years older than me and he was always the top goalscorer – someone I always looked up to. He was the top dog at Kirkby Boys and it was my ambition as a kid to play at that standard. I was the next generation coming through. He went to St Josephs and I was at Cherryfield. He lived just around the corner. I'd watched him from afar but our paths first crossed when I was sixteen and John was eighteen, playing Sunday league football. He'd signed for Burscough by then and he asked me to join him. Since then we've always been good friends. We played again together at Rhyl before John moved on to Morecambe when they were a Northern Premier League club and I went to Knowsley United. We both signed for Lancaster City and then Ashton United together. Right throughout our careers we'd phone each other after games and have a chat. If he'd scored two, I'd tell him that I'd scored two as well even if I hadn't – we were both as hungry as anything.

John: Starting out at Burscough was a tough education. We played up front together. We came from the Woodpecker, a Sunday league team. We'd also played for the Fantail for a bit as well – a very famous pub side in Kirkby. We must have been a pain in the arse to be around because we loved footy. I wouldn't say we were big-headed but we were confident. We probably rubbed people up the wrong way because we were very boisterous and we celebrated when we scored. We'd take the piss out of ourselves but we'd take no shit off the older players too. We both probably thought we were better than the level we were playing at. Burscough had more established players on contracts who were earning more than double our wages but they were in the stands because we were doing so well together. I think this environment cemented our friendship because we had a common goal and had similar personalities. I think we always played and conducted ourselves like we had a point to prove because the call never came from a Football League club and it was something we both wanted to happen so much. We craved to go full-time and even up to the age of thirty-odd, we believed someone might pick us up. It means the novelty of being in the Football League has never worn off for us. We see players who have never known a job. They've come straight from school, signed a youth contract and then become pro. Some become blasé about it all very quickly and it makes you scratch your head. I've never been like that and Jimmy's never been like that. This is a joy to us, we're getting paid for something we love doing. If we weren't managing Accrington and if nobody else would give us a job, we'd still want to run a Sunday league team. We'd do it for nothing.

Jimmy: The type of lads that don't care enough, they don't last long here. We try to educate them and make them appreciative of what they have. They soon get knocked into shape – not by us but by the rest of the team. It helps having a lot of Liverpool lads because one thing Liverpool lads are great for is, if someone needs picking up they'll put their arm around them. If someone needs knocking down, they'll knock them down. We've always been blessed by having good Liverpool lads in our squads. We don't have prima donnas here. Today we fell out with them for not tidying up after themselves at breakfast. They've got to wash their own plates, there's no one to do all that for them. We expect them to be nice people as well as good footballers.

John: If you stay at one club for any length of time you have to learn to build teams and dismantle them. Because of the level we're operating at, we have to get close to players – we can't be distant. We have to get inside their heads. As much as professionally you know you shouldn't because you'll have to let them go some day, they've got to become your mate because you have to get them to like you. At this level, they aren't getting paid a lot of money so there has to be another reason to sign for Accrington Stanley. If they like you, it's another reason for them to try – to run through a brick wall for you. But then, you've also got to make sure you don't make it like a holiday camp. You want them to enjoy their football but hard work has to be the priority.

Jimmy: I worked in an abattoir for seven years before becoming an electrician. John worked for Knowsley Council before becoming a primary school teacher. We were part-time at Accrington, then in 2003 we had a massive decision to make financially because we'd reached the Conference and the decision was taken to go full-time with the money earned from a good FA Cup run. Both of us had two wages coming in and the money at Accrington was all right. We could have stayed the way we were, as part-time Conference managers elsewhere earning more money combining two jobs. It would have been the safer thing to do. Full-time football meant my monthly wage would pretty much cut in half. But full-time football was irresistible. I just knew I'd have regretted it for the rest of my life if I didn't try. It paid off because within three years we'd won promotion into the Football League. To get Accrington back was an unbelievable moment in our lives. Nobody can take that away from us.

John: The FA Cup run changed everything. We beat Huddersfield, we beat Bournemouth and then got knocked out by Colchester. The run gave us the clout to go full-time. Eric Whalley was the chairman and getting into the Conference was the Holy Grail for him. Like Jimmy, I lost a bit of money too because the teaching wages were better than full-time football wages in the Conference. The biggest challenge was convincing players to come with us because they were in the same boat. Their logic was, well, Accrington should be paying what they were earning in their full-time jobs as well as what they were earning as a part-time footballer. Our argument was, 'Well, we're only paying you to do one job.' There were some difficult discussions and a lot of soul-searching.

Jimmy: When we first came to Accrington, John was player-manager and I was player-assistant. People were telling us it'd never work – we couldn't play and manage at the same time. I think it was beneficial, to tell you the truth. Both of us were coming towards the end of our careers but our will to win was just as evident as it was in the first game we played together as teenagers, if not more because we both knew the clock was ticking. I think it set the standards for the other players.

John: Getting sacked by Ashton United made us even more determined to succeed. When we took over at Ashton, a Manchester club, the team was seventeenth in the table. We finished eighth that season and got to the fourth round of the FA Trophy. The following season we finished third with a record number of points and won two cups. In the last season we finished third and won one cup. There were only two promotion places, the chairman had said we needed to get promotion, so he sacked us. One of the chairman's other reasons was he wanted both of us to stop playing – even though we were still good enough to play and even though we left ourselves out plenty of times to accommodate players so we didn't upset them.

Jimmy: The next day we got two job offers. One came from Leek Town and the other was from Accrington Stanley. Accrington had been relegated and Leek were in the league above. But we thought Accrington was a bigger club so we brought the entire Ashton team here and won the league the next season, which I know hurt Ashton.

John: In our first season at Accrington we both scored quite a few goals, even after the fella at Ashton said we had to pack in. I knew I could still do a job. But I suppose deep down you never want to stop playing. In the early days here we'd have murder with the other players in training sessions. There's also been times when we've stopped the car on the motorway because of disagreements – mainly because of players, how they've done. Challenging each other is important because your view can quite easily become blinkered. Sometimes once you've formed an opinion you find ways to validate that opinion. Sometimes you need someone to say, 'Listen, John – he's not doing it.' Jimmy is my best mate but it'd be pointless if he agreed with everything I said. He might as well not be here. I think there are too many managers that have that relationship with their assistant and it explains why they don't flourish as much as they might. I reckon there are no other managers in the Football League who has a mate as assistant manager, let alone his best mate. Because we are best mates we can have honest conversations. When you think about your family, how many times do you fall out? It's on a daily basis. It doesn't mean you won't go to war for them every single day of your life. Jimmy and I are close enough that we can fall out and carry on the next day.

Jimmy: We both think we're right all the time, we're very headstrong and that's why we clash. But what we try not to do is clash in front of the players.

They'll see it as a weakness then. You've got to be as thick as thieves when you're standing in front of a dressing room. You also realise as you get older you don't always have to say too much to players to force the reaction you want. Maybe we've mellowed a bit.

John: We've got a style of football that we've developed over the years and I think that's why we're not as angry as we used to be. We've had to add and take away but now we're comfortable with the way we play. For the last three or four years we've become very clear about our ethos. We're both football fans and we want to watch good football. There's no way we could set a team up and put five big lads at the back, three big lads in midfield, two big lads up front and lump it and hope that the second ball falls to us and we score. I'd rather walk away from football and do something else. I couldn't watch that.

Jimmy: Anyone who watches our teams knows that we like to play out from the back. We know too that you can't always do that. To earn the right to play out from the back you've got to win your little wars first, nudge ahead and then express yourself. At the end of a match John and I want to be able to say we've watched good, entertaining football. If we've been entertained in the pressure that we're under then surely the fans will feel that way as well.

John: It's very vogue now to play one up front. We were playing that twenty years ago. I was the lone striker and we had three midfielders bombing on behind me. It was 4–2–3–1 without anyone really talking about it. A lot of modern coaches think they have reinvented the wheel.

Jimmy: We're big fans of Graeme Souness as a pundit and as a speaker. If you listen to him talking about the Liverpool teams and the way they were set up, without the ball, Souness and Dalglish would drop a bit deeper and when they had the ball, they'd push back up. It was labelled 4–4–2 but, depending on possession, it was 4–2–3–1.

John: Back then the coaches and the managers were an aside, weren't they? They didn't have the prominence they have now. Can you imagine the spotlight Bob Paisley would have been under if he'd have achieved what he did then? His work would have put Mourinho to shame. As you can see, we're both massive Liverpool supporters but we're supporters of football first and foremost. We could name the winners of the FA Cup from '63 to '89 in a blink. Unfortunately, I couldn't name you the last five winners. Growing up, the FA Cup was the be-all and end-all. You looked forward to the final for four weeks. You were starved of live football on TV. The final coverage started at nine o'clock in the morning and finished at six in the evening and you didn't miss a blink of it.

You'd be glued to the telly for nine hours. Today, you could watch three live games a day from anywhere in the world. When we were kids, if you got an international game on it was a rarity – unless it was a World Cup. If you ate steak or lobster thermidor every day, you'd become bored of it. If you're exposed to something every day, you don't want it as much because you can have it. I haven't watched Match of the Day for eight years. If someone had said that to me as a kid, I'd have thought they were mad. It's the same with Football Focus. Television has changed football forever.

Jimmy: Football has become bland to a lot of people. It's not as exciting because it's there all the time. It's like being force-fed. I'd sooner watch Mansfield versus Notts County live at a football ground once a week than watch a Premier League, a La Liga or Serie A game every day. Unless Liverpool are playing on telly, I won't watch it. Bournemouth versus Arsenal? I've got no interest in it.

John: What I said before, though, about not having another manager in the Football League whose best mate is his assistant: you won't have another manager and assistant jumping up and down like we were when Liverpool scored the winner against Everton in the derby. I'm not sure whether many other managers and coaches are real football fans; if they are, they hide it well. Despite our frustrations with the game, we still love it more than ever. Now, you're getting 24-year-old coaches working at academies. What experience have they had in the game, let alone in life – good or bad that they can draw on, to be able to walk people through situations? I've got a lot of friends who are coaches at Premier League clubs and this is no slight on them, but there are too many situations where jobs are created and, to try and validate positions, they coach in a way that first and foremost reflects well on them rather than the primary focus being on the players or the team.

Jimmy: At Accrington's academy, we've brought coaches in who are the same ilk as us. When we first came back there were a few coaches who were coaching for themselves and did not share our ethos. We now have Andy Gray, who used to manage Prescot Cables and Burscough, and [former Everton midfielder] Paul Lodge, who we know from the Liverpool scene. They have the players cleaning the changing rooms, boots and toilets. It's a bit of a throw-back to the old days but it's teaching kids values about life – getting them to take responsibility for their work.

John: You might say it's because me and Jimmy aren't getting it, but the money involved at the top level has taken the game away from the common man. I remember it being a shilling to get into Anfield. As a teenager, it was forty pence.

At that time, my dad was earning forty quid a week – fifty if he was lucky, which is one hundred times what I was paying to go the match. My dad was the average working man. Now, a ticket costs fifty pounds. The average working man might only be on £500 a week if he's doing OK. So instead of it being a hundredth of your dad's salary, it's a tenth. If you think about how that has impacted upon the common man, football has become like opera. Likewise, my dad was on forty or fifty quid a week. Ian Callaghan was probably on around £150 – three times his wage. My dad could still say, 'Cally – the lucky bugger, he's doing something he loves.' But he wouldn't resent him. Footballers then were still superstars but they felt blessed they were earning three times the common man's wages. Now, you're talking four hundred, five hundred times the common man's wage. How can they relate to society? They can't. We have to count every penny at our club. There are plenty of League Two clubs who have finance directors. The finance directors at Accrington are me and Jimmy. We've got a budget that we have to work to and if there is a conversation to be had about money with a player, it will be us dealing with it – not a chief executive.

Jimmy: The toaster went missing the other day. We told the local newspaper that someone had pinched it and the story went viral. It's tongue in cheek but, deep down, we want people to think about that: what it really means. The reality is, that toaster needs replacing and it's going to end up coming out of our budget. Last month we spent a thousand pounds on strappings and a thousand pounds on protein bars. That's two grand a month. It's a player out of our budget. If I see a player taking a sip from a bottle of Lucozade before lashing the rest on the floor, I blow my top at him. Firstly, you'd never throw a bottle on the floor of your own home. Secondly, it's a waste. We played Liverpool Under-23s at Melwood a few weeks ago and our lads left their strappings, their bottles of water and banana peels behind. Someone from Liverpool went into the changing rooms afterwards, took a picture and sent it to our club asking whether it was acceptable. That hurt us big time. We were absolutely furious.

John: You hear people say that footballers have changed a lot in the last twenty years since the Premier League started. I've seen a big change in the last five years. As managers, we don't fundamentally change but we have to adapt. I think players are now seeing football more as a job. They don't see quite as much the overall package of enjoyment that football can give you. If I was a player now and a chairman came to me and said, 'Listen, I can pay you but I can't play you,' or, 'I can play you but I can't pay you,' it wouldn't even enter my head to choose not to play. I'd play every day and worry about not getting paid at a later date. If I said that to my players now there would be a few who'd play but not all. I think it's virtually impossible to create a team of players who'd all want to play. Don't get me wrong, the Football League is a hard grind. For seven years here especially, it was very hard indeed. We were close to going bust. We never went into administration when loads of other clubs did and we're proud of that. I think there are nearly fifty clubs that have gone down that route in their history and we haven't, even though we were prime for it. But there has been loads of times when me and Jimmy haven't been paid. The longest period was for three months. We've had to break it to the players that they weren't going to get paid. The new owner has alleviated that problem. You used to dread payday coming. It wasn't as bad for me and Jimmy because we were a bit older and our kids had grown up. For a lad who's twenty-six who's playing and got kids to feed when he's not on great money anyway, it's very hard to deal with. I've lost count of the number of times I've had to say, 'You won't get paid on Friday but you might get a bit on Monday and then some more the following Friday.' We've tried to use that to our advantage and create a siege mentality but you can only do it so many times.

Jimmy: That was why we left Accrington when we did [in 2012] for Rochdale. The club was in turmoil. Three people thought they owned the club and they were all fighting against each other and this meant the wages weren't getting paid. We weren't having to tell players lies but we were having to tell players things we didn't believe. A lot of management is kidology but we've prided ourselves on being honest with players.

John: The season before we'd finished in the play-offs with eight of the players having already signed for other clubs. One of them had agreed to join Stevenage – the team we got beat by in the semis. It meant that we had to rebuild the following season. There were a couple of tipping points. At Barnet, someone had forgotten to bring the left-back's shirt. So it had to travel on the supporters' coach and the supporters' coach was delayed on the motorway. The left-back was sitting in the changing rooms at five to three with no top. He ran on to the pitch wearing a jumper and the crowd threw the shirt on to him just as the game was about to kick off.

Jimmy: We then went to Aldershot. We hadn't been paid and were owed all kinds of money. We drew 0–0 and we were in the play-offs again. A young kid who's at Chorley now, Marcus Carver, was on the bench for the first time that day. They'd printed a junior boys' shirt for him. He tried to put it on and he couldn't move. After the game, the ex-chairman Peter Marsden asked to have a word with me and John. He told us that he was taking over as owner and chairman of the club but he didn't really want to do it and he didn't have a clue what he was doing. He said to me and John on the coach in front of the players, who must have been listening, 'Will you two run the club?' He was based in London and he wanted us to run it off the pitch as well as on, bearing in mind we were already in charge of the budget – a big strain. We looked at each other and knew then it was time to go. We'd sold Andy Procter, our captain, the day before to Preston and then the club got a few bob for me and John. That money more or less kept Accrington afloat for a few months. A lot of our fans didn't know how dire the situation was and we took a lot of stick for leaving.

John: I think we made the wrong move in choosing Rochdale. The club was a bigger one and the infrastructure was better but the cracks were the same. With Accrington, we knew where the cracks were. We were walking on ice and we could see the breaks, knowing as well we could go under at any time. At Rochdale the cracks weren't as visible but they were there.

Jimmy: Rochdale meant we had to rebuild our reputations. Our next job together was at Southport. I'd been working full-time at Port Vale on their staff when John got the call from Southport's chairman, Charlie Clapham. The risk going there for both of us was huge. Southport were in the relegation zone in the Conference.

John: I could have buried my career there and then. Southport were going down. It was a job for three or four months – a bit of pay. We had to ride Southport over the line like Tony McCoy. We managed to keep them up and that for me is still one of our biggest achievements. They were dead.

Jimmy: Southport is a difficult club to manage. They put out a statement saying they'd let us go when, really, we'd already decided to leave. We went to Sligo in Ireland and took them into the Europa League, beat a Lithuanian team 4–0 on aggregate then went to Rosenborg away and won there. The club had never won a European game before. Then the chance came to come back here. Leaving Accrington was a valuable experience. I think I learned more in those two years away from the club than I had in the rest of my time in football.

John: Not much has changed since our first spell aside from the financial stability, which simply makes work a lot easier. If you come and watch us train, you'll see Jimmy on my shoulders fixing the net to the crossbar. But we still don't have a training ground. Seeing the facilities at Premier League academies makes me envious. If they can afford facilities for players who aren't going to even play for the first team, why can't the Premier League build us something, which will then enhance the Premier League because you'll get more players coming through from this level. The best most academy players can hope for is a lower-league club, but academy players are not always prepared for lower-league football. In fact, very few are. Training at a Premier League academy only to find yourself in League Two or lower is like having an apprenticeship as a plumber only to become a spark. Nobody does anything particularly adventurous on the ball at academies. Every now and again they'll have a shot. The keeper never has to take a cross. The centre-half never has to head the ball. You come here and it's a totally different game. It's hurry-scurry and a million miles an hour. So they're getting coached to play a game that a lucky one per cent will end up playing. So what's the point? I don't get it. I just don't get it.

Jimmy: We train on a 4G pitch at Hyndburn. We try and get on our own pitch once a week and it's covered in ice at the moment. Half of the clubs in this league have their own training ground and the other half don't. They beg, steal and borrow. It's not ideal training on 4G because it's not the same as grass and grass is where the results are defined.

John: We've craved a training ground for years. It's one of our big bugbears. Every Premier League club has a nice academy. We're looking at a national team that isn't bringing players through because the top end is saturated with foreign players. The best way forward is for teams of our ilk to bring players through. Dele Alli came from MK Dons and his progression proves it can be done. It wouldn't be a blink out of the Premier League club's budgets – out of the billions the competition gets – to provide every Conference, League Two and League One club with a ring-fenced amount to build a training ground. Every professional football club in this country should have a training ground. If the FA had anything about them or the Premier League had anything about them, they could make it happen. They choose not to because they're only concerned with the top echelon where the most money is made. This is no disrespect to Liverpool, Everton or Stoke, but how can it be right that these clubs have eighteen pitches to be used on a daily basis and we only have one plastic pitch that we don't own? The money is there in the game but it isn't distributed in a way that is fair or sensible.

Jimmy: It's ridiculous. We're a professional club and we can't train on grass. I know John would be one hundred per cent against this but if they accepted plastic pitches in the Football League, I'd back it. Then, we'd have somewhere to play and somewhere to train. The community could use it and the club could take in extra revenue that way.

John: I just don't like plastic pitches full-stop. We broke the record last season to become the first professional team in England to have five successive home games called off because of the weather. We didn't play a home game for two months so there was no revenue through the turnstiles. Ultimately, there is enough money in the game to make sure the pitches are maintained properly. Am I right in saying half of the England team who played last year in Euro 2016 had spent time out on loan in the lower leagues? These players have seen how poor clubs really are, but are they perceptive enough to realise what needs to happen? We've just signed two lads on loan from Hull. They warmed up on the back field behind the terraces the other day and it was like the Derby had just been held on it. They must have been scratching their heads thinking, 'What have we come here for?'

Jimmy: I was embarrassed. I'd spoken to the lads on the phone. I'd sorted their accommodation and travel. I said to them, 'Training at the ground tomorrow.' They said, 'Oh, is that the training ground?' I said, 'No, just at the ground.' 'Where's the training ground.' 'Er, I'll just see you at the ground.' I couldn't tell them that we don't have a training ground. Today, we trained on the Astroturf because it was frozen. They still don't know we don't have a training ground. And they've been here a week . . .

Suddenly, it was time for John and Jimmy to go. They had an FA Cup match to prepare for at home against Luton Town the following day. A win would put them in the hat for the fourth round and the possibility of a draw against their beloved Liverpool. The prize money earned would keep Accrington running through the summer. It was winter's afternoon, it had warmed slightly, but half of the pitch at the Wham remained frozen.

CARLISLE UNITED

CARLISLE UNITED
PADDOCK
NORTH
PITCH
INVASION
MAY LEAD
TO ARREST
13
12
OPEN
NO TRANSFER
FROM PADDOCK
TO WARWICK
ROAD END
John & Kath

Derek Asamoah, Carlisle United.

Paul Casson, Holker Street, Barrow.

Jim Bentley, Globe Arena, Morecambe.

Bloomfield Road, Blackpool.

Dave Challinor and David Haythornthwaite, Mill Farm, Fylde.

Danny Rowe, Mill Farm, Fylde.

Peter Ridsdale, Deepdale, Preston.

Sean Dyche, Burnley.

John Coleman and Jimmy Bell, Wham Stadium, Accrington.

Haig Avenue, Southport.

Goodison Park, Everton.

Mayor Joe Anderson, Cunard Building, Liverpool.

Jürgen Klopp, Anfield, Liverpool.

YOU'LL NEVER WALK ALONE
LIVERPOOL
FOOTBALL CLUB
EST·1892

City of Liverpool, Delta Taxis Stadium, Bootle.

NORTH WEST

OLFC
1ST CHOICE SCAFFOLDING
NORTH WEST
SCARVES • T SHIRTS • PIN BADGES
KEYRINGS • MUGS • MORE

9

A VERY PRIVATE SHAME

ONE MORNING IN LATE JANUARY, SOUTHPORT FC CHANGED THEIR manager again. For the second time in the season, is one way of looking at it. Another would be, for the sixth time since John Coleman left the club two and a half years prior.

Steve Burr's record at Haig Avenue since replacing Andy Bishop four months earlier had been reasonable enough. Southport's board, however, discovered that Burr had failed in his application to take over at Wrexham. Southport's results had not been quite as good since: a hammering at home to fellow Conference National strugglers North Ferriby United came after defeat to Wealdstone from the Conference South in the FA Trophy. Directors began to wonder whether travelling to the north-west from Burr's home in Burton-upon-Trent in Staffordshire was becoming a strain, and on the journey back to Southport following a 3–1 loss at relegation rivals Bromley, chairman Charlie Clapham decided to intercept the spiral before it became terminal to Southport's survival hopes by acting, as he has done many times: Burr was dismissed. Liam Watson, the most successful manager in Southport's history was back – albeit only on an interim basis.

Watson had returned to Southport the previous September having been appointed with the title 'operations director', which in basic terms represented a sporting link between the boardroom, the dressing room and the manager's office. On resigning from his previous position at Stalybridge Celtic, Watson had claimed, 'You'll never see me in the dugout again. I'm retiring from management.'

Considering Southport's predicament, though, and considering Watson's experience, it made sense for him to step back into the breach. On the morning of Burr's exit, and his own temporary return Watson had turned his mobile phone on at 8.16 a.m. His plans for the day involved a morning swim in the gymnasium close to where he lives in Maghull and then an interview with me at a coffee shop in Crosby, yards away from the football ground of Marine AFC where he made his name as a whippet-quick non-league centre-forward.

By 3 p.m., the history on his phone reflected his demand: 76 incoming calls, many of them multiple attempts because he was busy speaking to someone else. The calls came from predictable groups of people: from out-of-work managers thinking Southport could be their next job and their agents; players wanting to know where they stood and their agents; local reporters sniffing out background on the latest development. John Cofie, who left Burnley for Manchester United in a deal worth £1million when he was fourteen years old, was one of those trying to find out what was going on.

'Cofie was going to be a superstar,' Watson says, using a tone that suggests the player's career path should be considered a warning to every young footballer. 'He's now a Southport player on loan at Chorley and I'd imagine he's ringing me to see what I want him to do tonight because we've got a Liverpool Senior Cup game at Widnes and his loan spell doesn't finish until midnight.'

The reaction to Burr's firing on social media had been swift. 'Absolute shambles of a football club,' wrote one observer less than a minute after Southport's official handle on Twitter released the news. 'Are you fucking joking?' asked someone else, almost as quickly. 'The best manager we've had in years. I was going to Gateshead but you can fuck that right off now.'

Southport's supporters did not know the full story but their frustration was understandable.

It had been an open secret that Watson originally left Southport in 2013 for AFC Telford because he thought the Shropshire club had more chance of developing into a Football League club, despite competing then at a lower level. Southport had tried all different types of managers since but whenever a relationship started to click, the manager would either get sacked or leave for a supposedly better job. The former Blackburn Rovers and Aston Villa left-back Alan Wright came first and was sacked after just a few months in charge. John Coleman, the Accrington Stanley legend, saved Southport from relegation in improbable circumstances but Clapham was unhappy, claiming his 'style of touchline behaviour' towards referees and assistants threatened the club's family values. Martin Foyle had played 533 Football League games, scoring 155 Football League goals, but he came and went quickly. Just as Gary Brabin seemed to be gaining a bit of momentum, taking Southport to within seconds of a replay only to lose to the Championship's Derby County in the FA Cup's third round, he decided to take a 'dream job' at Everton's academy, only to become manager of Tranmere Rovers soon after. There was Paul Carden, Dino Maamria and Bishop who came and went in the space of six months and then Burr, who was not universally the first-choice pick from four interviewees but was given the benefit of the doubt because of his experience managing in the Conference.

Portchat, the Internet fan forum, was in meltdown in the aftermath of Burr's surprise exit. 'It doesn't matter who we appoint, they'll only end up out the door in a few months,' suggested one pseudonymed complainant. 'How do the board expect us to support any manager? There really is no point to it.'

'I've seen dead sheep who could make better decisions,' wrote another angry Sandgrounder (as the locals call themselves), relocated to Gloucester. 'We need stability and Steve Burr could have built a team here. Well, Mr Clapham, that's gone. I'm just glad I've never worked for you or had to deal with you. In my opinion, your word is worth jack shit!'

There was a proposal that Southport should change its name to Poisoned Chalice AFC. An Albert Einstein quote was used too: 'The definition of insanity is doing the same thing over and over and expecting different results.'

The conversation soon moved on to Southport's new interim manager. 'Is this the same Liam Watson who steered Telford to relegation, almost did the same with Stalybridge and left them when they were rock-bottom the season after? Good appointment then.'

In the uncertainty, it seemed at least some Southport supporters had basic facts wrong, forgetting feats even at their own club. Watson, 46, was not only the most successful manager in Southport's history but the highest-achieving non-league manager in the north-west of England since the year 2000. In addition to his two promotions with Southport in 2005 and 2010, he accomplished the same feat with Telford in 2014. Somewhere in between, he'd also taken Burscough, a village club located near the market town of Ormskirk, out of the Northern Premier League and into the Conference North for the only time in its history. Telford were struggling when Watson was sacked there but he did not take them down and rather, at Stalybridge, he'd somehow kept them up in the 2014/15 season by embarking on remarkable run from the moment of his appointment.

He considered his choice to walk away from Bower Fold in September 2016 as an 'honourable decision', because he recognised that he'd taken a club with limited financial resources as far as he could. After nearly fifteen years of nonstop non-league management, he also wanted to devote more time to his son Niall, who at sixteen had just signed a scholarship with John Coleman and Jimmy Bell's Accrington Stanley youth team.

'It's not just Southport fans, it's all fans – they usually see only half of the reality but decide they can pass full judgements,' Watson says. 'It's the way society has gone so why should football be any different? Think something, scream about it on social media, make people follow you. It's worked for Donald Trump, hasn't it?'

*

An imaginative architectural historian has claimed that Napoleon III was so impressed by Lord Street in Southport, he ordered the great engineer Baron Haussmann to model the boulevards of Paris based around what he saw on his holidays in north-west England before the French Revolution of 1848.

Lord Street is, indeed, spacious and its cast-iron portico canopies could pass for belle époque. Southport, too, remains a handsome town with spacious thoroughfares, lengthy promenades and grand hotels.

And yet, if Southport was a person, it would probably be a granny. 'Plain talking, loves a good time, bit posh, magnificent frontage,' as the broadcaster Tom Dyckhoff wrote in the Guardian following a trip there in 2012. 'Southport hasn't declined, like so many here today, gone tomorrow seaside resorts,' he concluded. 'But it does have an air of a Britain shuffling off its mortal coil when the last of the pre-1970s package-holiday generation shuffles off with it.'

Perhaps Southport was saved from going the way of Blackpool and Morecambe because of its geography. The novelist Nathaniel Hawthorne said that in all his experience of Southport, having lived in nearby Liverpool as a consul for the United States, 'I have not yet seen the sea.'

Southport might have ice cream, roaming dunes and England's second-longest pier, built in 1860 by Sir James Brunlees, but strangely, while Blackpool's Tower is visible even on the greyest of days, reliably, you cannot see the sea from Southport's coastal road because the Mersey mudflats stretch so far out; and so, the aforementioned pier needs its 1,211 yards to get anywhere near the waters.

Southport, then, is best identified as a seaside town with a tourist industry but not necessarily a resort. It did not have as far to fall as Blackpool or Morecambe because it was always more of a place for the wealthy to live due to its closer proximity to the bigger cities of Liverpool by car and Manchester by train.

Southport is 21 miles up the coast from Liverpool and yet – though this is not an absolute rule – you could be in a different universe when it comes to a way of thinking, politically swinging between the Conservatives and Liberal Democrats. Southport is in the Sefton borough of Merseyside but, according to its postcode, it is an extension of Preston. Inhabitants tend to feel Lancastrian rather than Merseysiders and that is reflected by the accent Liverpudlians particularly label as 'wool'. On Sunday league football pitches, when kits have gone missing in the wash, you find more players wearing the shorts and socks of Manchester United rather than Liverpool or Everton, even though Manchester is further away.

Considering the affluence of Southport, considering its tree-lined avenues and big houses like those on Selworthy Road where Kenny Dalglish lives; considering too it is home to the world-famous Royal Birkdale golf course, the town probably thinks its football team should be doing better than it is and certainly should be more aspirational. There is a feeling of private shame towards Southport FC, the first professional team in the history of English football to adopt a sponsor in its name after a tyre company invested in 1918 and called it Southport Vulcan; the first team in the history of English football, indeed, from the old Third Division North to reach the quarter-finals of the FA Cup, as it did in 1931 only to lose 9–1 to Everton with Dixie Dean scoring four goals.

The shame might exist because of something that happened in 1978 and it has not been rectified: when Southport FC became the last club to be voted out of the Football League before automatic relegation was introduced in 1987. To make matters worse they were replaced by a club from a rugby town, one that had resigned from the league in 1931 as Wigan Borough and had seen repeated applications for re-entry rejected ever since.

Three-figure crowds, a dilapidated ground and an almost permanent residence near the foot of the table meant Southport went down. Rob Urwin, the club's statistician and unofficial historian, was at the Café Royal in London when Southport's fate was revealed. 'It was the only occasion when football reduced me to tears,' he said in 2015 ahead of Southport's third-round FA Cup tie at Derby. 'The W-word was a dirty one in our house for a long time after that, although I must admit Wigan took their chance and made something out of it.'

Frustration in Southport must surely be compounded by the fact that while the town's football team has remained in non-league, Wigan Athletic have since been to the Premier League, won the FA Cup and played in Europe, while other traditionally smaller clubs in the region like Fleetwood Town, Morecambe and Accrington Stanley have established themselves in the Football League. 'I was as pleased as everyone else to see them [Wigan] win the FA Cup. In all honesty, even in my wildest dreams I don't think I could ever envisage Southport doing that, but it is all about having money behind you,' Urwin continued. 'Wigan ended up with a chairman who pumped money into the club, and that is what you need to go up through the divisions. Fleetwood have done the same. I can remember not too long ago when they were two or three divisions below us; now they are in League One and going well. That is wholly down to Andy Pilley and the money he has put into the club, and you do wonder what might happen were he to change his mind and walk away, but that is a risk clubs have to take if they want to get ahead.'

Their most recent high in terms of position in the Football League standings had been in Division Three for three seasons in the late 1960s under Billy Bingham, the manager who would lead Northern Ireland to the last sixteen of the World Cup finals in 1982. Throughout that period, Southport held games on a Friday night to attract fans from the town who might otherwise consider travelling elsewhere to watch Preston North End or the big Merseyside and Manchester clubs on a Saturday afternoon.

'We obviously live in the shadow of Liverpool and Everton, but at one point a few seasons ago there were seven Premier League clubs on our doorstep,' Urwin said. 'Basically we've always had to hope people will consider supporting two clubs – we don't mind sharing spectators with some of the bigger teams. I just don't think we will ever get back into the league on that basis, unless a backer comes along. Towards the end of our time in the league, and for a few years afterwards when the club seemed to be dying every day, it was hard to see us making any progress at all.'

Southport FC was formed in 1881 as Southport Central and it was originally a rugby union club before its members reacted to a run of heavy defeats by deciding to try another sport. As Southport approached its centenary season, it was fighting for its existence with directors publishing a statement in the matchday programme of a game against Oswestry Town in September 1980 which pleaded for 'the people of Southport to support us at this difficult time'. This was after the board had judged it could not fulfil its duties and responsibilities effectively until the 'past affairs of the club have been looked into' by the Football

Association, who were asked to carry out a full and independent investigation into its own business affairs.

In November 1980 another statement was released, informing supporters that 'the most important and difficult decision in the club's history' had been made: Southport was going into liquidation, with the idea of clearing debts and re-forming. The statement told of 'the knockers, the people who stand on the sidelines and say how much better they could do things, and make suggestions when it is too late', adding that only three individuals had stepped forward to help following an extraordinary meeting of shareholders. 'These hard-working men found themselves in the hot seat, but they hoped, not without good reason, that other, more experienced people would come forward. This did not happen,' the statement concluded.

Though liquidation did not happen, the notes of secretary Geoff Clarke in the final match programme of the 1980/81 season reflected how close Southport had been to the edge, describing the previous months as 'the worst in the club's history', revealing too that at Christmas the league was on standby to receive Southport's resignation, thus preventing the visiting team from travelling.

By 1982 Southport languished in the Northern Premier League, playing in front of fewer than three hundred spectators. Charlie Clapham had moved to the town after relocating from the Midlands to develop his company, Palace Chemicals. 'I found it quite bizarre that all the reports on the club seemed to be on the front page,' Clapham remembered. 'I couldn't understand it – I thought they don't write about football clubs on the front page, they write about them on the back page.' His first game ended in victory over Gateshead in the FA Trophy and he enjoyed it so much that he decided to drive from Coventry to Spennymoor for the next round where Southport lost 5–0 and the players ended up playing in supporters' shoes because the pitch was frozen and it was too dangerous to wear boots.

Soon, Wigan Athletic would have Dave Whelan and they would emerge on the English football landscape. Southport, meanwhile, had Clapham, and though his chairmanship in the 35 years since has yielded three league titles, an appearance in an FA Trophy final at Wembley, numerous county cups as well as relative financial stability, a quick look at his Wikipedia page at the end of January 2017 revealed what at least one Southport supporter thought of him. His name supposedly? Charles 'The Con' Clapham.

Clubs the size of Southport have long been prey to suspicious-looking camel-coated businessmen holding big cigars and even bigger plans. When Liam Watson says Clapham is not one of those you are bound to think he is obliged to defend him; after all, he is employed by Clapham and this is his third spell working for him. But then, as Watson puts it, 'Bad men usually get found out pretty quickly in football.'

Watson was 33 years old when Clapham called for the first time to say, 'You have the Southport job.' In 2003, the club had dropped out of the Conference National into the Northern Premier League and Watson's pedigree was marked by three decent years at Runcorn, having become manager there aged just 29. Though he did not take Southport back up straight away, he did enough to make sure that when non-league's structure was altered, Southport finished halfway up the Northern Premier League table to ensure their participation in the newly created Conference North the following season. His earliest results at Southport, however, had been poor and within three months questions were already being asked about Watson's suitability. Southport's previous managers included Ronnie Moore and Mark Wright, ex-professional footballers with experience at higher levels.

Southport was a big step up from Runcorn, Watson's Football League playing career amounted to nine appearances for Preston North End before a knee injury curtailed his development, and supporters believed Clapham only decided to hire him because he was the cheapest option available. An injury-time equaliser on Boxing Day in the local derby at Marine came after some fans had arrived at the ground with the words 'Clapham Out' on their T-shirts. Within eighteen months, Southport had returned to the Conference, though Watson says Clapham only stayed with him through the challenging early stages because he could detect some form of a vision. 'The plan was to get rid of all the ageing pros on big Conference wages and replace them with hungry young players,' Watson remembers. 'It was a difficult decision to make because I'd played with some of these lads.

'There was luck involved as well and that's probably why Charlie stuck with me,' Watson says. 'The equaliser at Marine was like the Kevin Brock mistake for Oxford when Howard Kendall was on the verge of the sack as Everton's manager. Marine's right-back had just been announced as man of the match on the PA system. I think it caused him to lose concentration because within seconds he'd lost the ball and suddenly we had a chance.'

When he reflects upon his playing days, Liam Watson thinks most fondly of his time playing for Marine. Runs to the semi-final of the FA Trophy and the third round of the FA Cup had happened in the two years before he decided to join. Roly Howard was in charge and, aside from being recognised by Guinness World Records as the longest-serving manager in world football, he was a window cleaner in Southport by trade, with Kenny Dalglish his most famous client. Marine's team was full of powerful-looking men. Chris Camden, the Heineken Export-guzzling centre-forward who worked on the assembly line at the Vauxhall car plant in Ellesmere Port, was eighteen stone and nicknamed 'the Buffalo'.

Within the squad of fifteen players, Watson, at 25, was considered the runt of the litter. He was the best-looking, he had a lot to say for himself, but he had to speak up in order to survive because the atmosphere among the players was close and brutal. Had Marine's College Road ground not been only three-sided, Watson, Camden and the rest would have made it to the Conference after successive Northern Premier League titles in 1994 and 1995; instead, Leek Town and Morecambe went up.

Though individuals in their thirties like Camden had played in the Football League for Tranmere Rovers in their younger days, none had emerged through highly organised established academy systems like the ones we see now. Roly Howard might have banned his players from Sunday league football (and this explains why he decided to release John Coleman in 1984), but many of them, like the defender Andy Draper – who worked as a ditch digger and gave the impression that he would head bricks instead of footballs if he had to – had been amateurs before entering semi-professionalism; a competitive standard that many were proud to be at.

The rise of the professional football academies means routes into football now are standardised. Even the story of Jamie Vardy, whose emergence from non-league to Premier League champion and England international involves the moment where he was released by Sheffield Wednesday as a sixteen-year-old. In January 2017, every single member of Southport's squad had, at some point, been released by the academy of a Football League club.

'The dynamic of the game has changed massively in the last decade,' says Watson, who is dealing with players much younger than someone like Marine's Roly Howard was twenty years ago. Southport's oldest player was Neil Ashton at 32. Take him out of the squad and the average age dropped to 21.

'The players are different, we are now in the academy generation,' Watson continues. 'I've won four league titles in non-league football and if you look at the quality of the team that won the first one in 2005 to the last one in 2014, there had been a decline. The two Southport teams were very different in terms of the size and shape of the players as well as their ages and the way we played. In 2005, my two young ones were Michael Powell and Earl Davis. When we clinched the title on the last day of the season at Harrogate they were both on the bench. In 2010, they became the two experienced players: instrumental in helping us win the league again. The three young players from the 2010 team at Southport then followed me to Telford but by 2014, it had become more challenging to find that ilk of young person again, someone you can work with and help make better. Now you have academy lads who turn up with wash bags and fancy cars. Many of them are obsessed with image and can't handle a bollocking. I liken academy culture to taking lessons before your driving test. You take your lessons to pass but you don't always drive like that afterwards. You don't have the same driving instructor telling you what to do. The academy system is massively flawed because players are coached to play in the Premier League when there's probably more likelihood that a player will win the lottery than actually play in the Premier League.

'Traditionally, players let go by Everton would sign for Preston North End. Now, if you get let go by Everton there's a decent chance Prescot Cables will be your second club. And then, when you get to Prescot you spend the first twelve months being told not to do what you've been told to do for the last eight years. Are you going to be able to get the ball down and pass on Prescot's pitch? No way. It's all about winning the second ball. So it takes time to adapt. Only once you do that will the quality begin to shine through. Having the humility to play at Prescot after being at an academy is another issue altogether. When I played for Marine, I was delighted to tell people that Marine was my club: "Yeah, I play for Marine – we're top of the Northern Premier League. It's great." The kid now who has been released by Liverpool will say reluctantly, "I'm at Marine . . ." He'll be looking at the floor because he's been sold a dream and it hasn't happened.'

Watson would not let his son Niall sign forms for a professional club until he turned sixteen.

'There is an unhealthy rejection culture in football,' Watson explains. 'Nine-year-old kids go training at Liverpool for six weeks. One will get asked to stay on. Another will get told he's not good enough. How's he meant to understand that at nine, particularly if he was enjoying it? Lads at twenty-four or twenty-five, they can't get their heads around it when you release them, so what's a nine-year-old going to do? You'll get the coaches saying it toughens them up but it doesn't. It breaks them. It breaks the parents too. And in this world, they've got enough to worry about as it is.

'Niall must think I'm the worst [dad] in the world because I'm always telling him, "You're a kid, you should be cleaning the boots – learning your trade. Don't be thinking you're a footballer because you're not." I worked at Cammell Laird for four years after leaving school to learn a trade. I didn't turn pro until I was twenty-three. Niall has seven years on me. I hope he doesn't waste a day because it flies by. I see other parents and they're desperate to get their lad an agent at fourteen.

'Today, you speak to a young non-league player and you ask them what they do. "I'm a professional footballer." Who do you play for? "Southport." You're not a professional footballer then, are you, mate?

'Lots of young players want to say they are professional footballers because it sounds better than the reality. Everyone is chasing the dream.'

Watson recognises that the commitment required to survive at an academy often comes at the expense of an education, which contributes further towards occupational descriptions when players drop out of the Football League and into the Conference, where Southport are one of only seven part-time clubs in a league of 24 teams. But the other seventeen clubs share the same aim – earning promotion to League Two – and, given there are only two promotion places available, one of them through the play-offs, the competitive environment leaves a lot of potential for serious disappointment. By the end of the season as many as 22 managerial positions could be very vulnerable indeed.

Watson believes there will come a time not too far away where the Conference National will no longer be considered as non-league, and rather a fifth professional division of sorts; perhaps being split in two between north and south like it was forty years ago. The drive towards professionalism in the Conference National has affected the Conference North, with AFC Fylde, Nuneaton and Tamworth already full-time and Salford City and Harrogate Town announcing in the winter of 2016 they will follow them for the 2017/18 season, whether they earn promotion before then or not.

Conference clubs are taking risks which are potentially just as grave as the ones in the Premier League. Conference owners are aware that central funding for Football League clubs is almost twice as much as it is in the league below. Many clubs stand accused of spending money they don't even have in order to reach the promised land.

'Massive gambles are taking place,' Watson says. 'You also have clubs like Forest Green whose chairman has been putting more than a million pounds into the club for several years and it still hasn't happened for them. Forest Green are lucky that Dale Vince has a bottomless pit of money so he can keep doing it. Not every owner has a bottomless pit and not every owner is as patient as Dale Vince, though he's gone through a fair few managers.'

You can understand why Watson speaks of non-league losing its sense of tradition and soul. 'Everything that happens in the Premier League eventually gets mirrored further down,' he says. 'Now, because of the demand for instant success, if managers aren't getting sacked, they're choosing to walk away because of the pressure.

'The pressure on non-league managers is far greater than it was ten years ago,' he insists. 'I think it's a cultural problem which in sport is reflected by the power of the Premier League and attitudes towards it. I read an article which said the standard of the managers in the Premier League is the best it has ever been at the top with Conte, Wenger, Mourinho, Guardiola, Klopp and Pochettino. Well, two of them are going to end up failing because they won't qualify for the Champions League. Only four have the chance. Soon enough, two of them might get sacked because of the obsession with the Champions League and the money available there. If you have a sack culture at the top, it spreads across the game. In non-league, managers don't get time to turn it round. The sacking culture affects the players too. When I played, you'd sign for a manager knowing he'd be there for at least eighteen months. Now, players don't know how long a manager is going to be there for so they make more selfish decisions and move on a lot quicker if the money is slightly better elsewhere. Who can blame them? If a manager gets sacked, a player might find himself out of the next fella's plans. Because the Premier League looks after itself, everybody else has to and it means the mood around football isn't as happy as it used to be.'

Watson can only dream of signing someone for Southport and making his plans around the player for the next five years, as it had been at Marine when Roly Howard could rely on loyal servants like Jon Gautrey, Keith Proctor and Kevin O'Brien, the goalkeeper who now coaches Everton's academy players.

'A long-serving player now has been at a club for eighteen months,' Watson says. 'Having elder statesmen in teams helps young players maintain their standards for a lot longer. Again, you don't see any of this in the Premier League and the Premier League mirrors everything down. People don't realise just how much of an ultimate business machine it is. Club owners don't want older players because they have no resale value. It's as simple as that. They don't consider the professional benefits because the people making the key decisions are thinking of finance first and sport second.

'But do you honestly think foreign players want to live in England?' he asks. 'They don't, they come here for the money. Years ago, people went to Italy for the money – and look at the state of Serie A now, it's gone to the wall. Diego Costa is a great player. He's on eight million quid a year but because of British tax laws, fifty per cent of that is taken away. A Chinese club comes in and offers £32million net. He's getting a cheque to finish his career. Who really wants to live and play in China?

'All those years ago at Marine – when teams stayed together a lot longer – we used to joke that you'd get a P45 and a map to Oswestry. When players were finished, they'd take one final payday in the Welsh League. Now, the top players like Costa – at twenty-eight – are threatening to go elsewhere before their time is even up. It shows you that he's led by money. To be fair to Costa, he's not alone.'

Southport and the other six part-time clubs in the Conference are faced with two options: remain as they are and hope the fans understand why, or join the professional rat race and hope that somehow everything works out despite the huge financial risks.

The last time Southport did this in 2007, Watson decided to resign as manager because he had full-time employment as a nursing assistant at Ashworth Hospital and staying with Southport would have meant a cut in wages and the prospect of an unsecure future. Instead he accepted the job at Burscough and took most of Southport's players with him.

Watson says that in the summer of 2017, Southport will turn full-time again. He thinks it will remove an excuse culture at the club. At the moment, players train three mornings a week and it only doesn't interfere with any alternative full-time work because the majority consider themselves professional footballers anyway. Watson is adamant that he will be involved when the change happens, though not as manager – as the supporters might speculate – but as the director of operations, bringing some 'football knowledge and understanding to the boardroom'.

'Some people might see what's happened today and think that I've ended up back in the position I've always wanted, but the truth is, if I wanted to become Southport's manager again, I'd have taken the job in September when I left Stalybridge,' he says. 'I've got other aspects of my life that are more important now but that doesn't mean I won't do my best to help the club in the meantime. If I have to stick around for a day, a week or a month then so be it. If we get beaten 8–0 at Gateshead on Saturday, I might be back in the stands in my other role sooner than people think.'

Watson took Southport to within five points of the Conference play-offs during the 2011/12 season, finishing a commendable seventh considering the competition in the league involved Fleetwood as champions with Jamie Vardy up front. Luton Town, once of the old First Division, finished fifth that year.

'As a full-time club we have a better chance of reaching the play-offs,' Watson believes. 'Part-time in the Conference? You're working with your hands tied behind your back.'

INDEPENDENT LAND

10

MOVING HOME

THE HECKLE CAME FROM A SHADY-LOOKING INDIVIDUAL SKULKING near the timber yard. Paul Grimes was sat nervously in the passenger seat of a clapped-out car parked beside the Bramley-Moore dock, his heavy disguise failing him. Grimes, a former gangster, was filming a documentary with journalist Donal MacIntyre about Liverpool's criminal underworld. He had turned police informant when his son Jason died of a heroin overdose in 1992 at the age of 21. Grimes was in witness protection because his evidence had led to successful prosecutions against John Haase and Curtis Warren. His aim had been to bring down the dealers that he believed had destroyed his son's life. Grimes had since survived six assassination attempts and there was a £100,000 bounty on his head. The character near the timber yard recognised Grimes as a 'grass'.

Weaponry was uncovered, including a double-barrelled sawn-off shotgun and a Colt full-loading pistol, along with ammunition, when a search was made of Haase's Big Brother security firm, based a few hundred feet away in the largest brick building in the world, the old Stanley Dock tobacco warehouse. The police found a bath in the basement. It is said to have been filled with acid.

Haase used the site because it had been empty since 1985, like so many of the other buildings on the dock road as you travel north from the city centre to Seaforth, where the River Mersey oozes out into the Irish Sea. Before, the thoroughfare had been a significant one for Liverpool, a place that had been known as 'the New York of Europe' at its commercial peak, as well as 'the second city of the Empire', one that had grown rich off the slave trade. During the Second World War, from a secret bunker deep beneath the Western Approaches, the Battle of the Atlantic was planned at the operational command of the Royal Navy and Liverpool suffered a blitz second only to London's as a consequence, deeply affecting the dock area's strategic capabilities.

Following the Toxteth Riots in 1981, the Conservative chancellor Geoffrey Howe wrote to Margaret Thatcher, warning against public spending on cities like Liverpool because the Merseyside region would be 'the hardest nut to crack'. Howe suggested, 'I cannot help feeling that the option of managed decline [for Liverpool] is one which we should not forget altogether,' adding, 'We do not want to find ourselves concentrating all the limited cash that may have to be made available into Liverpool and having nothing left for possibly more promising areas such as the West Midlands or, even, the North East,' it felt like code: that Middle England is all to fight for and the Liverpool will always vote Labour.

There had been a history of militant trade unionism in Liverpool's docks because of the sheer number of men that worked there and the weight of money being made by the very few. In the boom years there had been as many as 43 active wharfs and each one was serviced by a couple of pubs at least, which are still there now but long closed; pubs with names like the Iron Horse, the Rubber Duck, the Bull and the Goat. By 1995, most of pubs were either gone or struggling and working conditions in the dockyards were getting worse. A dispute that began when five men were sacked and led to 500 losing their jobs became one of the longest-running in the world, finishing in 1998.

All of this has meant that the economies on the streets around Liverpool's eighteen docks have withered. Only a few like the Kings Dock and the famous Albert Dock have recovered and that is because of their geography close to Liverpool's city centre, which was transformed largely thanks to the European funding it received ahead of its 'Capital of Culture' year in 2008.

Many believe that Everton Football Club missed a trick here because five years before, plans to move to the Kings Dock fell through due to lack of funding. By 2021, though, Everton hope the Bramley-Moore Dock, less than two miles north of Kings, will be theirs. If this happens the ward's crime links will be in the past. The pubs might reopen. It is claimed the dynamic of Liverpool's docklands will change forever. Inevitably, so will Walton's.

*

Suspended above Neil Robinson on a telephone wire, a pair of Rockport boots are tied together by their laces next to some Crocs fastened by straps. To his side, rows of neatly appointed terraced houses face each other. Just behind him, as he stares in the direction of Walton Lane from Diana Street, is Goodison Park's ancient Bullens Road stand.

If asked to describe a classic image from one of Liverpool's inner-city boroughs, many would surely think of this. Not much has changed here since Everton moved in 124 years ago. Whenever Liverpool supporters enter through its narrow turnstiles, jokes are made about it being like going back in time. Jegsy Dodd, the performance poet and Anfield season-ticket holder, once compared the Bullens, with its many obstructed views, to a 'pirate's galleon', because of the timber and wood features that have helped tape the present structure in position since 1926. Of the four sides of the ground, only the Park End has been completely modernised in the Premier League era, an end of the ground which in the summer of 2016 received a refurbishment with its east corner filled in to ensure supporters sitting in the Gwladys Street end could not see Anfield's main stand rising in the distance, a reminder to Evertonians that their ground was being left behind; a reminder too that the site at Anfield was once theirs.

Everton's departure from Walton, however, would be of deep emotional consequence for many and, in a sporting sense, no one more so than Robinson, whose name will be inscribed into the history books forever as the Everton footballer who lived closest to Goodison Park as a child. He spent the first four years of his life with six brothers, a sister and as many as five other relatives in a rented four-bedroomed terrace at 45 Spellow Lane, pronounced locally as 'Spella', which is well known for its pub, which Evertonians still spill out of on match days.

Neil lives in Widnes now but it does not take much for the memories to flood back as I walk with him and one of his brothers, John, around the surrounding streets the morning after Everton have beaten Arsenal in a Premier League match. 'I love this place,' Neil says, pointing upwards at Goodison's three-tier main stand, which stoops over the smaller terraces like a grandfather shielding three innocents. Neil and John speak proudly about another sibling, Sir Ken Robinson, the world-renowned author and speaker on education. He lives in Los Angeles. 'I reckon we were all inspired by Everton in some way; living here, how couldn't you be?' Neil continues. 'We went to Gwladys Street Primary School, on the other side of the ground. We had everything we wanted in the world in one place as kids.'

Life was not easy for father Jim, though. An industrial accident saw him confined to the lower floor of Spellow Lane as a quadriplegic. This happened just a few years after he missed out on a job as permanent manager of the famous Winslow Hotel pub, just over the road from Goodison's main stand, because Norman Greenhalgh, Everton's left-back, had retired, the club had contacts at the brewery and this was not an era where football created a nest egg.

'Norman was appointed instead and it resulted in my dad working at the Kodak factory in Kirkby and that's where the accident happened,' Neil recalls. 'It was very difficult for him at Spellow Lane. All his mates used to walk past on their way to the game. They'd knock on the window. "Alright, Jim . . ." But he was stuck there . . .'

Jim Robinson saw his son play just one Everton reserve game live because there was only provision for five disabled people at Goodison Park when he broke into the first team and spaces then were filled by season-ticket holders, but there is no sense of resentment at all. 'It was his dream for one of us to play for Everton,' Neil reasons, recounting the moment he signed his first professional contract. 'The club sold Colin Harvey to Sheffield Wednesday on the same afternoon. We were all such huge Evertonians that I told my dad the news about Colin before my own. He was devastated and overjoyed at the same time – we both were.'

By the time we reach the end of the stadium where Robinson – a right-back – scored the only goal of his seventeen-game Everton career (the achievement was eclipsed that day in 1977 because Bob Latchford took his tally to thirty for the season during a 6–0 victory over Chelsea), he is thinking about the future and what leaving Goodison means both for the club he loves and for parades like County Road, where the survival of the shops and the pubs are linked to the existence of a major football team being based nearby. In front of him, there is rust on the corrugated metal that protects the brickwork on the back of the Gwladys Street stand. He wonders whether Everton could rebuild and remain, like their closest rivals Liverpool have done.

From the vast windows on the top-tier concourse of Anfield's new main stand, the views stretch across Merseyside and out as far as the wind turbines in Liverpool Bay. Goodison is much closer, less than a mile away: across Stanley Park, gently down the hill. When viewed from here, Goodison appears tiny. When viewed from Goodison, Anfield appears enormous.

The redevelopment of Anfield came at a considerable social cost, however. Two decades of delay has led to a wider decay. David Fairclough, who, like Robinson, grew up closest to the ground of the team he supported and ended up representing, tells stories about his early teenage years: hanging out at the petrol garage owned by Gordon Wallace and Peter Thompson – Liverpool first-team players, where Bobby Graham, the Scottish forward, once handed him a match programme. That land is flattened now and, sadly, in keeping with much of the waste ground nearby. Many of the roads around Anfield have simply been wiped off the map. 'Maybe the area can recover now they've finally got the main stand built,' Fairclough speculates. 'It was very important, though, that Liverpool stayed. Aside from all of the famous moments, the ashes of lots of people are buried underneath the pitch. Some things are sacred.'

Everton's decision to move was made nearly twenty years ago when former chairman Peter Johnson spoke of building a ground to rival the finest in Europe. It had been on the agenda of his successor Bill Kenwright ever since. In the 1960s Everton had been known as the 'Mersey Millionaires' because of the club's lavish spending in the transfer market but by the turn of the century – though Kenwright was a wealthy man – he did not have the money to find Everton a new home and keep a competitive team on the field at the same time, nor manage the debt that would follow in the years before any new ground would start paying for itself if attendances remained high. It was often believed that finding an appropriate site was Everton's biggest issue, but the club was already in the red and sales from season tickets were paying off the debt while income from television money helped pay wages. Kenwright was born into an Everton family and had seen the destruction of other clubs after they were sold to the wrong owner. Though he recognised the need for investment, it had to be from the right person – someone whose sporting interest in the club matched his business interest. He identified Farhad Moshiri, an Iranian-born steel magnate, as that person. Within a year of his arrival, the move to Bramley-Moore was announced as 'a once-in-a-lifetime opportunity to regenerate the Atlantic Corridor in north Liverpool'.

Neil Moore, the Everton player who grew up second-closest to Goodison Park behind Neil Robinson, has mixed feelings about the development. While Robinson had moved away from Spellow Lane by the time his Everton career started, Moore was still able to walk to Goodison Park. His journey began in his shirt and tie at his mother's house halfway down Shepston Avenue. He would turn right, cutting up Hans Road, which takes in junctions with Cowley Road, Bodmin Road, Milman Road and Bardsay Road. This was a time when the alleyways were not locked up by the council as they are now and this allowed him to bypass Leta Street and Mere Green altogether. At Gwladys Street, behind

Goodison Park's home end, a slight left would take him towards Bullens Road and the same primary school that Robinson went to. A right took him towards the player entrance of the main stand, past the Church of St Luke the Evangelist, where his mother, Vy, still works before matches serving tea to customers. The journey from home to workplace was complete in less than ten minutes.

Though he was selected to play against the great Manchester United side of the mid-1990s and marked Eric Cantona and Mark Hughes during a 1–0 defeat at Old Trafford, Moore's Everton career lasted only four games, and at the age of 28 he was marshalling Telford United's defence in the Conference alongside Jim Bentley, now the Everton-supporting Morecambe manager. Moore had grown up a Liverpudlian, attending matches with his father and uncles. 'Goodison Park was always in my line of vision but never in my thoughts,' he says. 'Football was a major part of the community around these streets, though. There were no Xboxes to distract kids and fewer cars on the road. We'd use the steel exit gates of the Gwladys Street end as a goal.'

As he looks at where the Blue House used to be, the pub where Everton's players and fans used to drink together before the club's megastore was built, Moore speaks of a 'sense of loss' when asked about the move to Bramley-Moore. 'The new site will be a blank canvas so I hope they don't get it wrong. Look at Goodison Park,' he says. "There's only one stand where you get a clear view of the pitch. You go in the upper Bullens and you need to crouch to see what's going on. But that's the beauty of the place. Loads of players have said how difficult it is to get a result here. Moving away will be tinged with sadness.'

Moore, who worked on a building site after finishing his playing career, is now employed by a taxi firm that scuttles Liverpool's talented young players between the Kirkby academy and first-team training ground, Melwood. He is not alone in being excited about the possibilities at Bramley-Moore but then, he stops to consider the impact on County Road pubs like the Black Horse, the Glebe, the Brick and Harlech Castle. After the announcement was made, some shops shut, almost overnight, and what does that mean for an area that already struggles?

'These businesses rely on Saturday afternoons when Everton are at home,' Moore says. 'I suppose it's not far from here to Bramley-Moore. Evertonians could walk it; it would take about twenty minutes. Bramley-Moore's not a million miles away. It's not like we're moving to Kirkby. I'm glad that didn't happen.'

*

Walton is the only constituency in England with two Premier League football clubs. It is also home to two of the most deprived social and economic wards in the country. It explains why Dave Kelly is currently leading a foodbank scheme where football supporters are encouraged to arrive at matches with essentials, dropping them off at points around Goodison Park and Anfield. Kelly is the chairman of the Blue Union, an Everton pressure group which works closely with Spirit of Shankly on such initiatives, and this relationship reflects that Liverpool is a city which will organically unite when a greater good is recognised.

It is because of the efforts of the Blue Union and Spirit of Shankly, indeed, that other progressive measures have been forced like the creation of Liverpool's Football Quarter, an area which aims at using the city's football clubs as an anchor for regeneration. The origins of both organisations lies in protest. While SOS formed in reaction to the growing fear that American businessmen Tom Hicks and George Gillett were leading Liverpool towards financial meltdown after failing to deliver on grand promises and quickly falling out, Blue Union's slogan, 'Support the team, oppose stagnation,' was a preventative one, coined following two decades of watching an unsuccessful side from decaying terraces during a period where the stadiums of so many other Premier League clubs modernised.

Kelly, a trade unionist, had previously helped lead the Keep Everton in Our City campaign, which had started in 2007 after it was announced Everton were planning on relocating from inner-city Walton to out-of-town Kirkby in a deal financed by supermarket chain Tesco.

The efforts of KEIOC led to a public inquiry and by 2009, Kelly was cross-examining barristers, solicitors and planning experts. Privately the inquiry team had voiced concerns about football supporters sitting in the gallery of what was essentially a courtroom for fear they might disrupt proceedings by chanting or singing. When the matter was eventually settled and the move quashed, the inquiry's chairman thanked KEIOC for the way they'd presented their case and how professional they'd been. 'There's a misconception of who football fans really are and what we can achieve,' reflects Kelly, sitting behind one of his hot-desks in the Unite offices in Liverpool city centre. 'We were vilified by many people for making a stand against Kirkby and we were a lone voice for a long time. By the end of the inquiry I took a great deal of satisfaction in seeing lots of residents groups, county councils and businesses opposed to the idea, saying exactly what we'd been telling everyone all along.'

The saga of Kirkby and the significance of what Kelly and KEIOC did to stop it happening surely ranks with the greatest demonstrations of fan activism in English football history. Yet the story was overshadowed at the time, not only because neighbours Liverpool were in turmoil and the words of Hicks and Gillett generated so many headlines, but also because the work of Kelly and others involved with KEIOC was anticipatory: they could see flaws in Everton's and Tesco's proposal that others didn't and because KEIOC ended up winning before the plan took off, the episode was never really allowed to become a crisis.

Kelly admits the romantic in him wants Everton to stay at Goodison Park forever but the pragmatist reminds him that his wish is an impossibility due to the geography of the ground.

'I watch Everton home and away and in the last eleven years I've missed only one game,' he says proudly. 'Of the seven ever-present clubs in the Premier League's history, we have been the least successful. While other clubs have invested lots of money in stadiums and infrastructure, we did nothing. Yet as Kirkby unravelled over weeks and months and years, it became clear the destination was not in the interests of the many and rather, the interests of the few, particularly Tesco. For Everton, it would have given a quick short-term fix to a long-standing problem, certainly not the long-term solution.'

The conversation about Goodison Park's suitability began in 1997 when then chairman Peter Johnson revealed plans for Everton to move to a 60,000 all-seater stadium which would stand four tiers high, each one divided by a strip of executive boxes. Johnson pitched it as 'the chance of a lifetime'.

'Goodison is and was a Grand Old Lady,' he said. 'But any club that had aspirations to be part of the European elite had to have a bigger and better stadium. I visited the likes of the San Siro and the Nou Camp and came away determined that Everton had to have something along those lines.'

Johnson had stressed that relocation was the only option because Goodison Park's location meant redevelopment was impossible, hemmed in on three sides by streets of terraced houses.

Johnson, who had grown up as a Liverpool supporter and had previously been the chairman of Tranmere Rovers, was an unpopular figure and he stepped down from his position in 1998 following an argument with manager Walter Smith over the sale of Duncan Ferguson. In his place, Bill Kenwright had long appreciated the need for Everton to move, but winning hearts and minds over the issue was a problem – as well as finding the finance to fund it. Though Kenwright is credited with bringing stability and care to Everton, especially at a time when businessmen with purely financial interests were eating into other Premier League clubs, the collapse of deals with companies like NTL and Fortress Sports Fund meant Everton missed out on new stadium opportunities like the Kings Dock site close to Liverpool's centre before the area was regenerated ahead of Liverpool's capital of culture year in 2008. By 2007, Everton were – instead – talking about moving elsewhere, and Kirkby would mean that the club's location would be further away from the city or town centre it represented than any other club competing in the Premier League – some five miles further out than the second farthest, Bolton Wanderers' ground in Horwich. Everton – like Bolton – would be playing in an identikit football stadium in the retail parklands. The mood was summarised by a letter from one supporter in the Liverpool Echo. 'They promised us a penthouse on the waterfront – now it's a council flat in Kirkby.'

Keith Wyness, Everton's former chief executive, had warned that 'serious' issues would arise if the club remained at Goodison for much longer. 'Attendance numbers will go down and then revenue will go down and when that happens you can't compete,' he said. 'We think within the next ten years there are going to be some very serious issues with regard to whether Goodison could even qualify for a safety certificate. Parts of the ground would require huge investment just to remain open. Kirkby is the only way forward. The deal of the century. There is no Plan B.'

The Destination Kirkby project had been announced at the Everton shareholders' AGM. As a shareholder, Kelly initially reacted positively to the news because he shared Wyness's view that change was needed. It was Wyness's claim, 'We will be getting a very nice stadium for a small amount of money,' that set alarm bells ringing, however. 'When something sounds too good to be true, it's because it usually is,' he says. 'It felt like we were vacating the city of our birth and we were handing over our city entirely to our neighbours from across the park, though that wasn't the sole reason for my objection to it. I'm a lifelong Evertonian and a more-or-less lifelong Kirkby resident. I've lived for fifty-five of my fifty-nine years in Kirkby. I've never believed you can force a quart into a pint pot. The reality is, the population of Kirkby would have increased by more than a hundred per cent on a match day. Its population was around 45,000 and the new stadium would have held 55,000. Kirkby is a relatively small town on the periphery of Liverpool. It would have meant that on match days the whole of the town would have become a no-parking zone. Though the plans claimed it would be served by a park-and-ride scheme they were dreadfully flawed. It was estimated that it would take fourteen seconds for a bus to park near the ground, for every fan to disembark the bus and then leave again reversing out.

'The transport plan was unrealistic,' he continues. 'I took great offence at the terminology being used, it was abhorrent. They were talking about "crush loading" fans onto trains [considering 96 Liverpool supporters were crushed to death at Hillsborough in 1989 and Kelly has long supported the affected families' campaign for justice]. They were talking about fans queuing for anything up to an hour and a half to get out of Kirkby after a match.

'The store that Tesco were proposing to build would have been the biggest in the UK but it would have been 107 per cent bigger than what they were legally entitled to. It would have dominated the town and other stores would probably have ended up closing as a result. It would have killed Kirkby town centre dead in the water. It was fundamentally flawed on so many different points. There was talk of cross-subsidies and finance coming in from different places but nobody could really explain how the ground was going to be funded.

'So I submitted a resolution to Liverpool City Council asking the council to support the campaign to keep Everton in Liverpool. I told them that if the city council allowed Everton to abandon Goodison Park and move to Kirkby it would have been akin to the decision to demolish the overhead railway, or to destroy the Cavern or to flatten one of the cathedrals. It would have been an act of urban vandalism. It would have been municipal neglect on a grand scale.

'People like us have long been referred to as the vocal minority. We shout the loudest. We're rent-a-mob. But we realised, it's all well and good getting out on the streets and making a big noise – you have to be organised to get what you really want in life. So we started a political party called First for Kirkby and stood as candidates in the town. Knowsley Council had sixty-two councillors at the time and sixty-two of them were Labour. Its MP had a 38,000 majority in parliament and Knowsley was the safest Labour seat in the country. But we came within sixteen votes of winning a [council] seat. If this had happened in any other town or city in the country, Kirkby First would probably have had people elected onto the council. I think this took fan activism and people defending football clubs to a new level. We took on the biggest retailer in Europe in the shape of Tesco. We took on our own local authority. We took on a Premier League football club. And we beat the three of them.'

KEIOC's campaign was endorsed by Liverpool City Council across all parties. The city's mayor, Joe Anderson, described the proposed Kirkby stadium as 'a glorified cowshed built in a small town outside Liverpool'. The councils of Sefton, St Helens and West Lancashire followed in their support. Kelly wonders what might have happened if Everton and Tesco had got their way, especially amid a worldwide financial crisis. 'I know of a council down south where Tesco had made a planning application. They started to build a big supermarket and then the recession kicked in. It caused Tesco to vacate the site. Would the same thing have happened to Kirkby?' Though the possibility was unlikely, it is understandable why Kelly warns, 'Goodison Park might have been bulldozed and Everton left without a home.'

Everton's future now seems to be at Bramley-Moore. Kelly says when discussions were taking place about the possibility of Everton buying the land in the Kings Dock in 2004, he was concerned because it would have meant Everton were moving from a landlocked stadium in Walton to one hemmed in by the River Mersey, and that this would render any further expansion impossible.

'I repeatedly get asked the question, what do you think about Moshiri? Well, nothing . . . at best I'm cautiously optimistic. The reality is, he's an investor. He's invested in Everton Football Club and he'll eventually look for a return on his investment. Who is going to pay for his investment? That's me, you and any other fella who goes through the turnstile. You can dress it up any way you want. He's not a Jack Walker, he's not a John Moores and he's not a David Moores. He's not doing it because he's a lifelong supporter. It's not Moshiri's club. He might own the club but without the fans, it would be worth nothing. Everton is my club, it's my kids' club. It's my grandchildren's club. That's why fans need to be consulted over the biggest decisions. That's why fans need to be a part of the thought and planning process, whoever holds the keys.'

On the wall of Joe Anderson's resplendent waterfront office is a copy of an oil painting by Walter Richards entitled Modern Liverpool, 1907. Amid the dark industrial colours of Victorian squalor, you can see St Nicholas's church and its green lawn where bodies were once buried in a plague pit. You can see the red bricks of the nearby Grade II listed Albion House – or the White Star building as it was – where five years later the names of Titanic's deceased were read out from a balcony, as a concerned public listened. Nearly all the notable landmarks are there too: the Albert Dock back when it was a working dock rather than a tourist destination as it is now, Lime Street Station and the railway lines leading out towards the soot-covered rooves of Wavertree; the magnificent St George's Hall and the overhead railway.

What isn't there is either of the city's two cathedrals, nor – most significantly – the Cunard Building, where Anderson's office is currently located. Anderson is taking me around the image, pointing out the changes. 'See, the two buildings next to an open plot of land where the Cunard is, are the Port of Liverpool and the Liver Building,' he tells me. 'When they went up people objected to them because they were too high. Now, the three buildings are called the Three Graces.'

The Three Graces helped Liverpool earn its label as a Maritime Mercantile City and six locations across the city are now regarded as World Heritage Sites by UNESCO.

'It shows you can create outstanding structures despite opposition and for future generations to appreciate them,' Anderson says. 'That's what I hope Everton do; the new stadium becoming a fine addition to our waterfront skyline, which is already recognised across the world. We can't wrap this city up in aspic. If we do, we might as well turn off the lights.'

In the month before I speak to Anderson, the New Statesman had described him as a character who 'inspires gratitude and loathing in equal measure' – not only a 'passionate and unapologetic defender of Liverpool on the national stage', but also a 'divisive figure in the city'. Anderson had worked as a merchant seaman, a pub landlord, a union convenor and a social worker before becoming the leader of Liverpool City Council when the Keep Everton in Our City campaign was in full swing. Elected mayor in 2012, his willingness to court private sector investment had fostered resentment and there were trust issues after a legal dispute where he took a school in neighbouring Sefton to an industrial tribunal after he was dismissed as a learning mentor. Blood on letters and excreta sent through the door, Anderson has seen it all over the years. His children had urged him to leave Twitter where he was often attacked for his appearance – though he's nowhere near as big or round as he's made out to be when you meet him. The abuse directed at him, particularly from Liverpool supporters, returned when Everton's move to Bramley-Moore was announced and it was revealed that Anderson – an outspoken Evertonian – had helped broker the deal between the club he supports and Peel Holdings, the owner of the land; especially when it emerged that Liverpool City Council would act as guarantors for the financing of the new stadium. Anderson subsequently was accused of favouritism.

Anderson begins by reminding me that he and Labour were in opposition to the Liberal Democrats when, under Warren Bradley, the council supported Liverpool's potential move from Anfield to Stanley Park in 2007. It would have been easy for him then to oppose a deal which would have meant the homes of Liverpool Football Club and Everton Football Club were separated by only a road but he backed it – amid fierce reaction from Evertonians – because he thought it was the right thing to do for the economic development of the city.

'I'll say it as it is, that's who I am and I don't particularly care what people think about me,' he says firmly, prodding his finger into the table that separates us. 'People say the council have bent over backwards to help Everton Football Club because I'm an Evertonian but that simply isn't true. When Liverpool made the decision to remain at Anfield and redevelop the main stand we supported it fully in the planning process, acquiring and buying properties in the area to give the club the space it needed to expand the main stand. Both Liverpool Football Club and Everton Football Club are crucial to the economy and the reputation of the city. Had Liverpool decided to move to the same location before Everton, we'd have backed it.

'I know Liverpool's owners really well and I've developed a great relationship with them over the last few years,' he continues. 'They've got plenty of money and have supported Liverpool financially. Above everything, though – especially in these uncertain and financially reckless times – you want stability and security around the club. Maybe fans would prefer a sugar daddy but when I think about Fenway and what they have brought to the club while trying to respect its history and acting responsibly in everything they do, it means that Liverpool has a strong foundation if somebody else comes along and wants to take it over. I think that's what we want for Everton: to have foundations that will secure the club's future for the next hundred years.

'A lot of people knock Bill Kenwright for his tenure as chair. I've got nothing but admiration for the guy. He's given the club his heart and soul over many years and has continued to do so even through a period where he's not been in the best of health – I think people know that. His passion for the football club and his desire to find the right investor has been admirable. For all we know he might have had more lucrative-sounding offers to take Everton off his hands but I know he was very wary about the wrong person taking it on and the impact it can have – just look at what Hicks and Gillett did at Liverpool and how David Moores, the former owner, ended up feeling about that – writing an open letter in a newspaper begging them to leave.'

As guarantors, Liverpool City Council will receive revenue of around £4million a year from Everton's stadium move and Anderson says this is the key reason behind his support for the project. Under Conservative rule, Liverpool

City Council has had £540million of funding stripped from its budget. It explains why he believes in what he calls the 'Invest to Earn' strategy that has led to criticism from Labour's far left because it involves agreements with private-sector companies that are often championed by the Tories. Such criticism came when the council paid £15million for the purchase and refurbishing of the Cunard Building. He argues the decision is vindicated by its value rising to £28million, added to the fact it now brings in £3million a year in revenue.

'Invest to Earn gives a socialist city council the opportunity to earn money from the private sector and invest in projects that will benefit the many rather than the few,' Anderson insists. 'Not only will Everton's new stadium generate income, it will transform an area of the city, create new businesses and new jobs, so that will mean a stronger local economy and more revenue for the council to act on things that need to be done in a socialist way. Yet you'll still get people criticising. "Why are you giving Everton and a multimillionaire a hand?" I'm doing it quite simply because it benefits the person asking the question!'

Anderson says the 58 per cent funding cut from central government since austerity was imposed in 2010 has placed immense pressure on Liverpool's ability to keep community venues like libraries and leisure centres open.

'I'm a socialist and proud but I get called a Red Tory,' he admits. 'I believe in redistribution of wealth but you've got to create wealth first. That's why we're setting up our own electricity company – a company that disrupts the market and gives cheaper energy to people. That's why we support the credit unions and put £4million into a fund to help the poorest in the city. In order to do that I've got to generate money. If people realise what we've had taken away and what we're trying to do, maybe they'll understand me a little bit more.'

During Anderson's time in office, Liverpool's city centre has undoubtedly become a more exciting and vibrant place. Here and in other prosperous areas of the city, the voting patterns from the EU referendum favoured Remain. It was recognised by its people that Liverpool had benefited from hundreds of millions of pounds in European funding when its own government did little to help it develop into the place it is today. Yet Remain's victory on Merseyside was closer than predicted, with outer boroughs like Knowsley backing Brexit.

Everton's stadium move from Walton will have implications for struggling zones like the County ward where there has long already been a feeling of detachment. It is fortunate that Everton has an excellent community department and the plan for Goodison Park is not to sell it to a developer for a profit but to leave the land to the guarantors – the council – as a legacy project, enabling the building of cheaper housing like on the Boot Estate in Norris Green, which had previously been boarded up. Having invested in derelict properties and made them affordable, the council now receives rental income and so – as Anderson puts it – 'everybody benefits'. Meanwhile, Everton's Free School on Spellow Lane (over the road from Neil Robinson's old house) will remain where it is and that means Everton certainly aren't abandoning the area completely. 'People say we shouldn't support free schools but this is a school that works with kids who didn't want to go to school,' Anderson adds. 'Now we're educating them. Now we're giving them hope. Now we're able to manage them. Everton have done that, a club that also provides accommodation for people with mental-health problems. This is an organisation that is perceived just as a football club but it isn't. It's far more than that.'

It gives Anderson great satisfaction helping solve a conundrum that has affected Everton across three decades. He had grown up in a tenement block called Kent Gardens a quarter of a mile away from the Pier Head. Aged 59, his association with Everton began 51 years before after he started watching games from the boys' pen. To fund his trips to Goodison Park, he sold lemonade in Norris Green on Thursday afternoons and Saturday mornings. The mother of Joe Royle, the legendary Everton centre-forward who we meet later in this book, gave him a two-shilling tip and this was enough to pay for the number 20 bus to County Road and enter the ground.

'I never thought I'd be able to have an active role in helping co-ordinate the future of the club I love,' he concludes, looking out through his office window where there are views across the River Mersey – a passage of water that will welcome 63 cruise liners in 2017. 'By 2021, we hope that figure will be double. By then, Bramley-Moore will be built and Liverpool will have a new skyline.'

11

RED THREAT

WHEN JOE ANDERSON MET THE MAYOR OF SHANGHAI DURING THE World Expo in 2010, the office of Han Zheng, who is now the Communist Party's secretary in the city as well as one of only 25 Politburo members that run China, was not really an office at all, and rather more of a grand hall decorated ornately with giant busts and paintings. Greeting Anderson, Zheng rose from his seat – more of a throne, in fact – and asked him the question, 'You, Mayor of Liverpool?' to which Anderson offered a confirmation. 'But you, Everton – why?' On Zheng's table was a photograph of Steven Gerrard.

Perhaps Zheng was aware of China's interest in the club he supported from across the other side of the world. There had been at least four movements from Chinese state vehicles to either buy or invest in Liverpool in 2016, though it is difficult to determine whether they were separate from one another or all part of the same plan. Each had links to the government in some way.

Through an unsolicited direct email Liverpool's owners were first approached by SinoFortone, a company that had committed £5.2billion to new infrastructure projects across the UK in the previous twelve months including a deal in conjunction with the China Railway Group which involved a green energy and affordable housing scheme that was signed off by Nicola Sturgeon, the SNP leader. SinoFortone had previously built roads, railways, airports, seaports and power stations across China and the Middle East. In Liverpool, home to reputedly Europe's oldest Chinese community, work on the £200million New Chinatown development had already begun less than a mile away from Liverpool's city centre. Though SinoFortone were not behind the project, plans had been presented to President Xi's delegation during a visit to Manchester.

Fenway Sports Group did not enter discussions with SinoFortone, nor did they speak to Liu Yiqian, a taxi driver turned fine-art collector who was said to be a Liverpool fan and, as China's 47th-richest man, believed to be worth £2.5billion.

Fenway were interested in selling a stake in Liverpool but only to the right partner for strategic reasons, surely recognising the potential dangers in having a more affluent minority stakeholder. That partner did not turn out to be China Everbright either, a corporation whose financial power stemmed from its association with China Investment Corporation (CIC), the country's main sovereign wealth fund, with assets estimated at around the £620billion mark.

With the year approaching its end, interest from China in Liverpool came again, though this time a story never appeared in the papers. CITIC, the biggest conglomerate in China, had appointed the New York-based Inner Circle Sports Group – a team of corporate finance directors, investment bankers and valuation advisors – to contact Fenway's intermediary, Allen & Co, to make enquiries about Fenway's position. As Inner Circle had helped Fenway in 2010 during their own takeover of Liverpool, it seemed to be the sensible way forward because a trust existed between the group and John W. Henry, Fenway's principal owner. Following the other failed approaches, CITIC appreciated that Henry would prefer to do it this way. By using respected middle-men, there was no paper trail and therefore it represented an opportunity to deny that contact had been made if it ever became a media headline.

It was believed the Chinese government had planned to use CITIC to buy Liverpool in the same way Everbright could have been used as a smaller vehicle for CIC a few months before, only this time CITIC would have acted for the Communist Youth League of China. Liverpool would be a gift to the future of China. The chances of this happening diminished in the New Year when concerns were raised from within the Communist Party about the impact of large-scale overseas acquisitions along with the phenomenon of China's domestic clubs burning money on inflated salaries for foreign players. China had wanted to play capitalism to display the power of its system and spread influence across the globe. Though a deal between AC Milan and Li Yonghong, a Chinese businessman, was later completed, those negotiations with the unpredictable Silvio Berlusconi had dragged since August. For symbolic reasons, the People's Republic of China realised it had to rein in its spending a little.

The story, nevertheless, illustrates the reach of Liverpool Football Club. When a team containing four retired players and fewer stars flew to Australia to play a post-season friendly to mark the beginning of the club's 125-year celebrations – a friendly which took place twelve time zones away and less than 66 hours after the final ball of the 2016/17 campaign had been kicked on Merseyside – nearly 80,000 spectators turned up in Sydney.

It is not just the ward of Walton that cares about Liverpool. It's not just Fenway who recognises the potential there either; a group that had taken control of Liverpool after the dreadful reign of Tom Hicks and George Gillett. Fenway were able to buy Liverpool on the cheap because of the debt incurred by Hicks and Gillett's leveraged buy-out in 2007. When the pair fell out, Liverpool started selling their best players and stopped spending the money accrued on adequate replacements. The club were not competing in the Champions League and was mid-table in the Premier League when Massachusetts-based Fenway made their move.

Liverpool's financial position may have improved but since then, the club have struggled to keep their best players long enough to sustain any reasonable amount of success and, while some supporters are appreciative of Fenway's steady but distant leadership considering the mess left behind by Hicks and Gillett, many are frustrated by the feeling Liverpool is an investment for Fenway rather than a priority, not to mention the wider pattern of sporting failure under American guidance. David Moores, whose great-uncle John Moores helped Everton earn the tag Mersey Millionaires in the 1960s, had sold to Hicks and Gillett in 2007; in the decade before that decision was taken, Liverpool won almost everything there was to win and even then, that was not enough – because the league title was not one of the trophies. Though they have reached other cup finals, Liverpool have won just one League Cup since 2007 and this era ultimately represents the club's leanest period since the 1950s.

Moores had sold up because he was afraid he would not be able to keep up with the new high finance of the Premier League and, like Bill Kenwright at Everton, believed he would not be able to afford the cost of the new stadium that Liverpool needed to compete in the long term while maintaining a winning culture on the field that would keep supporters coming through the gates. While Fenway have deeper pockets, they are not in the same league as Chelsea's Roman

Abramovich, nor Sheikh Mansour at Manchester City. Fenway arrived openly admitting they did not understand football culture in the way, as owners of the Boston Red Sox, they understood baseball. Equally, though there are similarities between the cities, to begin with they did not understand Liverpool in the way they understood Boston, and so it has taken Fenway time to get Liverpool anywhere near where they used to be.

By the end of the 2016/17 season, a campaign which began with the opening of a huge new main stand that took Anfield's capacity up to 54,000 (still 21,000 seats short of Manchester United's Old Trafford), Liverpool had qualified for the Champions League for only the second time in the six full seasons since Fenway's arrival. This had been achieved following Fenway's third managerial appointment. Having sacked Roy Hodgson a couple of months into their reign, club legend Kenny Dalglish was removed eighteen months later despite reaching two cup finals in his first full season in charge – winning Fenway's one and only trophy so far. Under Brendan Rodgers, Liverpool nearly won their first domestic championship in 24 years but less than eighteen months later again, Rodgers was gone. There were many elements that contributed towards the mood around the time of his exit but fundamentally the blame lay somewhere in the middle of a confused recruitment strategy and his failure to manage the unique expectations and idiosyncratic nature of a club that is a prisoner of its past, perhaps more than any other in the land.

This led Fenway to Jürgen Klopp, the German manager who lifted Borussia Dortmund from the foot of the Bundesliga to the title twice at the expense of Bayern Munich, despite the Bavarians' financial supremacy. After seven years in Dortmund, Klopp admitted to being tired of the job, but within six months he was suitably refreshed to become the highest-paid manager in Liverpool's history.

Jamie Carragher, the Bootle-born defender who is second on Liverpool's all-time appearance list having appeared in 737 games, played under six Liverpool managers across sixteen seasons. He thinks that the manager who arrives at Liverpool is not the same as the manager that leaves: the pressure which comes with attempting to win the league title reliably seeing an erosion of sensibilities. Liverpool is the intoxicating job that ends with managers being chewed and, eventually, spat out.

Roy Evans admitted he could not watch Liverpool for eighteen months after resigning as manager following 33 years' total service as player then coach, leaving

Gérard Houllier to operate alone. Houllier's end was nearly brought about two years before he actually went, having discovered a heart condition that nearly killed him. Houllier had become so paranoid in his final months as Liverpool's manager that it seemed as though he was having more public arguments with former players turned press critics than he had three points from victories. Next, Rafael Benítez turned power-mad having inspired Liverpool to the Champions League in improbable circumstances and then, having had to work with Hicks and Gillett; he ended up not knowing who to trust and perhaps himself contributing to a culture of suspicion that infested the club and eventually led towards his own departure. Brendan Rodgers was in place for three full seasons between 2012 and 2015 and his transformation was a visual one: by the end, he had new teeth, he had lost weight and, having left his wife, he had a new younger girlfriend.

Will Jürgen Klopp be different? Can he remain the same as he was before? Upon his presentation as Liverpool's manager in October 2015 he appeared in the Centenary Stand hospitality suite like a film star. No Liverpool manager had ever turned up to his unveiling tieless, wearing jeans and a blazer. Following a gloomy start to the season, his tanned face and floppy blond hair pointed towards the optimism of summer.

There were three differences between him and his predecessors and it related to experience. Klopp had played at a reasonably high level but not high enough to have earned the money that could have allowed him to slip into a quieter life. He had also remained loyal to his clubs, representing only two in Mainz and Borussia Dortmund through his 26-year career in playing and coaching. In Dortmund, indeed, because of his achievements and electric personality, he knew what it was like to be hero-worshipped. After Houllier, Benítez and Rodgers had dined on success and been told they were great, subsequent criticism became difficult to stomach. Because the three had forced their way into management despite limited playing careers, they had spent a lifetime trying to convince doubters that inexperience did not translate as a shortcoming. Klopp, though, had arrived at Anfield freely admitting that Liverpool was one of the few jobs outside Germany he could take, knowing his forte was guidance rather than tactics necessarily; that the Premier League would suit him because the power of words would hold resonance in English, a language he was comfortable with.

Klopp knows too that impressions count. I had only spoken to him before when others were around prior to and after matches. When it was suggested I arrive at Melwood for an interview one late spring morning, I found him already waiting despite being ten minutes early – and wearing his jeans.

Players have said that Klopp is a friend but certainly not a best friend. He balances being close but not too close. He is straight to the point and players appreciate that. He maintains a healthy distance between himself and the interviewer. He says things because he means them. He does not wish to necessarily impress but he appreciates – as a public figure – why it is important to try and influence listeners or readers with his thoughts. He is not Kenny Dalglish, who treated press meetings as an intrusion on his day.

Klopp talks quickly, he smiles as much as he curses, he has an opinion on most things and is willing to be forthright about the big issues, broader than football. And yet there is almost an innocence with some of Klopp's answers and that makes him endearing. Having spent his whole life living, playing and managing in Germany, he can admit the English Premier League has surprised him.

'One of the really interesting things is, there's only a little bit of water between our countries but when you move to a new league you realise how much you have become obsessed by your own life and how different things are elsewhere,' he says. 'I'm not sure if this is normal but I only knew about two English clubs as a child. That was Liverpool and Manchester United. This changed slightly when I became a manager. We played a few times against Arsenal and Manchester City while I was manager of Borussia Dortmund. You think you know a lot about the Premier League but really, you have to experience it to understand it properly. You recognise that, actually, you know nothing. Very quickly, I realised, you know what, this is really different – I had no idea about this.

'In Germany, for example, I never had a situation in games where wind had an influence on the game. In Germany we are not an island so we do not play close to the coast. There are maybe a few places in the north of the country but I've never been there. In England, Liverpool, Everton, Middlesbrough, Sunderland, Southampton, Newcastle and Hull are all close to the coast. It's a little thing but it can affect the way the game is played, especially when you play long-ball teams – so you have to consider it when preparing your team. You also have the intensity of the game here and importance of every single game. Wow, these players, these teams, these managers in League One and Two in cup matches – they test you a lot. No game is easy.

'And the result in England, of course, this comes above everything. Nobody cares about how you play and instead they prefer to see the three points – a clean sheet and all that stuff. You can play really well but nobody is interested if you don't get the result you deserve. You can say, "If we stick to this plan in a few weeks or months it will work," but it is harder getting that message across –

getting people to believe it. Instead, it is only about the last result and the next result. Each tool and each weapon, if you like, is legal as long as the outcome is a positive one for you. That's really different. It could happen in Germany that you are successful but because there is no plan and people don't like your football, the board decides to sack you. I don't think that is likely or possible here. The result excuses pretty much everything. That's not good or bad, it's only different – I must stress this. I am not complaining at all; only different.

'There are similarities, of course. It is interesting you are writing a book about the north-west. In Germany it is also the north-west with the most intense clubs, where football is the biggest of the three influences for people: family, work and football; where industries created the culture for football.

'I can only describe the situation from the inside. It's not about judging – saying good or bad, as I say. Because sometimes if you say something is different, it is viewed as a criticism rather than an observation. What I would say is, here everyone wants everything and so, there is surprise when the English national team cannot deliver in the summer – or sometimes when English clubs don't go as far in European competition. The Premier League is the most intense league in Europe, a hundred per cent and nearly all of the English national team play in the Premier League so there is an obvious link. You are playing an important tournament against players and teams with less games in their legs but we still expect they deliver in a perfect way. That's obviously very difficult. But nobody wants to say, OK – maybe one game less in the cups and make a penalty shoot-out instead of a replay. People want football, football, football, and we have to deliver – that's the situation. It's interesting to be in the middle of this. How could I have solutions straight away when I had never experienced this before? They tell you it is intense, let me tell you – it's even more intense than that. Now [eighteen months after arriving in England] we are much more used to it. But then, when we play young players in a cup competition and we lose like we did against Wolves, everyone says, "How can you disrespect this competition?" When you win like against Derby? "Everything is fine." I have never had a lack of respect for any football match because each football match is very important. I am a football maniac. I could play six times a week with my side but that is not physically possible.

'The winter? If you don't know about the benefits of a winter break, then you don't really miss it. But if you know about it, you would say it is a convenient thing to have: two weeks of calm in a period in the year when the rest of Europe is doing the same. I'm not saying this should happen around Christmas because football and Christmas is tradition in England and traditions are important. But in January, for example, where in Germany you have four weeks off – two weeks with the family and a mini pre-season in the other two weeks – in the Premier League this season we played ten games. That's a big difference, I would say!'

The demands at Dortmund required Klopp's full focus and the pressure that came in his final year meant the hiatus that followed involved more games of tennis than studying football elsewhere. Though they knew he was available, Liverpool insist they spoke to Klopp for the first time only after Brendan Rodgers was sacked. When it came to a decision between Italian Carlo Ancelotti and Klopp, having interviewed both in New York – and even though Fenway had been advised against the German because of his uncompromising public image – Klopp won because he simply blew them away with his hunger for the job, while also making them realise he is not just the caricature and is far more democratic than portrayed. It was thought that Klopp's personality would complement Liverpool's as a city. Perhaps Fenway recognised too that he would be able to show the passion they could not from thousands of miles away in Boston.

Klopp proceeds to tell a funny story about the reality of being a football manager switching between two big clubs in different countries, one that suggests again he is comfortable enough in himself to admit naivety. Not long after his appointment at Anfield, Liverpool had a Monday night game. Having trained at Melwood on Saturday morning, Klopp returned home to Formby. A few days before, Sky engineers had installed satellite television. At 3 p.m., as he lay on the couch, he realised there was no live football and thought it was unusual. Figuring he'd bought the wrong television package, he called BT and had their sports bundle installed as well. A few weeks later, Liverpool were playing on a Sunday afternoon at Anfield and so, when he returned to Formby he waited for the matches to start at 3 p.m. on BT. It was only then – after calling Liverpool's liaison officer and having not discussed it with anyone else before – that he realised no games in England were televised at 3 p.m. on a Saturday afternoon. 'I couldn't believe it!' he laughs. 'As I say, when you are in charge of Dortmund, you don't really think about England so much . . .'

Sky, of course, have had a profound impact on the way football is consumed in England. The sums of money involved have changed the way people feel about football. The costs of attending games regularly have led to demographic and therefore atmosphere shifts inside stadiums. At Anfield, for example, there are fewer if not any groups of young working class 'scallies' watching from the same section of the stadium; those whose spirit have traditionally generated the most noise. The cost of attending matches has also led to a sense of entitlement amongst the newer breed of fan while reducing the amount of patience. It must frustrate Klopp because he values atmosphere greatly. At Dortmund, he had the Yellow Wall behind one goal where it was affordable for younger groups which have marginalised from the English game. At Anfield, he has the Kop stand and an ageing fan base, frustrated by two and a half decades without a league title.

'Money, of course, is a big thing in football – there's no doubt about it, we cannot hide from it.' Klopp says. 'We can all say we are romantics about the game but we still earn a lot of money – that's how it is and, to some level, that's how people will judge us. For players I think it makes absolute sense players earn a lot of money because they waste the best time in their life for football. To become a footballer, you need total commitment and that means not going through the education systems that other people experience. If you earn enough money, of course, it's not a waste of time, but if you don't earn enough money it's a big sacrifice and you'd better have another career planned for the next part of life. Being a League One or League Two player for fifteen years means you have to work the day after you finish your football career and because of the commitment needed with football, players do not have the education to fall back on. Life after you are thirty-five – hopefully – will be longer than before.'

Klopp is sympathetic towards footballers because he was one. He can relate to the anxieties of a lower-league footballer in his early thirties, thinking about what follows.

'Absolutely. I remember the moment. I am not too smart but I am not silly, or whatever. I could have had a different career other than football player or football manager. The youth football system was different when I was a player because it allowed more time for education. I finished studying in 1995 when I was twenty-seven. I could have started working straight away but I couldn't because I loved the game too much even though the pay was only a few marks, as it was then. Before, it was always OK because even though I didn't earn a lot of money I didn't really need it to be happy. Very quickly it seemed, I was thirty-two – and now I realised I was an old player. I really started thinking about my future. I had a family. I finished my studies five or six years before. You cannot use it. You cannot go to a business and say, "Hello, here I am – I finished my studies five or six years ago but hey, do you still have a need or a use for me?" The world doesn't work like that. This was the situation for me. The feeling was bad. What do you do?'

Other than Sean Dyche, Klopp would be the only other active Premier League manager interviewed in this book. His level as a footballer had been similar to Dyche's and it is fair to say that Burnley has a bigger history than Mainz, the club Klopp played for and later managed. And yet while Dyche, at 45, remains Burnley's manager, Klopp has gone further – much further, earning a job aged forty at one of Germany's biggest clubs and now Liverpool, an institution with a global footprint.

Klopp, though, is nearly five years older than Dyche, he began his managerial career earlier and this is significant to Dyche's theory about why English managers do not get as much of a chance to progress as quickly, relating to the nationality of owners and the advisors they listen to. It is worth considering this: the season when Hicks and Gillett bought Liverpool in 2006/07 began with five foreign-owned Premier League clubs. In Klopp's first full season in charge of Liverpool and Dyche's second stint as a Premier League manager, that figure had risen to fourteen. Meanwhile, in Germany, when Klopp earned his big break at Dortmund in 2008/09, having impressed with his ability produce in Mainz a team that was worth more than the sum of its parts – much like Dyche at Burnley – all Bundesliga clubs were German-owned. The league employed sixteen German managers, two Swiss, a Slovenian and a Dutchman.

It might be a simplistic way of looking at trends but Klopp too in the past has spoken about finding the right owner to work for, admitting that the Liverpool job would not have been as attractive to him had it not been for Fenway, who he believes to be reasonable people that realise growth needs time, but are prepared to be ruthless if the need is there. Eighteen months before the sack, Brendan Rodgers had been rewarded with a five-year contract and in the summer of 2016, Klopp committed himself to Liverpool for the next six years. Though this offers security to both manager and club, such agreements are rare in football now.

'The business is much more intense than it was,' Klopp says. 'It has changed a lot, yes, of course. There is huge pressure, you can lose football games even when you do really well and the reaction consistently is about crisis when it does not need to be. It is a players' game and it is decided by the quality of the players and their decisions. Yes, you have to give them a plan; yes, you have to give them advice; yes, you tell them about common movements and ideas they should try together. You can do a lot. But if the players aren't good enough – or if the recruitment is wrong and the players do not fit your plan – that's really difficult and the pressure grows from there.

'What I do appreciate is all managers lose. Learning how to deal with losing is a part of every manager's responsibility. The pressure that comes with defeat is heavier the higher up you go because more people see it, more people are affected by it and more people want to say something. When I was a young manager, I found losing hard to deal with because I was still a player in the head. As a player it would frustrate me a lot. As a manager, everybody is looking for a reaction: the players mostly. So the challenge is to get your thoughts together quickly, to learn and to move on. Otherwise the players will see. The fans are very important, of course, but you need the players with you the most.

'When I started as a 33-year-old former player I had a feeling there was a lot of pressure because financially I had to make it work, though I loved football so much, so that made life a little easier. For young managers now it's really, really hard. Getting sacked is one thing. But what they say then about you, what people think about you could kill your whole career because PR affects football and the decisions that are made by other clubs that are looking for managers. So you have one chance – maybe you get a second one: done – find something else to do. Obviously in this era of "super-managers", as you call them, the super-managers don't have this problem. If Liverpool sacked me I could probably find another club. Not five times but maybe two or three. It means that sometimes there is less imagination at the top and more change at the bottom. So will managers stay in one position for twenty years? This will be more difficult.'

While fifteen foreign managers worked in the Premier League during 2016/17, the nine in the Bundesliga included seven who had spent a minimum of five years associated with clubs as a player or coach. Two of these were German-born from immigrant families but had chosen to represent Croatia and Turkey as players. During a season where clubs had given debuts to the smallest number of academy players since the Premier League's formation in 1992, the Bundesliga had offered the most in Europe. Klopp, whose Dortmund team included a core of players from the Ruhr Valley, believes identity is important but that does not necessarily mean a player has to come from Liverpool, a city with a fierce sense of self.

'I cannot make a difference where a good player comes from but I like it, for example, that Trent [Alexander-Arnold] has grown up around the corner from Melwood,' he says of Liverpool's exciting eighteen-year-old right-back who insiders predict will have a long career in the first team. 'For me, Ben Woodburn brings exactly the same excitement – though his grandfather, I think, is Welsh. You then have Ovie Ejaria, whose dad was a bus driver in London. He's been here for three or four years. Rhian Brewster – he's from London as well. So, do they need to be born in the city? Do they need to have spent lots of time in the youth system already? [Andres] Iniesta is one of Barcelona's greatest players and he is from another part of Spain.

'Our job, as I see it, is to create as many home-grown players as possible. By that, I mean players who have been with Liverpool since they were twelve, thirteen or younger – so they understand what the club is, what it means to people and their responsibilities as footballers. We have to educate them as good as possible. And then, we also need to make sure that if we can't use them, it does not mean they cannot have a decent career at another club, Premier League, Championship, League One, League Two, wherever. They all need to be ready. A Liverpool academy player of the future needs to have a professional future. If that doesn't happen, it's our fault because we are not making the right decisions early enough. If we see they do not have enough to play for Liverpool then we have to tell the boy, "Look . . ." It's about being honest, decisive and responsible. I'm not sure if it will happen while I'm still here but for the good of Liverpool and the good of football in general, this has to be our aim as a club.'

The issue of youth development relates to first-team recruitment because Liverpool will need to nurture the best players if they cannot afford to buy them ahead of the Manchester clubs or Chelsea. It seemed like a defeatist attitude or an excuse when Liverpool explained why they could not sign Alexis Sánchez from Barcelona in the summer of 2014 when Brendan Rodgers was manager and Ian Ayre, the former chief executive, was in charge of negotiations – citing that the Chilean simply wished to live in London. The explanation made Liverpool sound like an unimportant place, one that is not pushing boundaries to get where they want to be; setting a dangerous precedent. If you believe the reasoning it might also contribute towards thoughts about globalisation, reminding you that while the biggest cities become ever more important, the smaller diminish.

'Nobody has told me, "No, I won't come because it is in Liverpool – I want to go to London," though that does not mean it is not like this,' Klopp says, suddenly turning into an arm of Merseyside's tourist board, though his opinions are delivered so emphatically you believe him as absolutely genuine. 'What I will say is, if you come here first and you have no idea about Liverpool you will be surprised by how nice it is. That's the first thing all of my friends say when they come here for the first time. They go through the city and the region. They see the Mersey, the Albert Dock, the centre – out to Wales. "Yes, it's nice! You can do a lot here." It should not be an issue but maybe the image is sometimes. All I do know for certain is, I love being in a region where everything smells like football. I love it. I know there are much more important things in life but when you have the imagination and dreams of the fans, you have passion and hope. I never choose a club because of weather or something else. I choose where I go to work because of football.'

Klopp had mentioned Brexit a couple of times in press conferences, displaying shock at the outcome. I sensed he might wish to speak more about it. His message behind the issue relates to his management and the way he deals with players; people.

'It was last summer. I was on holiday. I woke up in the morning. The European Championships were being played in France. We had friends in the house,' he recalls. 'I walked into the kitchen and someone said, "England is out." I thought, good, our boys will be back earlier for pre-season . . . In this moment, I had forgotten that England did not have a game. It was a one-second reaction. Suddenly, "What?" I couldn't understand.

'Of course, everyone has the right to make a decision: left or right, that's the way it is. But is 51 per cent really enough to make an important decision, especially when only something like 70 per cent of the population voted? Why did the remaining 30 per cent not vote? For me, it's a misunderstanding of democracy. But, what I will say also is I'm really happy to be here at this moment of my life. I can see both sides. The way it is reported in England is different to Germany. I can see that the EU has not done a perfect job but I have always thought if you try to do things together you are stronger. If you do it alone, I'm not sure what happens.'

12

NEW ORDER

'Liverpool is a tourist club now. The top six in the Premier League are tourist clubs. It gets to Klopp. I think you can tell. When he shouts about the atmosphere, I think he's sick of people showing up at Liverpool and making a big song and dance about it: taking a few photos, using a selfie-stick at the game. If you were watching on the telly in your house and it was the 42nd minute and you were still going for that first goal, would you leave and make a brew? You wouldn't. But you see people with pizza boxes in the main stand. I just think, where has the club gone? Most football clubs now are sanitised and modern football is taking it away from its roots.'

Disenfranchised Liverpool supporter following his team's 1–0 home defeat to Southampton, January 2017.

Paul Manning's nickname in City of Liverpool FC circles is Chairmao. The nickname is semi-affectionate. Manning is a Liverpool supporter. Liverpool supporters adore Bill Shankly, who once stood before a huge crowd at St George's Plateau after his team had lost an FA Cup final saying, 'Chairman Mao had never seen the greatest show of red strength.' The idea of a football club called City of

Liverpool germinated because Manning had seen Anfield's famous atmosphere slip away, with tourists in the ground's famous Kop stand replacing the local community that once stood there. Shankly was a leader of a city. Mao was the leader of a country. Manning is the leader of a football club. Manning admits his approach is not always to everyone's taste.

'I'd like to think the dictatorial reputation I have isn't really a criticism,' Manning says. 'I hope they are taking the piss out of me in a good way. Our club is based on equality. But you always need someone to take control in order to get it off the ground and make it run.'

Manning had grown up watching Liverpool in its greatest era, when the sides of Bob Paisley and Joe Fagan lifted four European Cups in just seven years between 1977 and 1984.

'We knew nothing else other than complete and utter success and domination,' he recalls. 'We were completely and utterly spoilt on the joy of going to watch Liverpool win things.

'But the greatest privilege,' Manning continues, 'was being able to go with your mates on the bus and stand together on the Kop. That's what the Kop was: a disorganised band of homogeny, groups of five and ten lads from different areas of the city that somehow knew each other whether they were from Kirkdale, Hunt's Cross or Crosby. What brought us together was the Kop.'

By September 2014, months after Liverpool had gone closest to winning its first league title since 1990, Manning looked around the Kop in one of its quiet moments. Liverpool had not long scored and they were winning. The mood was sterile. 'There were more people sitting around me with bags of clothes. No groups of young lads. No groups of friends close together. Everyone was split up in different parts of the ground. The atmosphere had turned. I was sick of it.'

Manning went home and fired off an angry email to eight like-minded Anfield match-goers, urging a get-together. Of the eight who attended that first meeting only Manning and Peter Furmedge, his deputy, remain involved in City of Liverpool FC. When a second four-hour meeting involved twelve people, the discussions inevitably fell back towards frustrations with Liverpool. Manning had identified in the meantime that his frustrations, though primarily with Liverpool, were also with elite football in general. 'What Evertonians might be thinking never got a mention in the first meetings,' admits Manning. 'I realised that if we were going to do something about our frustrations, it shouldn't just be about Liverpool. It needed to be something new; something for everyone in this city.'

Manning learned that in the nine professional and semi-professional divisions below Liverpool and Everton in the Premier League, no clubs came from within the boundaries of Liverpool City Council. Just to the north, Sefton had five teams: Southport, Marine, Bootle, AFC Liverpool and Litherland REMYCA. Knowsley had one team in Prescot Cables. Wirral had Tranmere Rovers and Cammell Laird. Halton, which is nearby but not considered Merseyside, had Runcorn Linnets, Runcorn Town and Widnes FC. 'Somehow, the big blob in the middle – the centre of our universe – had nothing other than Liverpool and Everton, which is remarkable when you consider the appetite for football in the city.'

More emails led to more meetings. More meetings led to a social-media presence. A social-media presence led to a following. A following led to a name. City of Liverpool were in front of the application boards of the FA, presenting their case for entry to the North West Counties First Division for the 2016/17 season. When I meet Manning, City of Liverpool are midway through their debut season. They are in third position and holding a realistic chance of promotion.

This, however, is a simple description in its most basic form of the process involved. The human impact of setting up a football club is raw. The beauty of City of Liverpool is its membership elects its committee. Whether Manning is voted in again as chairman by that committee is irrelevant because he plans to step down.

'It's going to be quite soon,' he says. 'I can't keep doing what I'm doing. It's been a massive physical, mental and financial drain on me. If you're running a football club like ours you have to be prepared for a massive change to your lifestyle.'

Manning is married with three kids.

'Even before we kicked a ball, I was doing thirty to forty hours a week on City of Liverpool. When the games started, those responsibilities went through the roof. I was running round like a madman. I carry a lot of weight anyway. I was a heart attack waiting to happen.'

City of Liverpool is built on socialist principles, but to get there, a leader needed to emerge. And where there is leadership and true socialism, there is criticism. Where non-league football is concerned – when volunteers are involved – that criticism hurts even more.

'It really hurts because you're giving your time up for free, whether you make mistakes or not. You think, what have you done for this club? Ultimately, you've got to be a nutter to do it in the first place and a nutter to survive. Setting this club up has cost me a business because I became totally engrossed. I ran a call centre in accident and compensation claims. Don't get me wrong, it wasn't the biggest business in the world, but it was paying everyone involved a wage. I took my eye completely off the ball and focused on what had to be done with the county FA and various other authorities. And eventually my business withered on the vine because of football.'

*

The Delta Taxis Stadium is the home of Bootle FC. It is towards the end of January and City of Liverpool, playing at home, are drawing at half-time with Litherland REMYCA, the team just one position and one point above them in the North West Counties First Division. Litherland's ground, a sports park owned by Sefton Council, is the other side of a busy dual carriageway that runs out of Liverpool's north end into flat fields and, eventually, towards Skelmersdale and Wigan. If a true rivalry emerged here it would be known as the Dunnings Bridge Road derby.

The game had kicked off at 3 p.m. Liverpool had lost at home to Swansea City earlier in the day. The logistics department of City of Liverpool decided to lay on a coach to help those out who wanted to be at both Anfield and the Delta Taxis Stadium. I arrive late because of prior reporting duties and as soon as I open the doors of my car, having parked up in the forecourt of a new industrial warehouse that stores hair and beauty supplies, a cheer goes up that makes me think Litherland have taken the lead because it's not particularly loud and City of Liverpool's attendances have averaged over four hundred since agreeing a ground-share with Bootle.

The sun was setting on the coldest day of the year so far. The Mitre footballs being used were so dirty, their last clean had probably been in autumn. City of Liverpool 2, Litherland REMYCA 3 soon became City of Liverpool 2, Litherland REMYCA 4, when Christopher Lowe, a defender, scored a header in front of the Dodge Kop stand.

Despite the prospect of imminent defeat, the enjoyment was flowing as much as the Warsteiner lager being served from the chalet-style clubhouse and sunk on the two-step terrace, where the bulk of the 628 attendance stood huddled like penguins, singing despite City of Liverpool's demise.

The frustration is only small, with shouts of, 'Get Daley on,' in recognition of Daley Woods, the striker, whose day job is a policeman. The presence too of Michael Roberts in midfield is a reminder of how far a talented footballer can fall. Roberts, a lean figure, whose control of the ball is more advanced than any of the players around him, is 25 years old. At sixteen, Liverpool had taken him from Tranmere Rovers for £100,000. He had played for Liverpool's reserves beside Raheem Sterling but in 2012 was released and his only competitive games before signing for City of Liverpool had been for Bootle, the town where he lived.

Liverpool supporters are great believers that banners in football grounds should contain punchy messages or witty remarks and, accordingly, City of Liverpool are the same. 'Hated, adored, never ignored,' one reads. The supporter standing behind it, wearing a purple, white and gold-coloured bobble hat, proudly tells me he has given his Kop season ticket to someone else to follow 'The Purps'.

When the final whistle blows, Litherland REMYCA are victorious and the celebrations not only reflect the prospect that Litherland are a step closer to promotion, but also the fact that beating City of Liverpool is already viewed as a coup. The North West Counties First Division had not received much publicity in recent years, certainly not since FC United of Manchester began their rise out of the league more than a decade ago. City of Liverpool were the best-supported club in the division, their average home gate for the season standing at 422 while the rest fell somewhere below 100.

Paul Manning had told me that City of Liverpool were gaining in popularity because the club's priorities were clear. 'We don't exist because of what happens on the pitch,' Manning said. 'We don't care about players, the type who will leave you because they want an extra ten quid a week. We've already kicked out a few who think they are bigger than our club. We're looking at this from the fans' perspective. The reason why people are coming to the ground, seeing something different and feeling something different, is because it is different. The club is set up for the supporters: to create a supporter culture – to give supporters a voice in football, to make people come to a match and enjoy it; not to sit down and stay quiet or arrive at a ground and there's a seventy-year-old man with his flat cap and his dog and all you can hear is the players and the two teams shouting each other. It costs a fiver to get in and instead you'll experience a proper football-style atmosphere, something you don't always get at non-league level: people singing, shouting and screaming. The standard in front of you is decent. And most of all, you're amongst Scousers. OK, we've attracted a few foreigners and people from down south. But ninety per cent of the crowd are people that you know or faces that you recognise and if you don't know them you will soon. You don't feel lost or alone. It's a community.'

Though Manning says only positive things about FC United, the club formed in reaction to Malcolm Glazer's purchase of Manchester United, he was keen to stress a difference, that City of Liverpool is more of a progressive movement rather than a protest – or, indeed, a dying protest like AFC Liverpool seemed to be, the club born out of the disastrous ownership reign of Tom Hicks and George Gillett at Liverpool FC. While FC United have since moved into a new stadium after supporters raised £3.4million and were averaging attendances of more than 2,000, AFC Liverpool were paying Marine £500 a game to play at their rather more modest albeit tidy ground, with gates rarely rising above the hundred mark.

Despite the mood not being as positive as it once was over at FC United, with the 2015/16 season undermined by legal action, resignations, gagging orders and then average league performance, Manning views FC United as 'a complete and utter success story'.

'I think it's inevitable you'll have disagreements and splits at some point in a fan-owned club,' Manning says. 'People say, "Oh, look at all the trouble at FC United!" Yeah, that's after ten years of unparalleled sustained growth. They've raised £3.4million themselves and now they're in their own stadium. Any infighting that goes on is natural. People have a say and their football operation is a socialist democracy.'

It was during a meeting with the FC United board that Manning and Furmedge identified what they considered to be a flaw in the set-up at Broadhurst Park, however. Manning can remember someone making a comment about Manchester City's most recent victory; how lucky they supposedly were, emphasising how much disdain he still had for them. Manning looked at Furmedge. Furmedge looked at Manning. Manning speaks of it like a eureka moment. 'We realised that, as brilliant as their club is, it's a fault line,' he says. 'They've chopped their market in half. Anyone who wants anything, FC United are there to help – they do brilliant things in disabled football, for example. But – they hate Man City . . .'

Instantly, Manning and Furmedge decided to make their football club appeal to supporters across the city of Liverpool, rather than just Liverpool FC. It has since been a challenge convincing Evertonians that City of Liverpool FC is also for them. 'The attitude from Evertonians initially was, "It has Liverpool in the name, it's a breakaway Liverpool club . . ." It has been a hard task convincing people that City of Liverpool has nothing to do with Liverpool FC or Everton FC, we've got no history; this is a brand-new club for the whole city, everyone is welcome. "You can't have Liverpool in the title!" they'd continue.

'Where do you live, mate? "Liverpool . . ."

'What's your postcode? "Liverpool . . ."'

The fact the club's initials were CoLFC even made some Evertonians suspicious because it included the letters LFC.

'I don't think we've convinced Evertonians just yet,' Manning admits. 'At the moment we're around two thirds Liverpool, one third Everton. That's mainly because there's a culture at Liverpool for gangs of lads – or fellas – to go to the game together and that culture is not as widespread at Everton. I'd like to think at some point we'll touch Everton's hard-core support. It could be because they hate us but it could be because life isn't so bad for Evertonians yet. They can still get tickets, they can still take their kids to matches without the prices being through the roof. In the Kop, dad-and-lad season tickets are like gold dust.'

John Coleman, the Accrington manager, told me non-league clubs on Merseyside are up against it because Liverpool and Everton are so dominant in people's thoughts and Liverpool as a city is relatively small, so the fight for attention is more of a struggle than it is in Manchester. Coleman started his semi-professional career at Kirkby Town in the 1980s, the same decade South Liverpool were heading towards extinction, despite its history as the club to host the first match in British football history under permanently installed floodlights at their Holly Park ground in Garston. South Liverpool had provided Liverpool FC with two first-team players in Jimmy Case and John Aldridge. Coleman cited the demise of Kirkby Town and then its successor Knowsley United – as well as Stantondale, a club from the Orrell Park area, not far from the Delta Taxis Stadium where Bootle now play. Bootle had moved there after their old Bucks Park ground on Copy Lane fell into disrepair, a factor that contributed towards the club dropping into the Liverpool County Combination amateur league for six years before it started to rise again, re-entering the North West Counties First Division in 2006.

Manning believes the history of City of Liverpool will tell a different story because he has identified what other clubs have done wrong.

'Football's not about football at this level. If you are trying to attract people to come and watch a butcher, a baker, a candlestick maker, an accountant and an estate agent, and it's only about what happens on the pitch then that is why it's failing,' he says. 'Because you're not talking about kids, you're not talking about families, you're not talking about gangs of mates on the terraces, you're not talking about having a beer, you're not talking about having a laugh. Football at this level needs to be a spectator sport because football struggles with other interests. Does a parent want to take his son or daughter to watch football for the same price as it costs to go to the cinema? Non-league clubs are fighting for the entertainment dollar and they don't realise it.'

When AFC Liverpool formed in 2008, many Liverpool supporters were drawn like moths to a flame and Manning admits to being one of them. Alun Parry founded the club, saying, 'Many people have been priced out at Anfield. I do not blame Liverpool, their prices are low compared to other Premier League clubs. They are just too much for a lot of us.' Though AFC Liverpool are still competing, but only in the league above City of Liverpool, attendances have dropped after initial popularity and Manning believes this is a consequence of directors being unelected and therefore a misunderstanding about what supporters really want as an alternative to Premier League football: not just a place to watch matches, but rather somewhere they can influence the democracy of the club.

'We were only born five minutes ago and anything can happen in the future but we think we've found a niche for people in Liverpool to come and enjoy football again,' Manning says. 'At the forefront of everything we do we ask ourselves, what do the supporters want? The football is dragging on the coat-tails of the support, not the other way around.'

Manning's conviction is impressive. If there is one weakness to City of Liverpool's current arrangement, it might be geography. The Delta Taxis Stadium is in Bootle and Bootle is in the borough of Sefton. It means that within Liverpool's council boundary, the only professional or semi-professional clubs that exist remain Liverpool and Everton. Manning's agreement with Bootle, however, lasts for only two seasons and you can understand why they ended up playing there when he tells the story behind the move.

To apply for the North West Counties League, City of Liverpool needed to make its application by the end of 2015. At that point, Manning was led to believe that a home would be found at Wavertree's athletics grounds or Liverpool County FA on Walton Hall Park, where Everton considered relocating. While the deal for Wavertree fell through, the rejection letter for Walton Hall Park only arrived two months before the big deadline. 'By that time, we had five thousand people following us on Twitter, people who were interested in the club, potential members.' Manning had to decide whether to postpone the launch for a year or seek a ground-share. After emails were sent to every club in the area, the only ones that responded were Tranmere Rovers, Litherland REMYCA, Prescot Cables and finally Bootle – with just over a month to spare. 'We didn't have a league to play in, a kit, a manager, a ball or any supporters when we agreed a ground-share agreement with Bootle.'

Manning has since been criticised for the deal that was brokered, with Bootle benefitting greatly from keeping all the proceeds from sales at the bar. 'Bootle are the licensee of the bar so there was no other way around it,' Manning reasons. 'It's not the greatest deal this side of the Mississippi. But back then, did we think we were going to fill the bar with hundreds and hundreds of people swigging ale morning, noon and night? Yeah, we did, actually. Bootle certainly didn't.'

The challenge for Manning, then, is finding land for City of Liverpool to make a permanent home. He recognises that it must be within walking distance of a railway station for it to be accessible for people all across Liverpool – so they can have a drink at what also needs to be there, a clubhouse with a bar. He believes as well that the pitch must be 4G rather than grass so games never get called off and extra income can be made from it as a community facility.

The aim is to be away from Bootle by the start of the third season. 'We've made an offer to purchase a plot of land in Liverpool,' Manning reveals. 'We're not waiting for a handout from the council. As a community benefit society, we can borrow money like it's a mortgage and that should come in at around £1million. We then have to raise the deposit and the funds to build the stadium, which we'll do through community shares. I reckon we'll need close to the £500,000 mark for that. The new place, it won't be a Manchester City style training ground, it will be a cowshed somewhere in Liverpool.'

Two of the sites being considered were in Tuebrook and Speke. In theory, Tuebrook would symbolically be more appropriate because it would be closer to Liverpool's city centre than either Anfield or Goodison Park. Speke might be more practical because there is more space and the land is cheaper, though it is further out – and, perhaps, more of a risk because it is way to the south and this might result in some supporters from the north believing it's too far away. A bit like Everton and Kirkby, perhaps.

'I don't think the geography of the ground is going to be any problem for us whatsoever,' Manning insists. 'If we can win the league this year and announce our ground plans, I think the roof blows off in terms of the interest in our club. I think we'll be hitting a thousand attendances by the time we move to our new stadium. I believe we'll maintain it as well, because the thirst for change is there.'

13

SUPER BOWL

JIMMY VAUGHAN AND HIS SON JAMES ARE DISCUSSING FOOTBALL in the kitchen of their home in Clubmoor, Liverpool. Jimmy is the chairman of Home Bargains FC and James acts as secretary. Both have been involved since its formation as a junior side in 1988, when dad was manager and lad was player. While James, a car salesman, leans against a washing machine with a cup of tea in hand, Jimmy, a builder, is sitting opposite me. Both have been at work all day, they've been back an hour or so and Jimmy's wife is busy cleaning the plates from the sausage dinner they've just eaten.

It is Monday night and in six days Home Bargains will play in the quarter-final of the prestigious FA Sunday Cup for only the second time. Ferrybridge Social from the village in West Yorkshire known for its three coal-fired power stations and its motorway services will be the visitors and James has been told by Ferrybridge's secretary that they will be bringing two coachloads of supporters with them.

'We've heard they've got a giant centre-forward and they get it forward quickly,' Jimmy says with a nod which suggests he thinks he is letting you in on state secrets. Earlier in the competition Ferrybridge knocked out Pineapple, another Liverpool team, then in the previous round Oyster Martyrs from Croxteth – previous winners of the competition – met the same fate in Yorkshire.

'Some of the Oyster lads were quite vocal on social media afterwards, saying Ferrybridge didn't play any football and their pitch was a bog,' Jimmy continues. 'This will be their first away game – they've been lucky with the draw because we've already won games in Newcastle and Nottingham. We'll try and get it down and pass. But we're a Liverpool side; we know we have to win the physical battle first.'

James is itching to speak. He is 36 and does not play any more – describing himself not only as the secretary but the team's 'fourth-choice goalkeeper' in moments of desperation. Being on the touchline does not make him any less passionate, though. In one of the earlier rounds he was travelling around Australia. So desperate was he to keep a check on the team's progress he sat in a bar with Wi-Fi refreshing his feed every couple of minutes to see the scores on the official FA Sunday Cup Twitter feed.

'The competition is regarded really highly in this city,' James says. 'Last week we had twenty watching on the line. On Sunday there will be three hundred at least. People are interested. I go away on holiday with lads from Huyton. They play for The Eagle. They've been telling me, "We'll be there next Sunday." If you've played amateur football for any length of time, everyone knows each other and everyone knows which players and managers have won the National Cup. There's a fella called Billy Edwards and his three sons play for us. Billy won the National Cup with The Eagle in 1983. He still talks about it now, always reminding us that no current team would stand a chance of beating The Eagle. The National Cup, it's the pinnacle for us. In Liverpool it's like the Super Bowl.'

Aside from London, no other city has a history like Liverpool in the FA Sunday Cup. Between 1979 and 1983, Merseyside's domination was absolute with The Eagle being joined as champions by clubs with names like Lobster, Dingle Rail and Fantail – the team that Accrington Stanley's John Coleman and Jimmy Bell played for before entering the Football League through non-league. The next glory period came a decade later, and in the five years between 1989 and 1993, Almithak, Nicosia and Seymour lifted the trophy. Since 2011 there had been three Liverpool winners: Oyster Martyrs twice and then Campfield. Across half a century of Sunday league football, indeed, thirteen FA Sunday Cup winners have emerged from the fields on the banks of the river Mersey.

'To reach this stage, it makes us very proud,' Jimmy interjects, reminding me that the last time Home Bargains were there, in 2014, they lost to eventual winners Campfield. 'At the moment, we can say we're one of the best eight Sunday league teams in the country. There's not many players who can say they have a winners' medal. Imagine if we do it . . .'

Jimmy's mind trails off because he is thinking about football's importance, not just in terms of outcomes like results but the experiences it has given him. His thoughts are laced with concern because he thinks amateur football on Merseyside is not what it used to be.

'I played for Wavertree Town Hall in the Liverpool Sunday League,' he recalls. 'There were fifteen divisions and every game would have a referee. It's down to two divisions now. This was in the 1970s. Sefton Park was another breeding ground. On a Sunday morning you couldn't find a space on the grass. There was one changing room, one sink and no showers but the facilities didn't matter because everyone loved playing football. Now there's no football being played on Sefton Park whatsoever. The same has happened in Kirkby. At its height in Kirkby [there] were four different leagues and several divisions in each league. Fantail were from Kirkby and they had a winger called John O'Leary. Bobby Charlton said in his autobiography that John was the best amateur he'd ever seen play the game. I had to mark John one day when I was seventeen years old. "That's him there," one of the older players told me, because John's reputation went before him. This little chubby fella waddled out of the changing room. But I couldn't get anywhere near him.'

Jimmy says his passion for football is 'like a disease'. When he stopped playing, something remained inside him – an urge to wake up on a Sunday morning knowing there was a game to prepare for. Home Bargains started as St Brendan's Juniors. James went to Cardinal Heenan, the same high school as Steven Gerrard. One of the parents had links with Trinity Mirror and for a long time St Brendan's had the Daily Mirror as sponsors. Home Bargains FC was formed when one of the parents called into each of the stores in the Old Swan area of Liverpool looking for new backers. Tommy Morris, from the famous Scotland Road thoroughfare that leads into Liverpool's city centre, had opened Home Bargains in the Swan as a 21-year-old in 1976 when takings were less than £100 a week (though it was called Home and Bargain originally). Morris persevered and it wasn't long before the customers were flocking, enticed by the prospect of buying brands they recognised from other shops and the adverts on TV but selling at a lower price. Forty years later, there were 370 stores nationwide with turnover in 2014 of just under £1.3bn.

An early customer had been comedian Ken Dodd, who would often make the trip from his home in Knotty Ash to stock up on life's essentials. Legend has it he would often rummage to the bottom of the toilet-roll basket to make sure he got the biggest roll for his money. Dodd had a connection with the shop – one of the players' parents was his postman – and so it became easier to persuade him to present trophies at the end-of-season awards ceremony, which was always held at the Garfield pub (now a Wetherspoons rebranded as The Navigator).

'Tony, the postman, said at a committee meeting, "I deliver his letters – I can get Doddy to come along." I said, "OK, Tony, if you can – that'd be brilliant,"' Jimmy remembers. 'Tony then called us on the morning of the presentation. "Doddy's coming, he'll be there about one o'clock." I didn't really believe him. We got the presentation under way and next minute Ken Dodd marches through the doors with a bunch of tickling sticks. We couldn't get him off the stage! He took the microphone and started singing "Happiness". The whole place erupted!'

The memory prompts James to release an enormous laugh. 'We've always tried to get footballers or celebrities down for the presentation evening because it means a lot to the kids,' he says. 'I knew some of the cast in Hollyoaks and Brookside and they helped us out too. Phil Olivier [Tinhead] was one of them. Tranmere Rovers were always good to us. They sent players over. Les Parry was the physio and he was very helpful when he was there. If one of the Home Bargains players got injured Les would let us use Tranmere's facilities. We'd be sitting there on the treatment table next to John Aldridge and Pat Nevin. It was great. You could never get anything off Liverpool or Everton. I can understand it, because so many people are asking for so much off them. They can't cover everyone. Maybe they could have done more.'

Jimmy's interest in playing teams from other areas did not start with the FA Sunday Cup. As juniors Home Bargains would travel to Butlin's for the weekend to play friendly matches in towns like Harlech and Pwllheli. 'Our plaques are in pubs around north Wales,' he says proudly. With age, as the juniors turned into teenagers then young adults, the challenge became different. To ensure Home Bargains had enough players, Jimmy would drive to the famous 051 nightclub in Liverpool's city centre at 2 a.m. every Sunday to 'round up the lads'.

'They'd all pile into the back of the van and come back to ours and kip on the floor,' he smiles. 'They'd wake up groggy but at least we had a team. The problems came a bit later as they got older. Liverpool is a city of sheep so if a couple of lads do something, they all do it. They'd all go out on a Saturday night and I'd receive calls at five a.m. with one of them on the wind-up. "We're not coming!" I wasn't laughing along though.'

With players like James getting older at the same time, Home Bargains, which has teams under their banner all the way down to under-8s level, have been forced to look elsewhere for new blood in their senior side.

'The original gang are coming to the end now,' Jimmy sighs. 'One is now the manager, Anton Paul. I talked him into it a few years ago, because he wasn't so keen on taking the job at first. We've now got a few non-league players who aren't on contract with their clubs, which means they can play on a Sunday morning. Carl Peers is with Bootle. Mike Grogan plays for Marine. Dean Shacklock plays for Skelmersdale. We've also got John Couch, who was with Cammell Laird for years. Tom Owens is another one – he's doing very well at Witton Albion and they are near the top of the Evo-Stik First Division. Tom was meant to be going to live in Australia after Sunday's game with Ferrybridge. Witton have said to him, "If you stay until the end of the season we'll reimburse the cost of the flight." That shows you how much they think of him. It helps us too.

'Ten to fifteen years ago, more non-league players were playing Sunday football than there are today,' Jimmy continues. 'Now, many of the non-league clubs have players on contracts and that means they are forbidden from playing for anyone else. The lads that aren't on contract, they're being asked to train twice a week by their club then play on a Saturday. The boundaries of the non-league have stretched in the last decade so that means players are travelling further for away games. The non-contract lads are absolutely whacked by the time it comes to Sunday and it is stopping them playing. This has driven standards down because the better players are going where the money is and they aren't able to play on a Sunday where they used to do it for the enjoyment. Football is a lot more serious at every level than it used to be.'

James agrees: 'Our lads have improved with their discipline but we still see a lot of hostility towards referees. We live in a more aggressive society now. If you go out on a Saturday night, clubs are open until eight or nine o'clock in the morning. Years ago, you could cope with lads turning up hungover because two a.m. was just about manageable if you had six or seven hours' sleep. But you can't cope with drugs if that's what they've been up to all night. You get a sense that some lads are trying to prove themselves. Five or six years ago the trouble hit a bit of a low but things have improved because "going out" culture has taken on different times. Instead of getting home at two a.m., a lot of lads are going out at two a.m. It means it's impossible for them to show up for an eleven o'clock game on a Sunday morning. Gradually, that has weeded the troublemakers out.'

Jimmy tells another story: 'The old Coach and Horses, a pub that used to be on Lodge Lane – it's gone now – used to play Croxteth Legion, and you couldn't move in Sefton Park. It was heaving with people watching. The Pink Echo would come down and report on what happened. It was north Liverpool versus south Liverpool. You'd get fisticuffs. But at the end, everyone would go to the pub and have a pint. It has calmed down a bit in recent seasons but for a period, it was, "I'll come around to your house and blow your windows out."'

'A lot of the younger lads in our team don't even drink after games,' James reacts. 'Even when we've won, we'll go into the pub and they're all on Lucozade. Lads care about their appearance more now than they did before. They're obsessed by gyms and fitness. Gym culture has gone huge. It has affected the age of the people involved in amateur football. Because more and more players are really fit, it puts the older fellas off because they don't fancy running around after Usain Bolt all morning. This doesn't mean standards have increased, though. The players might be fitter but do they understand the game? I think a lot of young players are missing out on the type of guidance I received from the older fellas when I was their age.'

'It means that veterans' football has become very popular,' Jimmy says. 'The older fellas still want to play but they don't want the hassle of running round after kids – kids who have been doing God knows what the night before and are in the mood to prove themselves. Three veterans' teams use the same pitch as us, the over-35s, over-45s and the over-50s. They're all very competitive.'

Jimmy and James are talking between themselves now. I am listening. 'We're fortunate that in our team, we have the right balance of lads when it comes to age and I think that explains why we're more successful than other sides where they have younger more energetic players but don't always know what to do with their energy,' Jimmy continues. 'There's a good mix of fellas in their early to mid-thirties, a handful in their mid to late twenties and then a couple of teenagers. The youngest lad, Peter Mason, is seventeen years old and his dad played for us previously. Peter's been watching us since he was six.'

James: In recent years some of the Liverpool leagues have tried introducing under-18s and under-21 leagues. I think that's upset development as well because kids end up playing in a bubble for longer than they used to and it disrupts their development into adulthood. This is the FIFA generation: if there's a bump on the pitch or the ball isn't pumped up as much as it should they're whingeing about it. You still get a few off the street but we're finding more and more that the expectations are a lot higher. They show up on a Sunday morning with their hair done and their best gear on. They don't like it when their white trainers get a bit of dirt on.

Jimmy: The Premier League has too much power. If Liverpool have a one o'clock kick-off on a Sunday, four or five players go missing. Players ask if we can kick off at half-ten. We can, but then you have the issue of making sure everyone is awake and able to turn up. Also, the away team might be Evertonians, and so they turn the request down – knowing they'll have an easier game.

James: A lot of players have to work six days a week. If you're getting paid double-time at a weekend, you have to take it because there's a mortgage to pay. You're under pressure. Lots of the lads are self-employed, so can they take the risk getting injured at a Sunday match? In ten years, I don't think Sunday league football will exist. Honestly. Three teams in our league this season have disbanded already. Nicosia was one of them. They were two-time winners of the National Cup.

I ask what they think made Liverpool a hotbed of football talent in the first place. James responds first. 'The passion for football and the passion for drinking ale,' he says. 'Pubs used to give teams money. You'd have the name on the kit. All the lads would pile back to the pub, put money behind the bar on ale and then the pub would supply a buffet. There are fewer pubs these days, a lot of them have closed and the ones that are open are surviving by serving food. They're trying to attract families in rather than a boisterous gang of lads on a high after winning a football match. We used to drink in the Garfield but the first week it became a Wetherspoons the message was clear: "We don't want you here." We weren't their type of clientele, they thought we'd be too noisy.'

Jimmy and James are grateful to Home Bargains, 'supportive partners', who contribute £1,000 a year towards kits and annual pitch fees. The sum is small change when you consider how much it costs to send a side around the country playing in a national cup competition.

'It was £800 to get to Newcastle and £550 to get to Nottingham,' Jimmy says. The teams share the travelling costs and you win £300 for each round you get through but it takes ages to receive the winnings and you've got to pay the fees up front, including the officials.'

James has seen a change in the way the competition is scheduled. 'In the earliest rounds you don't go past Manchester for a game. I think the authorities like to regionalise it because the Liverpool teams are so strong and there's a possibility if they were kept a part, you'd get four Liverpool teams in the semi-finals every year and eventually the rest of the country would lose interest.'

'Social media has become a part of the routine in recent years,' he adds. 'I deal with our Twitter feed and the other teams are always trying to wind you up. It's only a bit of banter really but I don't think it's wise to react because you're asking for a fall. The team from Nottingham were called Attenborough Cavaliers. They were bragging on Twitter, saying they were unbeaten for four years. It's a bit embarrassing when you end up losing 4–0 as they did to us, isn't it?'

'We went to Newcastle in the round before last and the hospitality was great, there was chips, barms and curry,' Jimmy adds. 'Geordies and Liverpudlians are the same type of people. They invited us back to their pub, which is something we always do, win, lose or draw. The Newcastle team were said to be unbeaten – yes, another one. We were right up against it because we had to leave Liverpool at seven-thirty on a Sunday morning for a one o'clock kick-off. It was in December so a lot of the lads were at Christmas parties the night before. We were driving round West Derby dragging people out of bed and it meant that we went there five players short of our strongest team. It went to extra time and somehow we managed to pull through.'

Two years ago, Home Bargains played a team from Huddersfield. 'There were shouts of, "You robbing Scouse bastards",' James remembers. 'But we've learned to be disciplined. In the Sunday Cup, they appoint a higher standard of referees, but sometimes that disrupts the game because Sunday football is very different to professional football. It's not always a case of refereeing a game – it's knowing how to manage it, the ebb and flow. The referees are up-and-coming and looking to climb the ladder and they know they're being assessed. If you give them mouth they'll send you off. We always say to our lads, if you're going to complain do it with a smile. We've still got a couple of grumps who should know better but we've improved.'

'I always tell the lads, "If you complain to the referee, always do it with a smile,"' Jimmy says. 'Christ, I'd hate to get knocked out because one of the lads had lost their temper. James calls this potentially winning the Super Bowl. For me, it's the Holy Grail.'

14

WE'RE NOT SCOUSE

ON BOROUGH ROAD IN BIRKENHEAD A PARADE OF A DOZEN SHOPS have their windows boarded by plywood. The signs above are peeling but you can still make out that, once, these were stores that served the streets around them. There had been a launderette, a butcher, a florist and a cobbler. They all seem long-abandoned but when I talk to a resident, she tells me the last on the stretch only closed eighteen months or so ago, having clung on like grim death all alone for a few years. 'The Tesco Express up there killed it,' she says, head looking at the floor.

A couple of hundred feet away, from the top of the huge Kop grandstand at Prenton Park the scene stretches across the river Mersey. On a clear day, beyond the choppy brown waters you can see the old tobacco warehouse and the Bramley-Moore Dock where Everton's future stadium will be. The view rolls up the green hill that is Everton Valley and towards Anfield where the top of the new main stand, with its enormous cantilever roof, broods like a mechanical beast controlling an entire area.

How then do Tranmere Rovers survive in this environment, an environment where two of the biggest clubs in England are so close to you that soon enough you'll be able to see both of their grounds during your own home matches – especially when so many Liverpudlians and Evertonians live on Wirral?

How does Tranmere identify itself as different and is it possible to flourish in the modern financial era to the point that dips can happen without the club's existence being threatened? In a few days' time Tranmere will play Macclesfield Town in the semi-final of the FA Trophy, non-league's most prestigious cup competition. A quarter of a century ago, Tranmere had threatened to reach the Premier League, later embarking on remarkable cup runs – losing to Leicester City in a League Cup final when Tranmere was a second-tier club. It had taken fourteen seasons and three relegations to drop from the Championship into the Conference National. Is there a fear that a few more wrong turns might send Tranmere Rovers the same way as the empty shells on Borough Road?

Paul Casson, the Barrow chairman, had told me that Tranmere were under more pressure than any other club in the Conference to achieve promotion. Relegation from League Two triggers two seasons of parachute payments. Tranmere were second in a table with only one automatic promotion spot and facing the prospect of an extended campaign in the play-offs to avoid a third season as a non-league club without anywhere near as much central funding.

Only four places in the Conference table separated Barrow from Tranmere, but in terms of history, ground size and attendances there was a vast difference between the clubs. While I met Casson the day before Barrow's most important FA Cup match in years at a quiet Holker Street, Prenton Park in midweek was buzzing when I met Tranmere's owner and chairman, Mark Palios.

Palios, the former chief executive of the Football Association, had been a hard-working midfielder playing more than 400 games for Tranmere and Crewe Alexandra between 1973 and 1985, a period when Tranmere allowed him to be the only part-time player in the Football League due to his appetite for education. Having graduated from Manchester University with a psychology degree in 1974, he worked his way up through the ranks of the accountancy profession and on retiring from the game he became a partner in Arthur Young in 1986, moving to PricewaterhouseCoopers three years later where he proceeded to foster a reputation as a business-regeneration expert. His year with the FA was tumultuous: after banning Rio Ferdinand for missing a drugs test and narrowly avoiding a walk-out of players ahead of a key European Championship qualifier with Turkey, Palios – a single parent – resigned citing media intrusion on his four young girls aged between nine and fourteen after it emerged both he and England coach Sven-Goran Eriksson had separately conducted a relationship with an FA secretary, Faria Alam.

There are parallels with the task that Palios faced with the FA on his appointment in 2003 and the situation at Tranmere when, together with his wife Nicola, he bought the club eleven years later. One of his priorities with the FA had been to stabilise the organisation's dangerous economic situation by resolving the financing of the new Wembley Stadium. Despite a cash crisis, Palios was determined to solve it 'without selling the future'. The FA required a loan of £130million but by 'managing cash better, nailing down TV contracts, arranging cash flows – we managed to get by and solve the immediate crisis', to the point where the FA was debt-free.

On his entry at Tranmere there was also turmoil with medium-to-long-term implications and it explains why Prenton Park is very busy indeed when I visit him. The new executive lounges in the main stand are a sign of Palios's desire to diversify the club's income, particularly during the week. The total turnover from non-match-day income before had been £150,000 a year; having spent £300,000 investing in a makeover, income had risen to more than half a million in eighteen months. On an average Wednesday afternoon there were hundreds of children inside Prenton Park taking part in education and career workshops in connection with Wirral Borough Council, which for a long time had sponsored Tranmere before there was a separation of the ways and then a unification of interests thanks to Palios's vision. Having so many children around the place creates a vibrant and certainly non-corporate atmosphere – and it is part of Palios's plan to make Prenton Park what he calls a 'community resource'. Having given a place on the board to Ben Harrison, chairman of the Tranmere Rovers Trust, Palios sold the club's former Ingleborough Road training ground to pay off debts and Tranmere moved into a new five-pitch training ground, incorporating first team and academy, in nearby Leasowe. That decision was followed by a £120,000 investment in a futsal court outside Prenton Park which now makes money in the evenings and at weekends. Futsal had been a passion of Palios' during his time at the FA and he believes it will become an integral part of the education given to Tranmere's young players because the smaller-sided game offers five times as many touches of the ball and helps develop more technically gifted players.

It is a measure of the way Tranmere are thinking now, that one of the first things Palios tells me is that a Little Mix concert being held at Prenton Park as part of the Wirral Live festival might coincide with Tranmere's appearance in the FA Trophy final should they progress past Macclesfield. While success on the pitch might drive attendances up the following season by an extra thousand and create £200,000 worth of extra income over the course of a year, a single concert at Prenton Park could earn the club as much instantly. A return to the Football

League would mean Tranmere will break even but with a competitive budget in League Two.

Palios explains the reality.

'Our budget for players is £1.3million each year and with an average gate of five thousand every home game, it earns us £1million in revenue,' he says. 'That's before we've even started appointing management and staff. It also costs us a million pounds to live in Prenton Park in terms of running costs. This means we have to think differently. We want to become a community club that isn't afraid to use some corporate methods because there are so many other things we can do other than just the football to get the public's focus on Tranmere Rovers.'

He denies that Tranmere's future will be determined by hand-outs from the Football League.

'If you rely on central funding, you create undue pressure,' he says. 'This will be the third year of losses but we'll support it again whether we go up or not. Sooner or later, I'm confident we'll crack it. What's the alternative – put all your money into the team and hope to God you get all the luck? That would be a very risky strategy. The sensible thing to do is using the assets in order to provide a regular revenue stream that supplements the budget. When we dropped out of the Football League I said the following words: "It's devastating today but not disastrous tomorrow."

'I hate being called a non-league club but being one isn't going to kill us.'

There is a reason why the Boo Radleys from neighbouring Wallasey referenced Birkenhead in their song, 'Everything is Sorrow'. Here, unemployment runs at almost twice the national average. In the Ford, a sink estate, there has long been Wirral's cheapest housing; in 1985, when Howard Parker, a reader in social studies at Liverpool University, wrote a book called Living with Heroin observations were made about a 'lost generation', commenting, 'there was no purpose for those kids, no point'. Many of the case studies had come from the Ford.

This part of Wirral had suffered like Liverpool in the 1980s when cutbacks began at the Cammell Laird shipyard. The yard had provided tens of thousands of jobs for working-class men over generations. Among the famous vessels to slide down the old dock's great slipways and into the Mersey were the cruise liner Mauretania and the American Civil War Confederate raider, Alabama. A feeling remains that a deal between the British government, led by Margaret Thatcher, and the European Commission reduced British shipbuilding capacity in return for £140million, helping to sink both the yard and employment levels.

Mark Palios was at the end of his football career when this happened and he remembers the sight of former shipyard workers queuing up outside Birkenhead's dole office. He was born on the other side of the Mersey in Wavertree but was brought up in Wallasey and went to school in Birkenhead.

'Tranmere has given me a hell of a lot of momentum in life and that's why I decided to buy the club – not necessarily because I missed football,' he says. 'I came from a fairly thin background. I was in a foster home for a period and my parents weren't very affluent. A couple of things gave me stability. One was the school, St Anselm's. The other was sport, which I was reasonably good at. I played rugby until I was eighteen and didn't play football at all until I was fourteen. At sixteen, Tranmere picked me up. At different times in my life the club meant different things. As a kid it gave me tremendous confidence because suddenly I was playing for my local professional club and, for a quiet lad growing up on Merseyside without parents, it was a huge boost.

'Then as I became a young adult, the club was very understanding with me because I wanted to develop a career outside of football at the same time as my playing career was coming along, and they encouraged me all the way. Footballers who go to university were marked out as being different but Tranmere were always very supportive.

'A lot of people get submerged with the detritus of life: the job, the house and everything else,' he continues. 'I had the perfect balance because I was playing as a professional with Tranmere and becoming a chartered accountant at the same time. It meant that I was able to enjoy football to the maximum.

'Being part-time in the Football League was unusual. It meant that I'd leave work at five o'clock every night, wave goodbye to all the lads climbing up the greasy pole in the office and train mostly on my own. I was very appreciative of being able to play professional football and I encountered footballers who took it for granted because they had natural ability. Me? I had to work bloody hard to become a half-decent footballer. I trained alone most of the time and I was never coached anything.'

Palios says he had dreams of becoming a doctor but realised this would jeopardise his football career because he could not be in casualty at 4 a.m. then wake up the following day and compete effectively in a Football League match. When Panathinaikos offered £100,000 to sign him after hearing of his Greek ancestry – a move that could have made him an international footballer –

he turned it down because he was happy with the balance he had at Tranmere.

'Some players might have been suspicious but my background was probably quite similar to theirs. My dad was a Greek immigrant dock worker. When I was young there were times when there wasn't enough food in the house. When I first started playing, Brian Glanville at The Times rang me up. "What's it like on the [team] bus?" he asked. I told him the only difference was, most of the blokes turned up with the Daily Mirror for an away journey and I might have the Guardian. I remember on one of those journeys I overheard a conversation between some of the directors. I'd been messing around at the back of the bus and one of them said, "You wouldn't think Mark was training to be a chartered accountant, would you?" I laughed because it was a compliment, though I don't think he meant it as one.

'I loved the physicality of the game in the 1970s. When we famously beat Arsenal 1–0 [in a 1973 League Cup tie at Highbury], I was at university and the match report in the Guardian said that Palios would have received a booking inside the first minute except his tackle was so late it came after sixty-three seconds. [He had the job of marking Alan Ball, one of the best midfielders in the world, that night.] I was very team-focused and I'd have run through a brick wall to do my job. I'm half-Greek, half-Irish, so the warrior gene is there.'

Palios soon learned to be cautious about his education and his ability to articulate thoughts more quickly than other players. He speaks in a hushed even tone, with a suggestion of a Birkenhead accent, and has the level stare of a student in psychology.

'I never spoke up in the dressing room after a match except once later on in my career, because I was aware that managers might have seen me as a threat,' he says. 'Ray Mathias was a team-mate and he'd ask me for tax advice. I was accepted as a bit of an oddball, I'll admit. They'd hear I was an accountant and maybe think I wouldn't be able to handle the aggression of 1970s football.'

When Palios played for Tranmere they were at best a Division Three club. In the 1980s, they were on the verge of falling out of the Football League. The 90s was a rich period with semi-finals, cup finals and, almost, Premier League football. In the consciousness of many that's where Tranmere should be, because their achievements were featured on television and football on television in the 90s was new and absorbed in a way it isn't now, when so much is taken for granted. The reality is Tranmere is a club that for most of its history has struggled.

Palios was in retirement when he decided to get involved again. After leaving the Football Association he worked as a non-executive director at the British

Judo Association and acted as a member of the audit committee at Surrey Cricket Club. He was separating his time between homes in Winchester and Agen in France.

'Ronnie Moore, Tranmere's manager, had been sacked for betting. Some of the players had been arrested for alleged match-fixing. The club was relegated out of League One. The context financially was awful. We were losing a million pounds a year,' he remembers. 'I was driving through France with my wife, Nicky; the sun was shining and we were by the coast. It was a Saturday afternoon and Radio Five Live was on the radio. They were flicking from game to game. With ten minutes to go we conceded and Notts County scored. I said to Nicky, "That's it – we'll go down, we'll go down again and we'll end up in administration." She said, "Well, do something about it!" I said, "I will if you will." I knew what I'd be like. I'd be completely absorbed, so I needed to take her with me.

'The place was in a real mess,' he continues. 'It was a typical case of a club not receiving investment for ten to fifteen years and suffering as a consequence. If you are selling your house and don't put money into the way it looks, there's every chance you won't find a buyer. I could see that the lack of investment was tangible. The most pernicious thing was that everybody appeared beaten down by the circumstances. Nobody looked out of the window, and staff had stopped asking whether they could spend money on improving situations because they knew the answer would be no. At the same time there were lots of business practices where they were penny wise and pound foolish. They'd impale themselves on ridiculous contracts.'

Palios is aware of what some critical fans say about Peter Johnson, Tranmere's former owner, but he regards him as a friend and appreciates that it was under Johnson that Tranmere experienced some tremendous highs. Johnson was the Liverpool supporter who became Tranmere's chairman and then Everton's before selling to Bill Kenwright, largely due to supporter pressure. In buying Tranmere Palios persuaded Johnson to write off the debt owed him by the club and it in part explains why, today, a painting of Johnson remains hanging in Prenton Park's boardroom.

'You'll see history on the walls but a modern outlook in everything we do,' Palios says. 'There was a picture of Johnny King [the legendary manager] and it said, "We can't compete with Liverpool and Everton – we're like a deadly submarine." As soon as I arrived I asked for the top line to be taken away. I realise we can't compete with Liverpool and Everton at a product level at this point in time, but where we can compete with Liverpool and Everton is offering affordable live football. How many kids today only see football on a screen? It was Aristotle who said, "Give me the child until he is seven and I will show you the man." If you get a kid into Tranmere at five, I will show you the supporter.'

Palios thinks Tranmere can also play on their Wirral brand, 'but not too heavily' because he'd like us to attract fans from the other side of the river. For a long time Tranmere hosted games on a Friday night knowing many on the Wirral were Liverpool and Everton supporters and that earlier kick offs would leave the rest of the weekend for a focus on the big two. 'Ultimately, we can compete with Liverpool and Everton but we have to compete in a different way and in different areas,' he concludes. 'Saying we can't compete is simply too negative.'

It is claimed, though, that Birkenhead, with its Viking heritage, and Anglo-Saxon Liverpool are like oil and water. In Lewis's Topographical Dictionary of England Birkenhead's right of 'ferryage across the Mersey' granted by the charter in 1318 was the political hot potato of the nineteenth century as Liverpool sought growth by claiming the shipping lanes that led out towards the Irish Sea.

Separate councils still administer Liverpool and Birkenhead, Liverpool is in Merseyside and Birkenhead has a Cheshire postcode, and while followers of Tranmere Rovers regularly sing about not being Scousers, to older residents of Liverpool Birkenhead is derided as a 'one-eyed city', in the same way Mancunians view Salford or Geordies Gateshead.

'More than compete, you can have a symbiotic relationship with them,' Palios says of Liverpool and Everton. 'Liverpool have been very good to us and despite Everton being known as the People's Club it's Liverpool that have answered the call and supported us in a number of ways. Jürgen Klopp brought his first team here for a pre-season game and that was worth an extra £150,000-odd profit to us – it makes a difference on your million loss. Liverpool come here now and play their under-23 games at Prenton Park.

'What could be done is what we're trying to do here, by having grown-up relationships with other wealthier clubs without selling our birthright. The difficulty is finding the balance. Tranmere needs to migrate up the leagues before we can effectively use the players from other academies and that's just being pragmatic. The game tends to become more technical as you rise and at Premier League level the game is about technique and pace rather than power and aggression as it can sometimes be in the National League.

'We're the only nation in the world that has the football pyramid,' he continues. 'So long as the big clubs are sensitive to the rights of the fans from the smaller clubs, relationships can work. I was absolutely apoplectic when it was announced that under-23 teams would appear in the Johnstone's Paint Trophy. I publically said it was the worst idea I'd heard. My reasons for coming back to Tranmere are linked to this. How many people do you know that get up in the morning where 5,000 people are desperate for you to do well? There's probably as many as 150,000 people on Merseyside that notice what you're doing every day if you're the owner of Tranmere – even if it's through reading a small column about the club on a website. The strength and passion of the fans cannot be ignored if they are opposed to the governance of the game. Apathy would kill football. You can't disrespect that.'

Palios says it is too simplistic to say there needs to be less greed and a change at the top of football. He tells a story about going to a West Ham United game a few years ago. They were playing Chelsea at the start of the season and Chelsea were 2–0 up quickly, with fans accepting of the defeat. 'They were prepared to write the result off before the game and say their season begins after Chelsea's visit. In my day West Ham would have fancied their chances in a home game against any of the top clubs. There are very few headlines about redemption in sport. Every season should start with the chance of redemption. Not accepting you are going to lose to certain teams.'

He can explain why this happens.

'Teams can now go up and come straight back down, pocketing something like £175million inclusive of parachute payments. What if Tranmere, say, went into the Championship and their turnover is around the £10million mark? The Premier League has disturbed the competitive landscape by creating huge gaps. It means that clubs that have pocketed all that money are competing in the Championship with budgets that are way above their natural sustainable level. This is a contradiction in professional sport. If you have unbridled competition, the strongest will usually win. If football were a business and a business solely, many businessmen will say that it is their business to kill off the competition. If you look at other industries such as retail, you find monopolies. Supermarkets will consolidate to the point where there is only one supermarket left and that means they can do what they want with prices because there is nobody left to challenge them. So the consumer needs protection as well. That's where there needs to be intervention. The football administrators have a huge responsibility because their job should be to retain the integrity of the competition year on year. There's a need to rewrite the rule book otherwise you'll always get the same three or four teams at the top and everyone else struggling.'

Palios is optimistic about Tranmere's future, however.

'If there's any club capable of having a sustainable model in the lower leagues, it's Tranmere,' he says. 'I never spoke at the beginning about a five-year job to get us back to the Championship. The talk was about us creating an environment that within five years would allow us to compete in League One and have the ability to go into the Championship but not fall straight back down because of finances. Our turnover in League One was £3.8million of which there were player sales and hand-outs from the Football League, so the real turnover of the club was roughly £1.5million. Our turnover in the National League this year will be £6.5million and that's without the consideration of any hand-outs whatsoever. If we get promoted, that figure will increase. So already, there has been a big turnaround.

'Nobody has ever defined self-sustainable for a football club but I have tried to,' he continues. 'I define it as having a top-third budget in whatever league you're competing in with better than average support systems, while being able to break even. The theory goes that if you're top-third [budget] with average luck, an average manager and average injuries, you'll finish in the top third because there is a correlation between what you spend and what you get. If that's the case, you'll always be around the play-offs and that means you'll maximise your gate because there will always be interest in what you're doing.'

Palios says that for every thousand people that attend Tranmere matches over a season it is worth around £200,000 in revenue. Over the last ten years – through a largely fallow period in terms of success – attendances have averaged at 5,000. He appreciates for that number to increase, the product on the pitch must improve first and be maintained over a period of time.

'I think we've got the catchment area which is sufficient for our purposes if our horizon is the Championship,' he says. 'For me, the Championship is like the old Division One. Then, you only had to be one of the best players in England to play in the top flight. Now, you've got to be one of the best players in the world. I'm not limiting the club's ambition to the Championship because you should never limit ambition.

'In the Premier League, you cannot afford to rely solely on the local conurbation to build a team because the Premier League is really a world league that attracts players from across the globe. For us, that's fantastic, because there's a whole Merseyside diaspora that we can latch on to – players that don't get a chance at Liverpool or Everton. The majority of footballers I know – if they had the chance – would like to play at home and be around family and friends. Merseyside remains a hotbed of football and in terms of players it's a big catchment area. For Tranmere that's something exciting.'

Tranmere is reaching beyond its council boundaries for growth. The club has a memorandum of understanding with the Inner Mongolian government to develop coaching standards in the region's capital Hohhot. It meant that when Chinese coaches first visited Wirral to develop their skills with Tranmere, they invested in the area: in the shops of Cheshire Oaks, in hotels, in restaurants. He has since been told from the vice chairman of the Inner Mongolian Communist Party that by 2018, Hohhot will be sending 300 children with coaches to Prenton Park. Palios says it has been a challenge trying to get the message across to bodies like the local council, who used to sponsor Tranmere's shirts, that a vibrant business exists within their boundaries, though it is slowly getting through. 'It should say to hotels, to restaurants, "Get involved in Tranmere and we can all help each other."'

Palios wants Tranmere to become a Football League club again. He wants Tranmere to become a conference and events venue. He wants Tranmere to be a vocational college so young people are getting jobs at the end of their courses. He thinks all of these aims are fulfillable by 2020. Palios has also suffered from cancer since 2014 and that has meant four operations and eight weeks of radiotherapy. His recognition that 'We've also been relegated in that time so it hasn't been an easy existence,' feels like an understatement. Yet there are reasons beyond football why Tranmere stimulates him.

When Palios returned to Tranmere, the living and working arrangements of some supporters had changed to the point where they could still afford a season ticket but were not able to be there for games and they requested that the season tickets were given to good causes. Palios then asked Tranmere's supporters' trust to donate a further £3,000, and the players responded by relinquishing the same figure from their bonus pot. 'It meant that we were able to charge thirty-pound season tickets for children while the disadvantaged kids got in for nothing. It didn't cost the club a penny. We went to the relevant agencies and the council and said, "You find the right kids." This was an example of the goodwill of the supporters focused through the prism of the club doing good things in the community and creating future fans. What's not to like about that?'

Palios was thirteen years old when he was in a foster home. He becomes emotional, his eyes marbling with tears that don't quite run, when he tells a story about a thirteen-year-old girl who attended a Tranmere game. She later told her carer that she saw friends from her school class at the match and it made her feel 'normal'.

'I was taken to Wembley to watch Tranmere as a child, courtesy of Dave Bail, the manager of my football team, who knew of my personal circumstances which meant I was never able to afford attending a football match, let alone Wembley,' Palios recalls. 'I didn't tell anyone I was in a foster home when I was in school because the worst thing would be telling people when all you really wanted to be was normal, just like everyone else.

'But listen, I didn't want it to be about Mark Palios coming back on his white chariot to save the day because I wanted it to be about both of us – me and Nicky,' he concludes, explaining the great job his wife is doing leading Tranmere's excellent community initiatives having spent most of her working life in the field of law. 'Many of the businesses I worked with during my thirty years before returning to Tranmere, I didn't know much about because I wasn't an industry expert,' he admits. 'As an accountant going into British Steel and telling them their only child is ugly wasn't easy. "You're an accountant – what do you know?" they'd say, not really appreciating my skills in assessing situations and creating a path forward. Tranmere is the only work situation in my life where I'd consider myself to know the industry. And while my involvement is emotional, I believe it has a solid business base.'

PLAIN,
ORBIT AND CORE

15

OUT-OF-TOWNERS

THE ARCHITECTURE OF WINSFORD UNITED'S BARTON STADIUM IS brutal. There is a scene of steel and iron where lidless oil drums act as litter bins. The venue's rusting floodlights were built in the 1970s and their power is greater than standard football arenas because the ground began life as a dog track so there are wider spaces to cover. Beyond a two-step terrace with a tin roof which runs along one of the sides is a council estate and it was from the back window of one of these houses that Elfyn Edwards, Winsford's captain, was once shot by a youth with an air rifle, though Edwards, a tough defender, remained on the pitch until the end of the game, helping his team to victory and a clean sheet.

Overgrown grass now covers gravel where the greyhounds used to race. The sponsorship signs say this is the home of a side that plays in the Unibond League even though Winsford last played a match at that level seventeen years ago. On a dark Thursday evening Motörhead's 'Ace of Spades' blares through the public address system on repeat. You think it is over but it isn't. Lemmy always comes back. You have loose-change buckets raising money for the clubs that play here. Tonight, you have a Mid-Cheshire Senior Cup semi-final. You have 1874 Northwich hosting Witton Albion. You don't have Northwich Victoria even though they are in a higher league because 1874, the club founded by Vics supporters, would eventually beat them in the final a few months later.

Northwich, seven miles north of Winsford, must be the most dysfunctional football town in the country. At first there had been Northwich Victoria and Witton Albion, the big two. Northwich's history is richer and slightly longer and Witton, whose ground is actually outside Northwich in a village called Wincham, came to challenge them in the early 1990s having earned promotion from the Northern Premier League into the Conference. For one season Witton finished above Northwich but then fell out of the Conference and have never been back.

Aside from an FA Cup victory over Charlton Athletic and a couple of decent seasons the mood at Northwich Victoria has been bad ever since the decision was taken to sell the much-loved Drill Field ground in the town centre to Wain Homes for £2.4million. Clubs were starting to turn professional in the Conference and the league's administrators, emboldened by injections of money from rich club chairmen, ruled that members had to have 6,000 capacities with the possibility of enlargement to 10,000 in case of promotion of the Football League. Though the Conference reduced the rule to a slightly more reasonable 4,000 capacity requirement, Vics had already decided to leave by then.

The outcome has been catastrophic. The Victoria Stadium at the Wincham business park was built on the edge of Northwich but it never felt like home. When Vics were bought by Mike Connett, he registered the new ground under a separate company called Beaconet. When Beaconet went into liquidation the ground was suddenly owned by the bank. This allowed Jim Rushe, a go-cart track owner and property investor from Manchester, to take over a club in 2007 with massive debts and he proceeded to try and buy the ground back through another company called Northwich Victoria Developments Ltd. When that plan failed it allowed the chemical company next door to buy the land. In 2012 Northwich Victoria were made homeless.

Northwich Victoria have been on the road ever since, playing home games in places as far away as Stafford – 41 miles to the south. There were spells at Kidsgrove, Macclesfield, Leek and Flixton. For the time being they are tenants at Witton Albion's Wincham Park – as they were back when the doomed Victoria Stadium was being built.

Rushe, who was jailed for six years for his part in a £5million plot to supply cocaine in 2016, had in 2012 been declared bankrupt like Connett before him, and on the same day Paul Stockton, the chairman of the Northwich Victoria Supporters' Trust, chaired a meeting at a social club in Lostock Gralam near Northwich. The organisation had explored a possible community share issue with a view to raising funds to buy a stake in their stricken club. Now, it was being proposed that the supporters should break away and form their own team. Stockton describes the moment as 'an arrival of independence'. 1874 Northwich were born.

It had been an unusual period for 1874 when I went to meet Stockton. Ian Street, the manager since the club's formation, had resigned the weekend before and so Stockton, now 1874's chairman, was facing a situation he'd never experienced before. Street had decided to go after it became clear 1874 would not escape from the North West Counties Premier League, a demanding competition which has 22 teams and only one promotion place with no play-offs. Street had recently moved to Leigh, an hour's drive away.

'There is a sense of loss because Ian has been with us from the beginning,' Stockton tells me, standing near the gates of the Barton Stadium as the players begin to arrive for the game against Witton in their tracksuits. 'Ian helped us create something we're very happy with. But ultimately we have to accept that managers and players will come and go from the football club – though they'll always remain a part of our story. As a chairman and a board we're still learning how to deal with situations like these because we've never been through them before. We'll take some time to consider the next appointment because we appreciate the road rushed decisions can take you.'

Stockton, of course, is referring to what happened at Northwich Victoria, the club he used to support; the club he'd followed to Wembley for FA Trophy finals. Stockton, like the other 1874 fans I talk to, is reluctant to speak about the outlook at Vics, which had worsened since Jim Gannon's departure as manager in 2016. In a season where Vics reached the second round of the FA Cup, narrowly losing to Northampton Town, Gannon also nearly led them to promotion before deciding to return to Stockport County, a club across the other side of Cheshire, one he'd managed in League One.

By January 2017, with Gannon long gone and all of the players that had done so well for him following him out of the door, Northwich Victoria were placed into administration for the third time in a decade where demotion had been enforced on as many occasions, none as a consequence of on-pitch performances. The ten-point deduction that followed sent them bottom of the league, playing in front of crowds that were regularly lower than a hundred. To appreciate the context of that figure, consider that Northwich Victoria had attracted gates of more than 8,000 in the post-war years and were still averaging more than 1,200 less than a decade ago.

Listening to anyone associated with 1874, it seems as though Northwich

Victoria is now considered the feral child of a family, banished to a cellar of thoughts. 'Quite what's happening at that club, I don't know,' Stockton says in a way that is both pointed and somehow casual. 'What will happen with them will happen and it has nothing to do with us.'

Over a pint in the nearby Red Lion pub, James Wood, an 1874 board member, told me that the club's greatest challenge was not pulling away from Northwich Victoria emotionally but having the confidence to ignore doubters. He recalls how the chairmen that led Northwich Victoria into the darkness were dismissive of the supporters' capabilities. 'One of them said we couldn't run a football club from behind a computer,' he recalls. Stockton, Wood and all of the other volunteers that helped set up 1874 did all of the right things though, choosing to take advice from other clubs that had risen from the terraces.

'Up until the early 90s football supporters were treated as second-class citizens; you put up with what you get – certainly as far as Thatcher was concerned,' Wood says. 'Fanzine movements began to change the dynamic, showing that football supporters had strong feelings and were able to articulate them. We're not at the German model where so many clubs are owned by supporters but I'm hopeful owners now know that if they mess around with supporters they're risking something. Twenty to twenty-five years ago football supporters would put up with certain things happening but no longer. Fans believe in themselves. The people at AFC Wimbledon told us there'd be lots of put-downs: "You can't do this . . ." Wimbledon told us to ignore them – we could do it. It's hard work, long hours, but it has been liberating and very rewarding.'

Since the formation of 1874 Northwich, another club on the fringes of the town, Barnton, had emerged from the Cheshire leagues and are now competing in the same division. It means the greater Northwich area, which has a population of around 70,000, is serviced by four non-league football clubs, none of whom actually play in Northwich. For decades there had been suggestions that Northwich Victoria and Witton Albion should merge. 'I was in favour of the idea so long as the club was called Northwich Victoria and it played in green rather than red,' Wood jokes. He remembers the period in the 1970s and 1980s when the rivalry was at its fiercest – when there were pubs in Northwich that were no-go drinking zones for supporters of the other team.

'Witton were a bit like the noisy neighbours from down the road that you'd try and avoid if you ever had the misfortune of bumping into them,' Wood recalls. 'I can't say I've ever felt hatred towards them but in a very Cheshire way, I'd say there has always been an uneasiness between Northwich Victoria and

Witton Albion because the intensity of the rivalry was based around one ignoring the other.

'I have no idea what the plans for Northwich Victoria are now,' Wood adds, sighing. 'A merger between Vics and Witton was mentioned regularly throughout my childhood but I can't see it happening, not between 1874 and Witton anyway, because Witton is run by members and 1874 has shareholders. While Witton owns an asset – Wincham Park – 1874 has no assets at all, though we are in the black.'

Had 1874 decided to ground-share with Witton, it would have brought the club much closer to Northwich, but as it stands they will remain at Winsford until the end of the 2017/18 season because the rent at Wincham Park is considered too high. For Wood, the location of any new ground is key to 1874's identity, though he fears nothing will ever match the old Drill Field. He fears too that the land prices in central Northwich might prove too expensive as well.

'Drill Field was right in the town centre; close to all the pubs. Leaving was the biggest mistake Northwich Victoria ever made. Even though as a shareholder I voted to leave, like lots of other people did, I look back at the advice we were given at the time and realise it was erroneous. The Victoria Stadium was a soulless place.

'Winsford have been great to 1874,' he concludes. 'We have a lot to thank them for. But we can't progress with our long-term plans until we get back to Northwich. The clue is in the name. We are 1874 Northwich. We are not 1874 Winsford.'

Premier League footballers might live there but Cheshire football was at a low. Tranmere Rovers had been in the Championship and now they were facing a third year as a non-league club. Traditional rivals Chester City had gone out of existence and, though reformed, were finding life tough in the Conference. Historically, the grounds of Stalybridge Celtic and Altrincham had been in Cheshire and those clubs were positioned 21st and 22nd in the Conference North, heading towards relegation. Stockport County had fallen the furthest and they were now four promotions away from the level they had competed at not so long ago. Crewe Alexandra were at the foot of League Two, a club with its once-proud reputation for an ability to produce fine young footballers in tatters because of its links with paedophile Barry Bennell. Dario Gradi, the legendary manager that appointed Bennell, had been suspended by the Football Association.

Meanwhile, the future of Northwich Victoria was bleak. The 2016/17 season was only halfway through when it was announced the ground-share agreement with Witton Albion would not continue beyond the end of the campaign. 'The truth is they cannot afford to stay,' Albion chairman Mark Harris told the Northwich Guardian. 'And the harsh realities of football finance dictate we can't reduce the rent we currently charge to an amount they can pay.'

Harris had been Witton's chairman for nearly a decade. He is also the chairman of the Northern Premier League. Altrincham-born, he grew up supporting his local team, progressing from the terraces to the boardroom where he acted as chairman for a short period before being encouraged to join Witton. It is fair to assume Harris understands better than most the challenges of running football clubs in this area because he has done it for so long and has remained in the game. Though Witton supporters have been frustrated by the club's failure to progress beyond the Northern Premier League during his tenure it is widely accepted that, in contrast to Northwich Victoria, Witton has long operated with a strong sense of financial responsibility. It explains why Harris is keen for Northwich Victoria to remain at Wincham Park or for 1874 Northwich to replace them – if they can afford it.

'There is no reason not to ground-share providing your pitch can take it,' he says. 'Over the years people have asked me why don't we simply amalgamate all of the clubs in Northwich because they think it will get the town into the Football League. Number one, football doesn't work that way, because what actually happens, as fans of Oxford United, Reading and Swindon will tell you when Robert Maxwell tried to merge those clubs, not everyone wants it to happen. You'll never get universal approval and football supporters are intelligent and difficult to win over. You are risking alienating lots of people. The reality is there's a very good chance that if you merged the clubs in Northwich and managed to find success you'd be doing well if your attendances were around the thousand mark. Separately if those clubs were doing very well, the aggregate attendance might be closer to three or four thousand.'

Cheshire is the north-west's wealthiest county and yet its football teams are struggling. Altrincham has the highest concentration of net-worth individuals anywhere in the country outside of Mayfair and yet Altrincham – one of the great non-league names because of its giant-killing tradition; one that faced Liverpool in the FA Cup – will spend next season in non-league's third tier, a level they have not competed at since 1968 when they left the old Cheshire League. 'Do the high net-worth individuals in Altrincham watch Altrincham Football

Club? No they don't,' says Harris, who still lives in the town where he runs a travel company. He does not wish to speak about another club's positon and though it is clear Altrincham's decline is not due solely to finance, it is also clear that not all of the people that live in Altrincham were actually born there, so why should an affection for the town's football team naturally develop, particularly when families moving to the area because of work in Manchester might already have teams to support from elsewhere and there is so much Premier League football on television anyway?

Harris thinks some of Cheshire football's problems are related to geography, though. 'Cheshire sits outside the urban conurbations of Manchester and Liverpool,' he explains. 'We are stood here in Winsford, which is very much an overspill town. The footprint of Manchester and Liverpool has moved here – as has Warrington and Crewe. There aren't so many market towns any more and the trend towards urbanisation can have both a positive and negative effect with regards to recruitment, but usually a negative effect in terms of funding. For all the ambitions of a club wanting to install 4G pitches for the small community that surrounds it, funding is usually allocated to areas where there are more people, and so clubs like Witton need to bide their time to the point urbanisation comes to them and more houses are built. As football clubs, the challenge then is to tap into new people coming into the area – and make new residents with no emotional tie to football in Northwich want to come to you. From there, marketing becomes an issue as well as having a product that is going to capture their attention on a Saturday afternoon.

'Non-league football also has an ageing supporter base,' Harris continues. 'Traditionally, there was a clear profile of the traditional non-league's football fan. Children would originally get involved through a parent before attending matches – as I did at Altrincham when I was fourteen years old – on [their] own because non-league football is a safe environment. They discover booze, they get married, they have kids and then they come back. Volunteers are now getting older and there are fewer replacements because we're finding fewer people are coming back in adulthood. We've seen other clubs go out of existence because of this. It won't be because of a lack of money or support, it's because of the lack of people to run them. Whether that's because we're competing with Sky because there's so much more football on television, is difficult to say.'

Witton were aiming for promotion back to the Northern Premier League from its first division, which is split into two competitions in the north and south. Witton had controversially been placed in the southern league, a decision which impacted on the club financially, involving an extra £15,000 a year in travelling costs. The decision also impacted on recruitment because players were reluctant to commit to a team that would take up more of their time: time spent on the road when they could, instead, be with their families. The geography of the two-tier and three-competition Northern Premier League has altered significantly since the creation of the Conference North in 2005 because fewer Northern League clubs from the north-east of the country have been willing to seek entry to it due to the increased cost of travel, issues that had nearly driven Bishop Auckland, Whitley Bay, Durham City and Spennymoor out of existence. This has forced boundaries south and it explains why Witton, despite being located in the north, are facing extra travel pressures.

Harris thinks he has a solution and it is one that will be enforced from the start of the 2018/19 season, with the creation of a new midlands league at step three of the non-league pyramid to accompany the Northern Premier, the Southern and the Isthmian Leagues.

'I'm fully supportive of regionalised football,' Harris says. 'Not all of the problems non-league clubs face are financial. Many of them are personnel related. Players, supporters and officials are spending vast amounts of time on motorways. Nobody tends to think about this strain, not just from a financial perspective, but also the people involved getting time off work and the mental and physical stresses linked to that. I'm hoping this change will make the lives of everyone involved a little bit easier. It will also increase the number of derby matches.'

The reorganisation will impact on the North West Counties League and more promotion slots will become available. For the 2017/18 season, at least, 1874 Northwich versus Northwich Victoria might be one of those derby matches. It seems unlikely, however, that either of those fixtures will actually take place in Northwich.

16

FURTHEST FALL

JIM GANNON'S ASSOCIATION WITH STOCKPORT COUNTY STARTED in 1990 when he was 22 years old. Having played in 480 games for the club he became manager in 2005 and is now in his third spell in charge, taking what he describes as 'the call' after achieving success where no other manager was able to at the seemingly doomed Northwich Victoria.

'Football management becomes very difficult when a club is reeling backwards,' Gannon says. 'Like at Stockport, the situation at Northwich was one where the club was put into administration and lost ownership of the stadium. While Stockport remained at Edgeley Park, Northwich moved around: to Stafford, to Flixton, to Wincham. They lost some identity because they weren't playing in the town. It was a couple of enjoyable years, though. To achieve what we did, to reach the second round of the FA Cup, to develop players that are now playing very well three divisions above in the Conference National, to return to Northwich – to Wincham, anyway; it made it very difficult to leave. But my heart led me back to Stockport.'

Gannon had an unusual working arrangement. He was Northwich Victoria's manager while he was in charge of Stockport County's youth set-up, while his teaching job meant he also coached Stockport boys' school team. It meant he possessed a unique understanding of football talent in the area.

'I started my career at Dundalk and the football club was the hub of the community,' he says. 'I want Stockport to be that hub as well. Northwich was great but it wasn't my home. I understand what football means to this town. Everybody talks about the team, even in the bad times. In Stockport I felt as though I could play a huge role in re-energising positive passion for football in the town because I have lived here for such a long time with my family. Each week I don't engage just with twenty professionals. I engage with forty wannabe professionals and hundreds of kids who want to enjoy football. I'm a socialist at heart. I believe in the greater good. For me, there's no more important role or responsibility in bringing good results to six thousand County fans, knowing they will go home and the football club will affect their week. To be able to help the best local footballers progress, there's no greater privilege.

'My parents were hard-working working-class people,' he explains. 'They taught me that there is always someone less fortunate than you and if you've got the skills to help them you should. I've never been a greedy person or materialistic. If I've had any wealth I've tried to share it. I've always believed there is a greater value in giving than there is in taking. What I'm doing for Stockport, it's not for me. I see it as a community role. I think that anybody who goes into a football club and has a five-year agenda to achieve something for themselves will always fail. You always have to go in and do a good job for the people that employ you, the people that support you. All I want to do is a good job for Stockport County.'

Gannon had never played nor managed at non-league level until he was persuaded to join Northwich, initially as caretaker. It surprised him how much he enjoyed the role and the experience was re-energising following a dark period in management where he says attitudes of the people involved began to shift in the years after he was made redundant by Stockport.

'I never knock people who want to make money out of football but I don't take a great deal of satisfaction from that side of the game. I've never wanted to own a Porsche or to wear jewellery. I look at the Premier League and I don't relate to what's happening at that level. You have billionaire owners and millionaire players. Owners might have other altruistic activities where they share their wealth so I can't knock them. But for me, that's why I really enjoy non-league because I know I'm working with people that want the club to do well. They're not taking anything out of it except the satisfaction of delivering for the football club. Despite the massive amounts of money in football we should never lose sight of the idea that football has a huge role to play in the community.'

*

I had met with Jim Gannon at the Firbank Kitchen in Wythenshawe on a Thursday evening after Stockport County finished training at a nearby school. When his car was stolen from another part of Manchester and then found in Wythenshawe, Tony Coton, the former Manchester City goalkeeper, described the area in his autobiography as 'the kind of place where pit-bulls walk around in packs for their own safety'. Though the Firbank was hosting a comedy night and spirits were high as a compere told jokes into a mic, in 2015 the pub had been hit by arson attacks three times in as many months. The landlord was upstairs sleeping with his wife when offenders threw a paving slab through the window and hurled canisters inside at around 4.40 a.m. He was later told to pay £5,000 to make the attacks stop and three men were later jailed for blackmail.

Stockport trained in Wythenshawe following eviction from their crumbling Manor Farm facility in 2009. Of all the clubs to have dropped out of the Football League, Stockport's fall had been the most dramatic, especially when you consider that between 1997 and 2003 Stockport and Manchester City had met six times and Stockport were victorious in three, losing only once. For one season Stockport were in a higher division than their illustrious neighbours and a proud smile stretches across Gannon's face when he recounts the day he led the team out as captain at Maine Road and won.

Now, while City compete in the Champions League, Gannon prepares for derbies against Curzon Ashton, Stalybridge Celtic and FC United of Manchester. Stockport had long experienced ups and downs but no down had been as sharp as this, starting when Sale Sharks owner Brian Kennedy bought the club from Brendan Elwood, the person who Gannon says had 'driven the success of the 90s', though perhaps forgetting that one of Elwood's more unrealistic ideas had been to buy Maine Road when Manchester City moved to Eastlands and form 'Man-Stock County'. Kennedy brought Sale and Stockport together under the umbrella of Cheshire Sports and when he moved the rugby union side into Edgeley Park, Stockport effectively became second-class citizens. When Kennedy sold up in November 2005 to a supporters' trust for £1 he retained ownership of the ground, proceeding to charge Stockport £12,500 a month to play at a venue which had been home since 1902. Though the trust installed Gannon as manager, who saved the club from falling out of the Football League before achieving an improbable promotion mainly using young players, his efforts were being undermined by finance. County shared revenue raised from Edgeley Park with Sale Sharks, with 30 per cent going to Kennedy. To buy the club the trust had also agreed to give up a £1million-per-year profit from

Edgeley Park's conference and banqueting facilities in order to repay the debt owed to their former chairman.

That episode ended with redundancies – Gannon being one of them – and since then Stockport have been through nearly a dozen different managers and owners. In 2010, it was reported in the Manchester Evening News that Stockport County were weeks away from extinction and, though the club carried on until Gannon's third appointment as manager, its football operation has been suffering for a very long time.

'Stockport's story is a reminder that no matter how big you are you don't have a divine right to play at any level, history doesn't do you favours,' Gannon says. 'You look at Edgeley Park – an 11,000 all-seater stadium, you look at the fan base – we've just broken the attendance record in the Conference North. It has a Football League stadium and a Football League crowd. But as a business, it has retracted so much. Most of the problems associated with Stockport are related to the fact the club no longer owns the ground. It was owned by Sale Sharks and now it is owned by the council. So although the ground feels like an asset, it sometimes feels like a liability because we have to pay for it and maintain it. As a business we're not as big as the crowd and the ground suggest and the budget isn't as healthy as you'd imagine. This has been a problem for us on the terraces and when negotiating with players that we want to sign, they believe that we have a huge amount of money to spend but we don't.

'You only have to look at what's happened at Fleetwood, what's starting to happen at Barrow and now Fylde to understand the pressures we face,' he continues. 'These are new-money clubs with wealthy investors. Clubs like Stockport and Darlington have bigger fan bases but are in a poorer business position, which explains [why] the Fyldes and Fleetwoods are ahead of us. Stockport is a club that shouldn't be at this level but we have to accept it has fallen to this level before we start to grow again, because the potential is there to grow into a club that operates in a better way than it is now. It's a big wheel and it will take big arms to make it turn.

'Next season you could have York at our level. Kidderminster and Nuneaton are already full-time. Fylde have a Football League set-up and then Salford have millionaire backers and are going to be professional too; Harrogate the same. Above us, the Conference is more or less a professional league and that is reflected by the way the FA impose transfer windows similar to the Football League. As a football club we can only go so far part-time. We have huge strides to make before returning to the Football League is a possibility and we have to commit to a stronger full-time set-up. This is the next phase for me. At the moment I'm trying to make us as competitive as possible as a part-time club. I still believe a good part-time side can get promoted from this level and stay in the Conference. But to be competitive in the Conference and stand any chance of promotion into the Football League, you do really need to be full-time. That's our challenge in the medium term.

'When you get into the Football League you experience a huge financial boost. It means you can invest more in your infrastructure, you can have a bigger squad and you can build a development squad to grow players. That's what we did in my first stint when we got players from non-league like Ashley Williams and Liam Dickinson, who we sold for several hundred thousands of pounds. And then we had our own players from our academy – Tommy Rowe, James Tunnicliffe and Josh Thompson; players we sold for six figures.

'I've always been a builder rather than a buyer,' he adds. 'When we played in the League Two play-offs [in 2008] I think the only fee we paid out for any player in that team was £20,000 for Gary Dicker. Gary played brilliantly that day and went on to captain Brighton to the Championship. There is always a risk playing young players in lower-league football or in non-league but for any club to flourish and for the game in general you've got to give young players a chance. Even at Northwich, we took players from lower levels and tried to make them better players. Jordan Williams and Richard Bennett went from the Evo-Stik North to full-time with Barrow in the Conference and they are doing very well indeed. That gives me great satisfaction, knowing you've played some part in helping someone improve themselves – even if it's just by giving them a platform.

'I finished my playing career at Crewe under Dario Gradi and did my pro-licence there. My aim was to emulate what they did: signing players, coaching players, selling players; reinvesting the money and making the structure stronger, repeating the process. For two or three years that's what we managed to do. We built a good young team playing a great brand of football, winning fair-play awards, developing players and selling players that went on to become full internationals. The aim is to return to that model but for the time being we just want to be a very good non-league club.'

At well over six feet tall Gannon is an imposing figure. His posture means he hangs over people when they listen. His voice is a curious hybrid of Mancunian and Cockney having made family connections in each of those places, and though his Irish upbringing rounds the edge off his accent with a smooth assurance, there remains an intensity about him – the way he delivers his thoughts with authority – which has had consequences in a managerial career where falling out with chairmen, directors, referees and opponents has been a theme. Few non-league managers would have the confidence to name Valeriy Lobanovskyi as an inspiration – especially over Johan Cruyff – but Gannon does, because Lobanovskyi paid respect to set-pieces. I had watched Stockport train earlier that evening and for twenty minutes out of the hour-long session, the same drill was rehearsed: Danny Lloyd, the exciting forward taking a corner, one of the team's powerful midfielders winning the near-post flick, with the aim of a big centre-half thundering in a header having made a run from deep. The same routine was practised from throw-ins and though the description may sound basic, Gannon's thoughts about the way the game should be played are far more complex.

He tells me that the latest player he has hopes for is in fact Lloyd, the 25-year-old Stockport signed from AFC Fylde the previous summer. Lloyd had a reasonably paid job at a waste-management company in Liverpool when Fylde went full-time and Stockport managed to capitalise on his determination not to rely totally on football for an income by offering him a part-time contract to play in front of the biggest crowds in the Conference North at a club where the slump has been arrested, with Stockport pushing for promotion under Gannon. Gannon had got the best out of Lloyd by reducing his defensive responsibilities and in early March his goalscoring achievements were attracting attention from the Football League. Gannon reminds me that he also gave Fraser Forster and Wayne Hennessey, now Premier League goalkeepers, their Football League debuts as loanees.

'I've always tried to develop players who are effective,' he says. 'It's a very hard thing to achieve because you're teaching players what the game is about and how to win football matches, then working backwards. I like the saying, "Give a man a fish, you'll feed him for a day; teach a man to fish and you'll feed him for a lifetime." I want to give my players the skills so they can affect the outcome of a game.

'I'm not saying coaching is prescriptive, that we do too many drills, that we copy too many people and we're not open-minded enough or free-thinking to allow players to express themselves. But I'd like to think there are no lost causes in football – that we as coaches can still add value to players whether they are eighteen years old released by Football League clubs or twenty-eight years old and considered at their peak as a non-league player. I don't see myself as anyone special, just someone who thinks clearly, talks straight and explains things in a way that players can embrace it and take it on to a pitch.'

Gannon is not overly critical of academy football but the socialist in him says young players should earn less and have their pay incentivised. He believes academies teach players to be better players rather than winners and this is a glaring inconsistency because professional football is defined by winning and losing.

'It's a massive conundrum for the game of football,' he says. 'Of course we want players to take care of the ball because if you have the ball the opposition can't score and you can build attacks. But ultimately football is an invasion game where you have to find a way to get the ball from one end of the pitch into the net at the other end. Leicester City won the Premier League and they did it in a very efficient way, proving it can be done. What we have to do as coaches is embrace modern concepts of possession, skill, flair and creativity but always with the mind-set of creating opportunities, scoring goals and winning games. Sometimes we hide behind good coaching, allowing players to develop without finding the right balance for the team. I see this in school on games' day. There are no winners and no losers in sport even though there are kids who will fight if they lose a game of Monopoly. We've got to embrace natural competitiveness to be able to win and to learn how to recover from defeat.'

Gannon is pragmatic rather dogmatic. Aside from Gradi, renowned for his passing style at Crewe, Gannon has been influenced by other strong-minded managers. There was Turlough O'Connor at Dundalk, Dave Bassett at Sheffield United; then Danny Bergara, Dave Jones and Gary Megson at Stockport. Though it was Uruguayan Bergara who he related to the most – because he came from another country and, like Gannon, was trying to gain a 'sense of where he was at in his life' – each one had different ideas about the way football should be played.

'I was once told that without technique there's no tactics,' he says. 'You can't talk tactics if the players can't pass or deliver a corner. Every player at each level will have some technique so you can therefore impose some tactics. When you play long ball and make long runs your techniques become complicated and your tactics simple.

'In England you have teams that are physical, you have teams that have flair, you have pitches that are poor, you have bowling greens. You've got windy days, you've got wet days, you've got all sorts of conditions. Therefore, as a manager and as players, we have to be multi-skilled in recognising what needs to be done.

'The real measure of a manager is whether he can get his team to play effective football at different levels,' he believes. 'I've competed in the Europa League and the SPL with Motherwell, League One, Two and the Evo-Stik North. There are three things a manager needs to consider: his own principles, the players he has and their skill sets, then what works at the level he is operating at. From that he has to find the right way to play. At Sheffield United I played for Dave Bassett and it was route one, set-play orientated. I finished at Crewe with Dario Gradi and he had the opposite beliefs. I can't criticise one or the other because both have produced winning teams and international players. To be able to be successful in the Europa League and the Evo-Stik North shows an ability to adapt and accept what the level is. Ultimately, you have to find a way to hurt the opposition. If they find a way of stopping you, it's sensible to find another way of overcoming them. Then, finally, you have true winners.'

17

PINCH ME

'THE MOST IMPORTANT PART OF MANAGEMENT IS HOW YOU recruit,' Joe Royle says without a second's thought, as we sit in the kitchen of his magnificent home in the market town of Ormskirk, West Lancashire. 'Second is man-management,' he continues. 'Third is coaching – we've made coaching far too important in this country. It's actually recruitment and basic talent that's most important. It doesn't matter how good the coaching is if the raw product isn't there, does it? You'll only go so far.'

Royle is now 68 years old and works as an advisor to David Unsworth, Everton's Under-23 manager. His chief responsibility is to watch the young players Everton have sent out on loan and report back with his observations. His last full-time job in football, at Ipswich Town, was over a decade ago and so it is easy to forget his achievements in the game. It was his ability to judge talent and character, to see value where others did not, that ensured he became manager of two of the north-west's biggest clubs in Everton and Manchester City, clubs where he'd also played. He remains the last Everton manager to win a trophy, the FA Cup in 1995. It was his achievements at Oldham Athletic, though, that set him on the path back to Goodison Park, the stadium where he'd spent half of his playing career, where he was top scorer in the team that won the First Division championship in 1970; a team, indeed, that included the Holy Trinity midfield of Colin Harvey, Howard Kendall and Alan Ball.

Oldham Athletic was Royle's first job as a manager. He was loyal to Oldham and remained there for twelve years until Everton, the club he'd also supported as a boy, asked him to take over from Mike Walker, the manager who had almost led Everton to relegation. While Wimbledon and Watford's stories in the 1980s are well documented and perhaps enriched by both including FA Cup final dates, Oldham's is just as remarkable. In 1994 Oldham were seconds away from reaching an FA Cup final of their own only to have the opportunity snatched away from them by a Mark Hughes goal for Manchester United in the last minute of extra time. Shattered emotionally and physically, Oldham lost the replay 4–1 at Maine Road three days later.

'In 1982, I became the youngest manager in the Football League,' Royle says. 'Harry Wilde, Oldham's chairman, told me that although the board didn't really know me personally, they liked the way I interviewed. "You've got the job on a one-year contract on fifteen thousand pounds for the year. Oh, and by the way, you've gotta sell someone quick 'cos we're skint . . ."

'I'd seen Oldham play the season before when I was at Norwich as a player. I realised they had some good kids with a blend of experience; players like Rodger Wylde, Jim Steel, Paul Futcher and Kenny Clements – I'd played with Kenny at Manchester City.

'We finished the first season seventh in the Second Division. That summer, I was told again, "Joe, we need to sell." It was a trend that was maintained throughout my time Oldham, over and over again. We were always susceptible to a bid for a player.'

This stark financial landscape placed an emphasis on recruitment because sooner or later Oldham and Royle knew they would have to enter the transfer market for new signings.

'When you have less, it's even more important that your recruitment is right because you can't afford to make mistakes,' Royle says. 'It was easier to get players in to start with because we could afford the wages. We took Denis Irwin from Leeds, then Andy Linighan, Andy Ritchie and Tommy Wright. Moves like that, they don't happen now. The difference in wages being offered in the First and Second Divisions weren't so big. Now, you have players in the academies you've never heard of and the Championship clubs can't afford them financially. They only drop down on loan or because they think it aids their development for a very short period of time.

'Leeds were a much bigger club than Oldham but we were able to give players a few quid more with the guarantee of an opportunity. That was a word I'd emphasise when trying to convince them, opportunity. They usually appreciated that Oldham had to sell to keep afloat so players saw us as a springboard. Building sides was like a game of snakes and ladders. By the time I left Oldham I was probably on my sixth team.'

Royle signed Denis Irwin for free and sold him to Manchester United for £625,000, where he remained for the next dozen years, winning everything there was to win.

'I read articles where they say Zlatan Ibrahimovic is the greatest free transfer of all time. They list all the others and I think, someone has forgotten Denis . . .

'Sir Alex [Ferguson] says Denis was one of the best value-for-money buys he ever made. Any Manchester United team from Alex's era would have Denis in it. He was the complete full-back; could get forward, get crosses in and defend without giving any fouls away.'

Royle says his relationship with Jim Cassell, who would later become a very successful youth academy officer at Manchester City, was the most important relationship at Oldham because recruitment was such a significant matter; he appreciated his relationship with the chairman above him lived and died by it. Contacts were also key; knowing what was happening at other clubs, which players were available and who was due to move where. Royle had spies working for him.

'I worked out that I could get to twenty-eight clubs within an hour and a half's drive from Oldham. Oldham's location was ideal for scouting and seeing opponents as well because so many clubs from the north of England were in the top two divisions back then. Jim and I soon realised it was a good idea to saturate our scouting on the two big clubs from Liverpool, the two big clubs from Manchester and then Leeds. Occasionally, we'd go to Halifax, and that's where we first saw Rick Holden [although they eventually signed Holden from Watford]. Jim and I felt that we knew as much about the players of all these clubs as the people in charge there did – we prided ourselves on that. It meant we were able to raid them successfully. Aside from the four from Leeds we took Neil Adams and Ian Marshall from Everton. We took Paul Warhurst and Earl Barrett from Man City, kids who weren't going to get in their first team that we could afford to pay. All these lads did well for us and we made a big profit on them.'

It is the signing of Irwin from which he takes the most satisfaction, though.

'Little Billy Bremner was a great player and a great man too, we got on like a house on fire. He was in charge of Leeds and decided that the team needed a clear-out. God knows why but he thought it was a good idea to let Denis go.

Towards the end of the season I received a call from Pete Gunby, who was the head of youth at Leeds. He said, "Joe, I can't believe this – they're letting Denis go . . ."

'I said, "What?"

'"Yes, Joe; they're letting Denis go . . ."

'Denis had played something like sixty games for Leeds and Pete knew how much I liked him. I kept looking at him and concluded that he was Peter Lorimer's stuntman. I don't mean that disrespectfully to Peter. Peter stood on the halfway line, Denis would give him the ball and then run round him to receive it again. When it was lost, Denis would run all the way back. Peter was the senior player with marvellous quality and Denis had a good appreciation of space and responsibility as well.

'When Pete Gunby told me I got straight on to my chairman and said, "I think we can make money on this one, Mr Chairman . . ." Music to his ears, of course.'

Irwin was due to sign for Chesterfield. 'I ambushed that deal and got him to Oldham instead,' Royle says, grinning. He realised that other players were turned on by ambitious swoops like this one. 'If you got one player, you often got two. Andy Linighan was Denis's team-mate at Leeds and he didn't want to leave Leeds. But with Denis coming to us, that drive with Denis every day across the M62 didn't seem so bad.

'Eventually, it started to work against us,' Royle admits. 'Howard Wilkinson got the Leeds job. I asked him about a young kid who was in their youth team that kept getting sent off. He said, "Joe, there will be no more bargains for you at this club from now on." So we never got David Batty.'

While Batty helped Wilkinson and Leeds seal promotion to the First Division under Wilkinson in 1990, Royle experienced his 'pinch-me season' at Oldham.

'We'd seen off Arsenal, who were First Division champions, in the League Cup in November, Southampton in the January then Aston Villa in the FA Cup the following March. After games, we went for drinks with the directors in the Old Grey Mare pub as usual and a fan came up to me and said, "Just pinch me . . . I'm in wonderland."

'The town was rocking. I always said, "If you plugged into Oldham, you could have lit Blackpool up." There was so much excitement. We built a souvenir store at Boundary Park and the board were concerned how long it might take to pay for it, "two, maybe three years?" The store paid for itself in months. The town was going crazy for Oldham Athletic.

Home Bargains, Alder Sports Club, Liverpool.

STANNO
bargains

Tranmere Rovers, Prenton Park, Birkenhead.

RIDEHALGH
3
NORTH STAR
ENVIRONMENTAL LTD
KOP STAND

90:00 TRANMERE
ALDERSHOT
NORTH STAR
ENVIRONMENTAL LTD
KOP STAND
SUPPORT
TEAM

1874 Northwich, Barton Stadium, Winsford.

NO STANDING

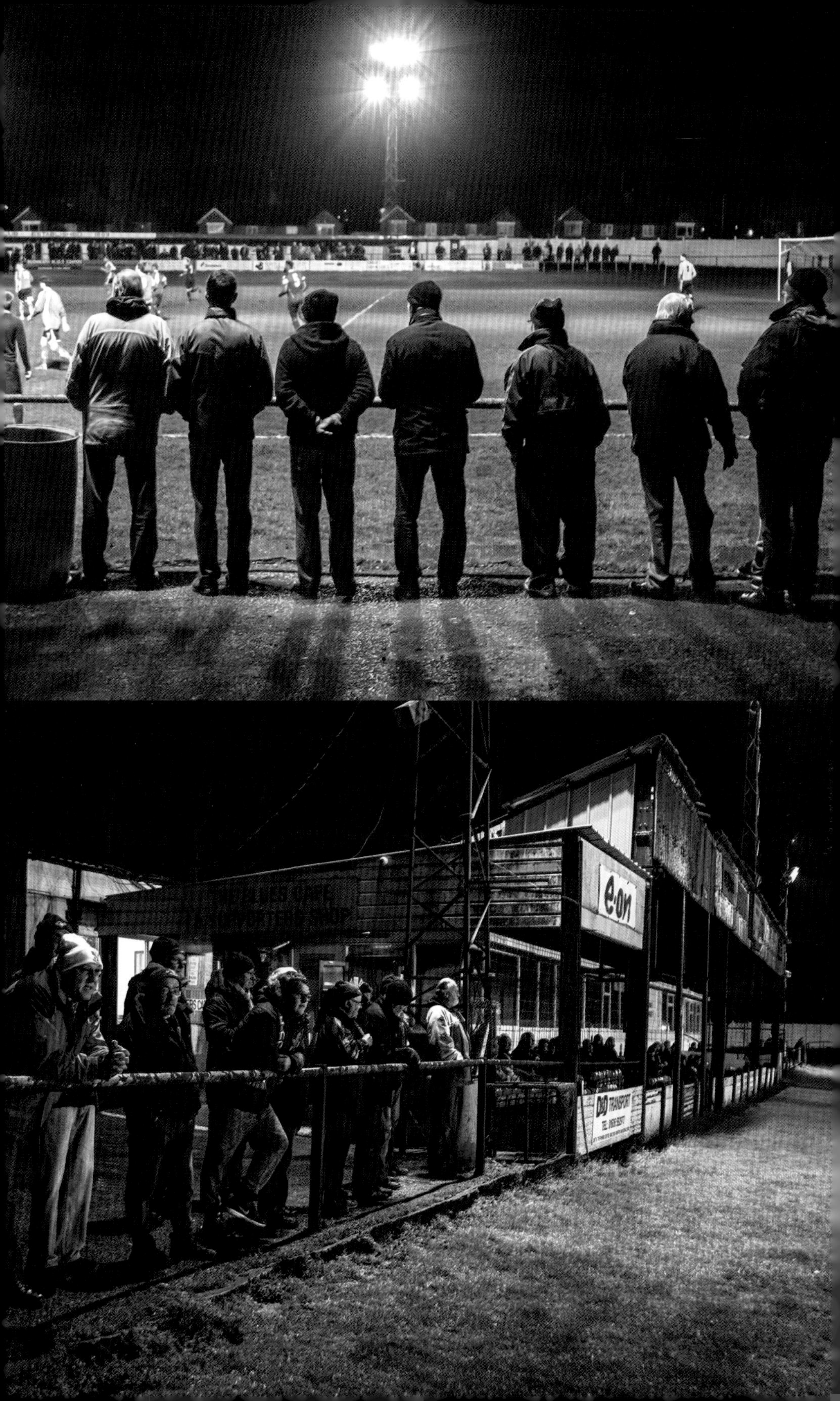
e·on
TRANSPORT

Stockport County, Edgeley Park, Greater Manchester.

Joe Royle, Ormskirk, Lancashire.

Tommy Banks, Farnworth, Greater Manchester.

Gary Neville, Moor Lane, Salford.

Butcher's Arms, Droylsden.

Dave Horrocks, Fletcher Moss Rangers, Didsbury

Etihad Stadium, Manchester City.

C
Sold Out
LEEDS UNITED

'I always tried to be the first in amongst the staff. One day, I got there at eight a.m. and three queues had already formed outside Boundary Park. The fans were waiting for tickets; one for the next FA Cup tie, one for the next League Cup tie, and another for the next league game. We had a tiny ticket office with two windows and the poor girls on the desks were run off their feet. We had a ridiculous situation where there were cardboard boxes full of money being kept in the boardroom with just one guard manning the door. We had such a great year. The cash was rolling in. Soon, little Oldham Athletic were in the Premier League, for God's sake!'

Oldham is a place that feels like it is perched between light and darkness. To the west stands glorious Manchester, with its glass buildings, its famous music scene, its fashion, its restaurants, its bars, its universities and its powerful football clubs. To the east, there is the bleak desolation of Saddleworth Moor, up grey tracks where during winter the craggy outcrops, gullies and hollows are deep-crusted in snow; where the vegetation is molested by nature and the terrain's austerity makes you conscious of the violence of geological processes.

The area's unsympathetic moorland winds ability to bring tears to the eyes means Oldham Athletic's Boundary Park, the third-highest football ground in England, is also considered the chilliest. Joe Royle called it 'Ice Station Zebra' after the Cold War espionage movie set in the North Pole. 'Oldham . . .' Brian Clough said before pausing to think what to say next for once, '. . . the place scares me to death.'

It was partly because of the bad weather in Oldham that a decision was taken in 1986 to equip Boundary Park with a plastic pitch, a pitch they were still playing on five years later when Oldham were crowned as Second Division champions.

'You don't go up on your home record alone but our home record was pretty damn terrific,' Royle admits. 'I wasn't even keen on the idea before it was suggested. But then I realised our training facilities were so bad, it needed one downpour and the pitch was flooded. I spent a lot of time – too much time, in fact – looking around Manchester for alternative training venues, including school grounds. Creating a plastic pitch at Boundary Park gave us a huge advantage because it meant we had somewhere to train every day, somewhere to pass a ball rather than go running around the streets. The other side of it was the revenue. We could rent the pitch out in the evenings and over the summer months. They even played cricket on there, cricketers like Carl Hooper smacking the ball over the stands. Community-wise, it was very good because it brought Oldham residents closer to the club. There's no doubt about it, the plastic pitch helped put us on the map – but also because we were bloody good on it.

'We were playing Ipswich Town one winter's night,' he continues. 'I always liked to watch the opposition in the warm-up. Psychologically many sides came with preconceived ideas of how difficult it was to play at Oldham. All four corner flags were blowing in different directions. It seemed to be snowing in one half and raining in the other. I could see their players digging their heels in the plastic. They clearly didn't fancy it. We were 4–0 up inside twenty minutes.'

Defeated managers used to complain about the harsh environment of Boundary Park, saying it gave the home team an unfair advantage. Upon entry to the top flight Oldham were informed they must return the pitch to a natural state of grass. Royle does not think the ruling affected Oldham's performances because they remained in the First Division and then the Premier League as it became for the next three seasons. He believes, though, it simply became harder for Oldham to trade because of exposure. When Oldham were in the Second Division, few of the games were televised. In the Premier League everybody would get to know what they were up to.

'We found it harder to get the bargains because our wages weren't as competitive as they once were with all of the clubs suddenly having huge injections of cash from the TV deal,' he says. 'But to some extent as well, you can't go on forever selling big and buying cheap because eventually other clubs get wise to you.'

Royle knew the game was almost up when he was approached to become the manager of Manchester City. Though he would go to City later in his career, this offer was one he rejected. 'We'd taken Barrett and Warhurst from them and at the end of the meeting Peter Swales, the City chairman, said, "Just one more thing, Joe . . . are there any more of our kids you think have got a great chance? Because we'll keep them if you think they do." It was a big compliment but it shows you that other clubs were well and truly on to us.'

Like Stockport, Oldham had become a significant place during the Industrial Revolution as an international centre of textile manufacture. At its peak, it had become the most productive cotton-spinning mill town in the world, producing more cotton than France and Germany combined. By 1998, the town's last mill had closed and eighteen years later Oldham was named by the Office for National Statistics as the most deprived area in England. Though the skyline is still dominated by the cotton mills which once marked Oldham as a powerhouse of the north, many of those mills now sit derelict and in disrepair; a reminder of Oldham's lost industry and why more than 60 per cent of the borough voted to leave during the EU referendum.

Football has not offered an escape. In 1994, Oldham Athletic were relegated from the Premier League. By 1997, they were in English football's third tier and that is where they have remained for the last twenty years. In 1999 Oldham's outlook had appeared so bleak so quickly that their chairman Ian Stott suggested a merger between Oldham and its closest rivals, Bury and Rochdale, creating a Manchester North End. Stott was forced to resign following the hostile response from fans.

The geographical and economic predicament of the three clubs has since not been helped by Manchester City's relocation east in 2003, providing an attractive and easily accessible option for the floating casual supporter. A simple Venn diagram that includes a combination of geography, economic circumstance and the presence of two massive Premier League clubs can explain why the futures of Oldham, Bury and Rochdale appear challenging. It is economic backgrounds that compound the state of the football clubs. In areas of low incomes, pitch performances would have to change dramatically for any substantial, sustained increase in match-day attendances. Because of the closure of the mills – and subsequent unemployment – the people of Oldham have more pressing things to do with their money.

'My son lives in Oldham. We've spoken to several investors trying to get some money into the place but it's a hard sell in the current climate, with a new stand that's not been finished and a team struggling at the bottom with no finances,' Royle says. 'To be fair to Simon Corney, the owner, and his partners they've put a lot of money in over the years to keep the club going but they want to get out and I can understand why.

'My first game in charge of Oldham was against Shrewsbury Town and we won 1–0. The gate was around 2,900. In the glory days, we sometimes got close to 18,000. We became a lot of people's second club, not just because of the brand of football we were playing but because we were successful as well. I hope those days return. A lot will have to change for that to happen, though.'

18

GRAVEL RASH

IT WAS J.B. PRIESTLEY WHO SUMMED UP THE TERRAIN BETWEEN Manchester and Bolton by writing, 'The ugliness is so complete it is almost exhilarating, it challenges you to live there.'

But live there people always have, particularly in Priestley's time and particularly because of mining when street names such as Coal Pit Road and Colliers Row gave a clue as to the number of quarries that had been active.

'Twenty-eight in Darcy Lever, Great Lever and Little Lever alone,' Tommy Banks tells me as we sip coffee made by his second wife, Rita, in the front living room of their home in Farnworth, a town where the people are so proud of their identity they claim to be Farnworthian rather than Boltonian even though many admit there is little to separate them. 'In fact,' Banks continues, 'when I were a nipper, I remember my mother telling me there had been 110 in total across the Bolton area. Me, I was at Mosley Common.' On releasing that information, he slurps away contentedly, nodding his head.

I had decided to meet Banks because, at nearly 88 years old, he is the only person alive that connects the distant past of Bolton Wanderers with the present day. Before becoming a footballer, he had been a pitman and had served in the army. He played with Nat Lofthouse, one of football's great Corinthians and almost certainly Bolton's greatest player; Banks won the FA Cup in 1958, the same summer he represented England at a World Cup, and when his career was coming to an end he campaigned for the maximum wage to be abolished – a decision that cost him his job. When you consider the finance involved now in football and how Bolton had fallen into English football's third tier having committed too much money towards players in their Premier League days without thinking seriously about the consequences of the lucrative contracts being distributed if they slipped out of the top flight, I simply wondered what Banks made of it all – if he can relate to what Bolton Wanderers are today: a struggling third-tier club playing in a half-empty modern ground on the edge of town. I wondered whether Banks recognises the game he retired from as a professional in 1961.

Banks had suffered a mini-stroke in 2015 and though his memories are lucid, the words he wants to use don't always arrive in the time he expects. Sometimes his thoughts dart from one to the next. He tells me he used to enjoy the challenge of the Daily Mirror crossword, though it's something he can't complete any more. 'I used to be able to tell you everything about everybody . . .' he says ruefully, though you can tell straight away that he is a stoic by the way he delivers his next line. 'Never felt sorry for me'self, me. Never.'

In 2012 he had helped with the release of his biography, the wonderfully titled Ah'm Tellin' Thee, where Gordon Taylor, the chief executive of the Professional Footballers' Association, had written in the foreword, 'Today's multi-millionaire footballers owe a great debt to the son of Farnworth who might well have been formed out of the very coal pits which featured in that area as he was granite-like, a great player, great person and a great character.'

Banks's voice is present in the story which is evocatively told using his local dialect. Conversations are recalled authentically between Banks, who was Bolton's left-sided defender, and Roy Hartle, the Boltonian who was equally tenacious on the right, so when Banks tells Hartle, 'Roy, when thee's dun wi yon mon wilt chip im o'er 'ere un ah'll si if 'ee leeks gravel rash?' Banks is really asking Hartle whether he fancies sending Mark Pearson the Manchester United winger in his direction, so he can find out what Pearson thinks of Burnden Park's infamous trackside gravel near him. Banks and Hartle are described as 'a loveable gruesome twosome' and while Bobby Charlton remembers how the pair 'epitomised how a potent mix of honest endeavour and passion, sprinkled with a fair degree of skill' could take a team a long way, Jimmy Greaves's memories were less fond. 'Bolton was a place where men were truly men and we feared their sheer brute force,' he admitted. 'They regarded us as Southern Softies and there was no more daunting place to visit.'

The best insight comes in Chapter 17 when there is an examination of Banks's role in the abolition of the maximum wage, a campaign that had started almost from the game's inception but had accelerated at the start of the twentieth century when Billy Meredith, the Manchester United winger, revitalised the players' union after his Welsh international team-mate Di Jones had died having cut his knee on a shard of broken glass during a pre-season match only for the wound to become infected. In response his club Manchester City refused to accept liability because Jones was only playing in a friendly, with the officials maintaining his contract didn't mention anything about involvement in non-competitive matches and therefore he was 'not working'. There was no insurance cover in place, so Jones's wife and children did not receive compensation.

Banks's career was coming to an end by the time members of the PFA gathered at Manchester's Grand Hotel more than half a century later but that did not matter to someone who had recognised the wrongs of contracts in professional football and was determined, as he says, to 'purrit reet'.

It was Banks's speech that changed the mood of the room. Stanley Matthews, whose career spanned both the pre-war and post-war eras, was unsympathetic towards the union's position as the dispute flared in 1961, only to change his mind when he encountered widespread feeling in one place. 'I've done well out of the game, but could I ignore the injustice to my colleagues?' he recalled. 'Loyalty to the players won. My hand went up.'

Even Bob Lord, the outspoken Burnley chairman, suddenly conceded there should be no wage-ceiling. In contrast, his counterpart at nearby Blackburn Rovers, Jim Wilkinson, argued that even a £30 maximum (a 50 per cent increase) must be opposed as 'it would be suicide for many clubs'.

Banks had risen to his feet chiming, 'Ah think it's neaw time ah spokk Mr Chairmon.'

Then he cleared his throat and began to make his point by delivering first the famous words, 'Ah'm tellin' thee . . .'

When I meet Tommy Banks, it is fifty-six years and two months exactly since he walked through the doors of the Grand Hotel wearing a mackintosh coat, a trilby, a suit, a shirt and a tie. Despite his health taking a turn for the worse, despite the fact he cannot walk as much as he would like to these days, and despite the fact he cannot speak as quickly as he used to, he remains as passionate about workers'

rights now as he did then.

'Sit up, love,' Rita asks him, as he slowly begins to tell me what life was like for him and Nat Lofthouse before they became footballers.

'When I left school,' he begins, 'my father said, "You won't be going down th'pit." Well, what else will I do? I thought. I'm the youngest of eight, y'see: three brothers and four sisters. Th'pit was unavoidable, though. All roads led to th'pit. My father knew a fella with a horse. I was horse mad – loved horses. Even the horse worked at th'pit. At fourteen I became a coal bagger moving six tons a day and then joined the army at twenty-one where I played football for my regiment. I was a lucky bugger because most of the lads went to Korea but my colonel said to me, "You're staying 'ere, Banks – to play football."

'Lofty was a few years older than me. He didn't have to join the army because Bolton had a director who owned one of the four mines at Little Lever. The director persuaded th'army that Lofty was needed down th'pit. Of course, Lofty was needed for th'football – for Bolton.

'The work were 'ard – nonstop. I was in charge of moving th'coal to the surface of th'mine. You couldn't see for smoke upstairs. Long days, they were. The bus stop was a couple of hundred yards from our house and you had to catch two buses to th'pit. We'd be there at seven. If you were late and missed the last cage, the bosses would drop you like a stone. There'd be no work. You'd have to walk home with your tail between your legs because there were no buses home until the evening when everyone clocked off. Very few folk missed the cage.'

Army work did not broaden Banks's horizons. Before, he had only left Farnworth for Bolton and he had only left Bolton for away matches or for the annual week-long holiday in Blackpool during the summer.

'My mother used to ask, "Where are you playing today, Thomas?" If it was, say, Coventry, she wouldn't have known where it was. So I just used to say t'other side of Manchester. When we went to play a team in Spain – one of their best teams – I went home and told everyone we were going abroad. My mother asked where and then she said, "Don't tell me, t'other side of Manchester?"

'Aye, it weren't a bad bringing-up,' Banks continues. 'I had a good mother. Kids now have it very different. All of my football as a junior was played on ash pitches by the side of th'mine. You'd go home with bloody knees every time because there was no grass. I was seven year old when I won my first medal. The rest of the lads were eleven year old. It taught me to rattle into them. Aye, this helped me when I became a professional player. I was never frightened by anyone. I were never big. But I were never frightened. I were only a nipper but

I think the other players were frightened of me.'

Banks, indeed, played with Nat Lofthouse. He played against Stanley Matthews many times. But it was Tom Finney who made the greatest impression on him.

'Apart from this Messi, Tom was the best footballer that ever lived. Messi – he's only twenty-nine now and he must have played a thousand games. He's fantastic – and smaller than me! But my man is Tom Finney. He were a good 'un – he were a good 'un! He was a left-footer and they played him on the right so he'd dribble inside me and I couldn't stop him.

'Matthews? Don't forget he were forty-odd year old and so he was in his mid-thirties the first time I met him. I didn't get picked for the '53 FA Cup final when Bolton lost and I think I'd have been able to stop him. My brother, Ralph, played and it would have been beautiful for my mother to see her two boys out on the pitch at Wembley.

'Jimmy Armfield used to say to me, "Tommy, Stan trains like nobody else trains." He used to have his own ways of training. He used to run on sand when t'others were on the gravel. That made him stronger. He was very determined. I remember being told a story about him being asked to guest in an all-star match in Brazil. They told him he'd be substitute. "You mightn't play," they said. "I jolly well will!" he told them. "I'm not coming if I don't play." He were his own man, Stan. He used to ask me, "Are you going mad?" because I used to rattle into him at Burnden Park – which was a homers pitch – 'orrible to play on. There were a drop of about three foot from the terraces to the grass. You'd have red shale on the side and if you fell there, you'd need stitches. Aye, Stan were a good 'un. But he weren't as good as Tom. Tom was a gentleman. We played for England together and they always put me and Tom in the same room 'cos he was the only one that understood me. The London boys? It was like I was speaking a different language.'

Banks found out he was selected in England's 1958 World Cup squad on the same day he won the FA Cup final by beating Manchester United. It meant that he missed the celebratory parade on an open-top bus through Bolton's town centre. In his absence, his mother stepped forward to shake the hand of the mayor.

'I don't think I'd have been capped if it wasn't for the Munich crash a few months earlier,' he admits, with further fortune coming at the expense of someone else because the other England left-back, Jeff Hall, contracted polio around this time and subsequently died a year later. 'In my humble opinion Roger Byrne wasn't better than me, though. He had Duncan Edwards playing in front of him – a wonderful player he was, that lad. Six foot or five-eleven and thirteen stone, boy, he could play. I think he'd have made me seem a better player like he did with Roger, he could head 'em all day, he could tackle 'em all day. Don't get me wrong, Roger Byrne was a good player. But Edwards made it seem like he was a cracker.'

Growing up in Farnworth, Banks describes Manchester as 'New York'. After Saturday games, he would go there for a drink with the other players and their wives, though 'Lofthouse never came with us so much'. It has always been a much bigger and fancier place than Bolton but in May 1958 – because of what happened on the runway in Munich, Manchester United were the neutrals' choice over Bolton, the smaller club.

'Anyone who said they wanted United to lose – even the Manchester City lads – they were telling lies,' Banks says. 'It was a tricky game for us to play in. If Munich hadn't have happened, United would have been the favourites because they had such a good team. That team was the best I'd faced. They beat us at Old Trafford and it was one of those games where I think some of our players were already beaten before they set foot on the pitch because of the reputation. United played good football, they bought good footballers and they always had a good crowd.'

The FA Cup success meant Banks was selected to play for England at the World Cup a month later. He was not long home following a disappointing tournament where England exited at the group stages when a letter arrived through the post from Jimmy Hill, the chairman of the PFA, detailing that he had been approached by a company to provide a candidate for a lucrative advertisement: Gillette razors wanted someone to appear on their billboards across the country. A few weeks later, Banks can remember having a drink in his local pub, the Egerton, when a familiar long-distance lorry driver collared him, explaining that he'd nearly crashed as he'd entered Heathrow Airport. 'There was a big bloody billboard with your bloody mug on it saying "Men Shave with Gillette"!' the driver laughed.

Banks says he pocketed more than £300 from his work with Gillette and that his 'hundred-pound win bonus from the FA Cup was much harder to earn'. This contributed towards his conviction that footballers were earning less than they should be.

'Y'see, they were getting paid more money than us down th'pit. Now who wants to go down pit and who wants to play football, was my point? We weren't paid enough. Twenty-five thousand was a bad crowd. They were all paying the entrance fee, which was bigger than it was before the war. In 1922 when Bolton won the FA Cup for the first time, they got two pounds for a win and a pound for a draw. That's fair enough – it was a lot of money, there's no doubt about that. Nearly forty years later, though, the bonus was the same even though crowds had gone up and it was more expensive to get in. Where were all the money going? They were all businessmen, these directors, these owners.

'Looking back, I had a lot to say. Maybe I shouldn't. It was difficult to make everyone realise the problem. Lofty – we got on – but he'd say, "We're all right really . . ." Of course he was all right because he was the best player, the captain, and he was on more money than the rest of us, I'm sure of it.'

For being outspoken, Bolton effectively sacked Banks, though they retained his Football League registration, which meant that any other club that wanted to sign him would have to pay a fee. It transpired that fourten years' service mattered very little to Bolton's directors, who would not grant him the dignity of an easy move elsewhere.

'Jack Rowley [had been] a centre-forward at United and he was in charge of Oldham. He called me and said, "Tommy, will you come to us?" I said, "Aye, course I will, Jack." A week later he came back to me and said he had no chance of getting me because Oldham had no money and Bolton wanted the earth. The clubs had all the power. That was another thing I didn't like at all.'

It should not really be a surprise that one of the loudest voices when it came to the threat of strike action was that of Tommy Banks. Where there were mines, there was Labour, and where there was Labour, there were unions. Industrial Bolton had become a centre of grime and the conditions were appalling, with dust hanging in the air and lung disease affecting the lives of many. The industrialists were ruthless by nature and became involved at boardroom level at clubs like Bolton Wanderers. 'They treated us players the same as workers,' Banks says. His mother had worked in the same cotton mill for 52 years and her chemist was the local Labour MP. Banks spent his childhood listening to his words of wisdom from over the counter. 'He made me realise it was a waste of time for the Tories in this area and that as workers, we should look after one another.'

Banks, though, cannot believe the financial trajectory football has taken since the abolition of the maximum wage, with 'the football players looking more and more after themselves'. As a union man and a Labour voter, all he wanted was equality in his industry – equality for everyone.

'It's terrible, it really is. I had no idea it would go this way,' he concludes.

'Football has changed completely. It's not the same game at all – to me it's not anyway. It's gone through the door. It's over with. I'm pleased these lads are paid well but it has gone too far. I know Messi's a bloody good 'un but even he's paid too much. What's he on – twenty thousand pound a day or something? Too many outside people are making too much money out of it to really care about the idea that it has lost touch with reality. I was Tommy Banks. No different to t'other lads. No different at all.

'The money has made the FA Cup go down the drain too and that makes me sad because I know how proud I was to win it. Christ, what a competition it was. And we did it with a lot of local lads in the team . . .'

After a pause, he adds: '. . . The others, like Dennis Stevens and Ray Parry: they were foreigners to me.'

Stevens came from Dudley in the Black Country to play for Bolton.

Parry came from Derby.

Bill 'Nibbler' Ridding was the manager of Bolton Wanderers for eighteen years. In 1958 he assembled a side capable of winning the FA Cup for £110. While Nat Lofthouse and Roy Hartle were Boltonians, Tommy Banks came from Farnworth – as did Tommy Lawton and Alan Ball, who were rejected by Bolton as teenagers. Bryan Edwards was from Leeds but he spent his entire career at Bolton and stayed in the town after retirement. There was Eddie Hopkinson, the goalkeeper, from Co Durham, John Higgins from Bakewell, Brian Birch from Southport, Doug Holden from Manchester and then the 'foreigners', Ray Parry and Dennis Stevens: Derby and Dudley's finest. Ridding? Wirral-born. Played for Tranmere Rovers. Played for both Manchester clubs. But for a short spell at Northampton Town where he did not play a game, Ridding spent his entire professional life in the north-west.

By the time Sam Allardyce was finished as Bolton's manager 49 years later, there were thirteen nationalities in Bolton's match-day squad against Chelsea. The club had been in line to finish fifth, their highest position ever in the Premier League era, when Allardyce resigned with two games left to play citing a strained relationship with chairman Phil Gartside, who refused to sanction greater spending to finance a push for Champions League qualification. Three players were English – though none from Bolton – there was one Welshman, two had come from Spain, there was a Finn, an Ivorian, a Jamaican, a Slovak, an Iranian, a Portuguese, an Israeli, a Frenchman, a Pole and a back-up goalkeeper from Oman. Ten years later, the only person that still lives in the area is Allardyce.

'Sam was the master at resurrecting careers, just like Kevin Davies up there,' says one of Allardyce's former players, Jimmy Phillips, who is pointing at the wall of an executive suite at the Marcron Stadium, where the photographs of players leave clues as to where Bolton has been and where it currently is. Beside Fernando Hierro, the former captain of Real Madrid, you have Liam Trotter, Bolton's midfielder, whose only winners medal at the age of 28 has been that of the FA Youth Cup when he was a teenager at Ipswich Town.

Phil Gartside died in early 2016 and by then the position of Bolton Wanderers was perilous, with the club facing a winding-up order after Eddie Davies, the Farnworth-born owner, had still not sold up despite deciding to do so eighteen months earlier. Gartside had been trusted for many years to steer the ship in Davies's absence but when Gartside fell ill and was forced to stand down from his duties, the rate at which the financial turmoil at Bolton unfolded was rapid.

Davies had arrived in 2003 supposedly as Bolton's saviour, with the club encouraging shareholders into voting him in, in turn rendering their own shares worthless. When a consortium fronted by ex-Bolton striker Dean Holdsworth and Inner Circle, a company owned by businessman Ken Anderson, took control of Davies's share of Burnden Leisure, the club was in a worse position than when Davies first arrived.

I had decided to meet Phillips because he is Bolton Wanderers through and through. He had grown up in the Sharples district of the town, he had walked through the turnstiles as a season-ticket holder at Burnden Park for the first time as a nine-year-old, he had played more than a hundred games for the club before being transferred to Glasgow Rangers when he was happy staying where he was, and, upon returning six years later after a spell at Middlesbrough, he had played a couple of hundred more games before retiring at the age of 35. Phillips has since been a coach, a caretaker manager on a couple of occasions and is now leading the academy as its director. Jimmy Phillips, I had thought, sounds like he might have been a defender for Bolton Wanderers – a bit like Tommy Banks. Maybe even Eddie Davies.

Phillips is already there, waiting patiently in a seat next to the reception when I arrive at the stadium they now call the Macron after the Italian sportswear manufacturer that sponsors it. For seventeen seasons it had been the Reebok, a company with roots in Bolton after J.W. Foster and Sons started making running shoes in 1895.

By 2014 it was decided Bolton and Reebok should go their separate ways but for the previous nine years there had been parallels in the modern tales between club and company, with high optimism followed by crushing experiences: 2005 was the year Reebok was bought by rival German group Adidas for £3bn as part of an aggressive new strategy to dominate the global sportswear market, only to find its units shrink by a third.

In the Premier League's race for absolute global attention, Bolton had fallen away and, similarly, the global markets had not been kind to Reebok under foreign ownership. As in other parts of the north-west where football is intrinsically linked to the way people feel, should it really be a surprise that 58.3 per cent of voters in Bolton elect to leave the European Union when market forces across the world have in some way had a negative impact on local institutions valued so dearly?

Phillips speaks proudly about his background. When asked about his association with Bolton and the area, memories tumble out without there being need for a break.

'I was born in the town fifty-one years ago,' he begins. 'I studied at a local secondary school and played football for a Sunday league team called Moss Bank. Before the academy structure was in place players from Moss Bank were traditionally invited to train with Bolton Wanderers during the school holidays from the age of fourteen. I was one of the lucky four to be invited in.

'My mum was a school teacher and my dad, a management consultant in computer programming, was a Liverpool supporter,' he continues. 'Dad was born in Birkenhead and had a Kop season ticket along with a couple of pals in the 1960s until one famous day when my mother was completely fed up with him disappearing off to the football every other Saturday and threw his season ticket into the fire.

'I watched Bolton because by the time I was big enough to start watching live games, my dad had long since stopped going to Anfield. I'd seen them gain promotion in '78 to the old First Division. Frank Worthington was one of my heroes. Before him there was Peter Thompson. It was the team where Peter Reid patrolled the midfield. In my first year as an apprentice Peter was still at the club before he went to Everton. More recently, me and Peter teamed up together to take the first team for the final ten games of last season.

'I left school at sixteen and served what many would say was an old-style apprenticeship while doing my A levels at a college half a mile up the road from Burnden Park. It was a time when the club had no money – completely skint. Bolton had dropped into Division Three and there was a real struggle. John

McGovern was the manager and three years previously he'd raised the European Cup as the captain of Nottingham Forest. John gave me a great insight as to what you had to do to be a professional footballer in terms of dedication, enthusiasm and professionalism. He oversaw a very difficult period for the club when he was running marathons to raise the funds to pay the wages. Any players who had a value to the club were sold and Reidy was one of them. John was having to replace the experienced players with non-league signings, most notably Tony Caldwell who came in from Horwich RMI and famously scored five goals in one game against Walsall.

'We used to have an old ash pitch round the back from Burnden Park and it only got used when the other training fields were out of action because of the rain. The ash had huge puddles on it one day. I remember John misplacing a pass during a seven-a-side game and he disappeared to the side of the pitch where he proceeded to do twenty press-ups. I gave him a strange look and so he said to me, "You've got to have standards, son. That was a crap pass." John had great pride in his own game.

'I got transferred to Glasgow Rangers in 1987. The fee was £75,000 and that kept the club going for the next six months, which shows you how little we were getting paid as players. Phil Neal was my manager and one Thursday afternoon his car was on my mum and dad's driveway at home. I was thinking to myself, what have I done wrong here?

'He was sat in the front room and he said, "Right, I'm selling you – you're going to Glasgow Rangers." He'd booked me a ticket on the six o'clock train from Preston to Glasgow. I was twenty-one years of age, there was no agent involved and it was a simple case of, "Right, you're off." Graeme Souness was the Rangers manager and the station master had allowed him to park his nice Jaguar on the platform at Glasgow Central. Graeme and Phil knew each other from their Liverpool days but it was the managers doing all the running about.

'The club has always been up and down,' Phillips adds. 'In the 1970s we missed out on promotion from the Third Division into the Second Division twice before finally sealing it on the last day of the season. We later had a year in the First Division then went back down. During my time as a player here we had two promotions into the Premier League and two relegations. It wasn't until Sam Allardyce that we had the sustained period in the Premiership.'

It is, of course, the Premier League now rather than the Premiership – a competition that takes brand so seriously, it employs spotters to read through every match-day programme of every club competing to make sure its name is referred to correctly, even in direct speech from interviews. Phillips was Middlesbrough's left-back when the First Division gave way to the embryonic Premiership in 1992 and the first changes he remembers were small. 'Ayresome Park had quite a big shale run off from the pitch to the stand and Sky erected a train track for the camera to run up and down following the play,' Phillips remembers. Within a couple of seasons, players like Phillips were sharing pitches with highly paid superstars hired from the greatest league in the world, Italy's Serie A. 'To be able to have a go against legends like Ruud Gullit and Gianluca Vialli was very exciting. Many of the rest of us were just normal people making a living by playing football.'

There were no superstars at Bolton initially. Instead, there was a focus on the Scandinavian market, with some success recruiting particularly from Iceland. 'From this part of the world, the players had a similar mentality: work rate, train hard – would enjoy a beer after a game, though in the right proportions. Plus, they had a greater technical ability and tactical knowledge compared to the way we were brought up playing 4–4–2. Gradually, tactics were changing.'

Bolton's first big foreign signing was Saša Ćurčić, a Serbian international from Partizan Belgrade. Phillips describes him as 'a great, great talent but a real one-off, a loose cannon'.

'I remember him dribbling past five Chelsea players from the halfway line at Stamford Bridge and sticking the ball in the back of the net. No one else on our team could have done that. But I also remember times when he should have squared a pass to someone else for a tap-in into an empty net but refused to do so. He did what he felt was right but you couldn't change him. We had to change tactics to get Saša into the team because we knew that off the ball he wasn't going to be running around but on the ball, he could create something out of nothing.'

More clubs were looking towards the continent for signings. Money was flooding into the Premier League and it contributed towards England becoming more of an attractive place for foreign players to play.

'Richard Sneekes was another signing Bolton made – someone who was beyond our means a decade before. He was a very talented midfielder that had played in the same Ajax academy as Dennis Bergkamp. As well as being a nice guy, Richard was opinionated about football. He admitted to me that his opinions resulted in him falling out with the Ajax coach too many times and that was why he ended up leaving. He came to us from the Swiss club, Locarno, and now lives in the Midlands where he manages Sutton Coldfield Town. We still talk from time to time.'

Phillips believes there have been two phases since these exciting days, when surnames like Ćurčić and Sneekes were exotic and mysterious to the folk of Bolton. The first phase involved many clubs believing they could capitalise on the wealth of the money coming in from the Premier League by signing younger – less heralded – versions of the Gullits and the Viallis before anyone noticed by giving them wages that 'didn't always reflect their levels of ability'.

'This,' Phillips says pointedly, 'has created a culture of players who are earning not far off the top wages but in terms of performance are far below the standard that the top end set. The money has created an elite environment when a lot don't deserve to be described as an elite player.' From there, a second phase came when clubs were taken over by foreign owners keen to board the gravy train, and the new businessmen deemed it savvy to invest money in the very best young players rather than proven ability because, theoretically, if the player emerged as expected it would be a better financial investment in the long term rather than spending considerable sums on players at the peak of their game, albeit ones who might not have any sell-on value. 'It has resulted in a lopsided economy where more money than ever is being spent on the youngest players even though many are nowhere near the highest standard,' Phillips says. 'Many end up earning too much money too quickly and fizzle out.'

Bolton's journey under Allardyce was different to many clubs in that he was seven years late to the party when it came to signing familiar big names from the continent, with France's Youri Djorkaeff at 34 and Hierro at 36 having the same sort of impact at Bolton from 2002 onwards that Gullit and Vialli had at Chelsea around 1995 and 1996. It was only when Allardyce left and Bolton moved their recruitment in keeping with modern trends that the situation really began to unravel.

Bolton had reacted to the Premier League's popularity and the growing demand for sheen by deciding to move from their old Burnden Park ground in the town centre to the Reebok Stadium in 1997. Officials appreciated the club had more reason than most to heed the all-seater directives of the Taylor Report, released in the aftermath of the Hillsborough disaster in 1989. Burnden Park had suffered its own tragedy in 1946 when 33 supporters were crushed to death and 500 more were injured as a cup match with a Stoke City side that included Stanley Matthews kicked off.

When the move was first suggested in 1994, Phillips was as apprehensive as he was excited. After leaving Rangers in 1988, he had played two seasons at

Oxford United and he began to appreciate the virtues of a place like the Manor Ground where the pitch had a huge slope and the dressing rooms were cramped and dank.

'The big clubs would turn up and in the tunnel you'd see the players' faces and think, "Bloody 'ell, they don't fancy it here today, we're 1–0 up already." It concerned me when Bolton decided to move that we'd lose something because, similarly, nobody liked coming to Burnden Park. Between 1992 and 1995, we beat a lot of the big teams. They'd turn up, take one look at the pitch and the old dressing rooms, see a ground certainly in decay, and decide they didn't really fancy it too much. Playing on home soil gave us a head start against clubs like Liverpool, Arsenal and Everton.

'We were going into the unknown. The new stadium had its fantastic facilities, but it became more of an even playing field for the opposition. They arrived at the Reebok and there wasn't as much to fear. They knew there was a great pitch and knew they could play their football.'

Bolton were the first north-west Premier League club to move grounds. The Reebok looked much nicer than Burnden Park and was more attractive to corporates. There is a sense, though, that the new stadium had wanted to be everything to everybody and ended up being nothing particularly special to anyone. To get there, you have to follow signs for Preston and Wigan, bypassing Bolton altogether as you drive from Manchester before arriving at Horwich, a separate town with its own football history where the club ended up disbanding after relocating from its sloping Grundy Hill ground to nearby Leigh. Overnight Horwich RMI became Leigh RMI. Leigh RMI later became Leigh Genesis and in 2011, having moved again to a new modern facility named the Leigh Sports Village – and some sixteen years after leaving Horwich – the club folded.

Horwich's plight should act as a historical warning to owners thinking about making radical changes. Bolton's move to Horwich had, indeed, been viewed as radical in 1997, with fans not only unhappy about its location but also its name. There had been a campaign to call it simply the New Burnden Park, and though the Reebok as a title came to be regarded semi-affectionately by locals due to the fact Reebok came from Bolton, the Macron does not have quite the same ring to it. Today, the Macron rests in the centre of the identikit Middlebrook Retail Park, with only the hills behind it giving a clue as to where you are in the country. Fancy a McDonalds, a Subway, a KFC or a Harvester roast dinner with your football? You've got it.

If anything, the Macron is more convenient for away fans than it is for home fans due to its close proximity to the M61 motorway. It means visitors don't have to fight their way through traffic heading towards Bolton's town centre on the Manchester road, nor do they have to worry about car parking due to the space in the retail park, even with Bolton deciding to sell much of that land off to raise funds amid their financial crisis. I imagine Bolton's ground to be tolerable when the times are good but when it turns, the out-of-town location makes the woes of the club easier to ignore.

'I'd agree with that,' Phillips says. 'I think the fans miss not being able to get the bus into Bolton, having a drink in the town centre and making the twenty-minute walk to the ground. Everybody drives here now and very few people use the public transport so you lose the sense of camaraderie between your own supporters. People would arrive at Burnden in great spirits whereas they arrive here in dribs and drabs from wherever they've driven from. In the Premier League era, this didn't seem to matter because everyone was desperate to see Premier League football and be a part of the show. When you drop out of the Premier League and hit a financial hardship, it suddenly becomes inaccessible. Whereas at Burnden Park you could pop down on the day if you fancied it, here more planning is required.'

Bolton is eleven miles north-west from Manchester and 35 miles east of Liverpool. Like Tommy Banks before him, Jimmy Phillips considered Manchester to be a very different place to Bolton. 'It certainly wasn't a place I ever ventured to,' he says. 'Now, a lot of Boltonians will go there for a night out instead of staying in the town.' It means that Manchester's economy gets bigger and the high streets of Bolton suffer as a consequence. Though accents are very different – as well as attitudes – there is a danger that Manchester is swallowing Bolton and again economic realities contribute some way towards the Brexit vote – while Bolton elected to leave, Manchester – overwhelmingly – did not want to.

As far as Phillips is aware, there were no conversations in the early Premier League years with players like Mark Fish, the South African defender, or Arnar Gunnlaugsson, the Icelandic forward, about having the pleasureland of Manchester on Bolton's doorstep. The mid to late 1990s, he says, was a time when most of Bolton's players lived in Bolton and socialised in Bolton. By the time he left for Glasgow Rangers in 1987, Phillips was being paid £110 a week, or 'less than many working men'. He would spend much of his earnings in Bolton and, because he wasn't alone in the squad in doing so, being seen around the town fostered more of an understanding between the players and the fans, and therefore there was more of a feeling that the representatives of Bolton Wanderers were also representative of the town it existed in.

As the Millennium passed, however, Phillips says, 'you began to see more players signing for Bolton because not only were they attracted to the competition of the Premier League, they were attracted to the money of the Premier League and, because they had the means to do so, many of them ended up living in Cheshire or Manchester – which rediscovered itself especially after the Commonwealth Games of 2002.'

It is the word 'competition' here that is key because not only does it reflect why moods began to change, it hints at where it might be going if we're not careful. In 2011 Liverpool's former chief executive Ian Ayre proposed that Premier League clubs should be able to negotiate their own television deals abroad and break from the system now where the finance breaks down equally. Ayre compared Liverpool against Bolton, and by saying that Liverpool interest more people in Asia, he was also saying Asia doesn't really care about Bolton; it ended up in a public slanging match and Liverpool's owner John W. Henry contacting Bolton's chairman Phil Gartside, expressing his regret at Ayre's comments.

'It is true that the Liverpools and the Manchester Uniteds have bigger followings elsewhere in the world,' Phillips admits. 'You have to ask the question, though, why are so many people across the planet tuned in to Premier League football? When you hear people say it's the best league in the world, they are saying it because it's the most competitive league in the world. It is competitive because money is consistently distributed equally, otherwise you'll see the top clubs pulling away and the spectacle just won't be as interesting eventually because it will become predictable. The way clubs like Bolton used to be able to give Liverpool or United a game – being able to beat them – is the beauty of English football and that is what I think makes the league so attractive.'

Phillips believes too many decisions have been made by football's authorities that benefit the television companies first and the match-going fans second, with televised games making it more challenging for lower-league clubs like Bolton to win support back.

'There is a whole generation of fans used to watching games from their living rooms,' he says. 'I remember sitting at a Premier League meeting where they were saying the brand is growing seventeen per cent year on year because of the demand in Asia. This is happening while there's an economic depression in the place where the so-called product is being produced. Ticket prices haven't fallen so there's an unhealthy balance. It's cheaper and more convenient to watch football at home than it is live and at the stadium – even outside of the Premier League, because there's a lot of Football League games on TV as well. If this continues to happen eventually attendances will fall and English football won't be the spectacle it used to be.

'Football on TV is at the overkill stage now,' Phillips says. 'I remember having my season ticket and small arguments in pubs happening about whether a goal was offside or not. There were no replays so nobody could really prove it. The camera angles in the football coverage has taken some of the beauty of the game away because small arguments are now presented as scandalous stories on the back pages of newspapers – it's made everything sound very serious indeed.'

The themes of Liverpool, Manchester, geography, finance and an unnecessary mood of seriousness are a feature of Phillips's daily work at Bolton's academy, where he is trying to develop players that are good enough to play for the first team. Two of them, Rob Holding and Zach Clough, were given debuts by Neil Lennon and their subsequent sales to Arsenal and Nottingham Forest have meant 'we still have a club', according to Phillips.

In the summer of 2016, Bolton dropped from being considered a category-one academy to category two after assessments by Double Pass, the company from Belgium that audits academies on behalf of the Premier League, which had in 2012 launched the Elite Player Performance Plan (EPPP) with the aim of improving the quality of home-grown players by the top English clubs.

Clubs with fewer financial means have argued it has become easier for wealthier clubs to lure away their best players without significant financial penalty and there is a belief that, as a consequence, EPPP is now being used as a device for recruitment rather than improvement. Before EPPP, the only time a rival club would be able to see another team's players was during games when they played each other. For access now all they have to do is send email notification 24 hours before any fixture to be allowed in.

'It means that our club is open for any other club to watch our games from under-9 level all the way up to under-23,' Phillips says ruefully. 'We had a terrific little player from the age of seven. He was one of the best players in the north-west of his age. When he was ten, we lost him to one of the category-one clubs. The system is set up for the cat-one clubs to sweep up all the best talent. I believe it's based on the model in Holland where there's three huge clubs that get all the better talent and develop it. If the talent doesn't work in their first team, it then filters back to the other teams. But what happens when the biggest clubs get greedy and take too many players? There's a drain of talent.

'A lot of the bigger clubs have their first-team squad then they have an elite development squad, then they've got another development squad. It means that they have too many players. Whereas in the past they'd have sixteen young players pushing for the first team, they now have forty. It means clubs like Bolton are finding it harder because that's twenty-four players unavailable to us that might have been otherwise. It's making it harder for smaller clubs generally to find the raw materials we need because the category-one clubs are flooding the local leagues with talent-spotting at a time when we're cutting our cloth accordingly.'

Bolton is close to Manchester and Liverpool geographically and they are left in a vulnerable position. Phillips has been working hard developing a relationship with the Bolton and Bury Junior League, trying to convince players and parents that Bolton provides a greater opportunity at first-team level. It is a hard argument to support, especially when Manchester City nearby are offering full-time contracts with education at private schools, which means players have better career prospects whether it's as a footballer or something else.

'I speak to people involved in German football and they all tell me they are delighted by the latest English TV deal because it means they'll try and buy German players for twice as much and then they can reinvest it in their structure and create more players that they can sell on again. German football regenerates itself and English football does not and I think that's ultimately why German football seems to be a happier place than English football, because opportunities for young players are always there. Where does all the money from the transfer fees go here – is it the agents? It's a difficult time for youth football. Opportunity is key. Going from three subs to five subs to seven subs means that managers need bigger squads. When the pressure is on and the money is there, they'll go and get experience.'

The latest Premier League initiative has been the rolling out of the Performance Management Application (PMA), a device which, according to the authorities, allows coaches and players to monitor progress through a 'performance clock'.

'The player gets match reports, training targets for the year split into six-week blocks, as well as targets for games,' Phillips explains. 'You tend to find that parents soon get involved and it takes over a player's life. That's where the system breaks down, it puts too much pressure on the player to play well when perhaps he's in need of a break from football. I find that the better players in our system are the ones who respond to the coaches' comments themselves rather than the parents. They progress well because they've got an understanding of the game and an understanding of what is required from them. Being able to work it out in your own time is really important and these lads obviously haven't been put under pressure at home where every minute of every day football is being talked about.

'Ultimately, players need to learn how to play in an environment that can be hostile, but sometimes the environment is created that way too soon at too young an age when players aren't equipped emotionally to deal with it. The real sad story is the one about the players who get released by academies at sixteen, seventeen and eighteen years of age and they've fallen out of love with the game to the point where they stop playing altogether. That never used to happen in my day. Now, a lot of players disappear off the radar.'

At the height of Bolton's financial problems in 2016, many of their young professionals were released because Bolton could not afford them, even though some were potentially good enough to play for the first team. Subsequently, two signed for Premier League clubs, one League One and two others at League Two. Phillips's son, Nathaniel, went to Liverpool. 'I suppose it shows we must have been doing something right,' Phillips says. 'It's annoying we had to let them go and it's put us back a couple of years, but at least we still have a football club.'

19

SALFORD LADS' CLUB

GARY NEVILLE IS SITTING IN THE ANCIENT STONE DUGOUTS OF Salford City's Moor Lane football ground, looking across a pitch that slopes sideways and dramatically towards him. Over on the opposite touchline, cold rain is battering the metal shell of a new stand and a digger behind it is making noise.

'That over there . . .' Neville points, jolting forward suddenly, '. . . it has to be finished by the end of the month.' Breaking from the interview, Neville shouts a question at a lone construction worker wearing a hard hat. When he asks, 'Are we on schedule?' it seems like more of a demand and, though positive, the construction worker's response is not the most convincing. It is the start of March. If the stand isn't completed by the end of March, Salford will be thrown out of the Conference North, so Neville is quickly counting days using his fingers. 'One . . . two . . . four weeks, isn't it? Christ . . .'

A critical discussion follows, or – as those who know him best might call it – a classic Neville confrontation. Neville spent nineteen seasons as Manchester United's right-back and his manager throughout that time, Sir Alex Ferguson, knew how to deal with him. 'Gary, go and annoy someone else,' he used to say. 'We always said of Gary he woke up angry,' Ferguson wrote in his 2013 autobiography. 'Where he sees flaws, sees errors, he attacks. His instinct was not to negotiate himself through an impasse, but strike hard with his opinions.' Neville, according to Ferguson, 'would answer his shadow back – he has to have an argument every day'.

While other teenagers were trying to manoeuvre their way past the doormen at the famous Haçienda nightclub on a Friday night, living the acid-rave hedonism of the early 1990s, Neville was tucked up away in bed – preparing himself for a junior game the following day. He had made the decision to distance himself from his old friends in Bury, old friends that might lead him astray – he was desperate in wanting to be a footballer but by retreating socially, it did not leave him cosseted.

His honesty, energy and fearlessness means that he is not always popular and yet Neville's driven personality explains why he played 602 games for United and 85 times for England; why he was able to help win eight Premier League titles, two Champions Leagues, three FA Cups and two League Cups. It also explains why he is here at Salford six years after retirement, doing his own thing albeit with the help of four former team-mates. While Tommy Banks worked on building sites after his retirement as a footballer, Neville has accrued enough wealth to help a club that had nothing, aim instead for the Football League.

On the day I met Neville, there had been stories in the papers about another one of his projects in Manchester's city centre near to the town hall and Central Library, where a controversial £200 million blueprint to build luxury apartments, a five-star hotel, restaurants and offices inside two bronze skyscrapers would mean the demolition of a 1950s synagogue, a 1930s police station and an eighteenth-century pub believed to be the only nearby building with a direct link to the 1819 Peterloo Massacre.

The previous September, Neville had outlined his vision 'to deliver the biggest statement in architecture and development that Manchester has seen in modern times', only for heritage groups to react by urging ministers to intervene, describing it as a 'planning disaster of a magnitude not seen in decades'.

When Neville and his brother Phil, Ryan Giggs, Paul Scholes and Nicky Butt bought Salford City in 2014, the decision was viewed with similar suspicion, albeit on a much smaller scale because not many people really cared for Salford, a club where not all of the 35 season-ticket holders even turned up every week.

Why, then, were five millionaires made rich by their success as footballers really interested in a club that had never been higher than the fourth-highest division in non-league football – one where the ground was rotting, the pitch was rutted and Old Trafford, despite being in the next borough to the south, felt very far away indeed?

While travelling together on a train, Neville and Giggs were discussing what to do next with their careers. Neville was retired and Giggs not far off. They were both motivated by competition. 'The conversation initially was about building a soccer school or an academy,' Neville remembers. 'Then we realised we didn't want to be babysitting: you have the kids Monday to Friday, there's no game at the end of it and then they go home. We realised we needed to run a club – the only question was, which club? In this area you have Bury, Oldham, Rochdale and Macclesfield. It might have been cheaper to buy either one of those clubs because when you start at the bottom as we have, there is so much to pay for if you want to meet your ambitions. In the Football League, a basic infrastructure is already in place. But then, we appreciated as players that owners never really own football clubs. It's the fans that matter most because without fans you have nothing. When we decided on Salford, there were thirty-five season-ticket holders and fourteen committee members. We wanted to build a club in our own name, for us to be accountable for what happens.

'Salford felt right because Giggsy lived here for thirty years, Scholesy was born here before moving to Oldham and I had my first trial for United here – just two hundred yards away on Littleton Road when I was ten years old. The Cliff, United's old training ground, is in Salford, so Butty was in and out of here for years too. It's where we all grew up.'

In buying Salford, Neville and co. would be able to make mistakes and learn as they went without the controversy that arrives when you are high-profile, in control of a bigger club and there are more people around to complain when it goes wrong. A dozen or so Salford supporters did not renew their season tickets when they arrived – fearing the purchase was a pursuit of vanity, fearing too that everything would change, that nothing would be the same again. The sight of diggers and stadium developments says that things are changing at Salford, especially when you look at the Conference North table and see they have achieved two promotions in as many seasons and could make it three in three if they go up through the play-offs this time around, as AFC Fylde's healthy lead at the top when I talk to Neville means they are likely to finish as champions.

The club's emergence has been rapid. Salford were soon to announce that joint-managers Anthony Johnson and Bernard Morley had agreed new two-year contracts, which means that whatever league the team is competing in, football will give them full-time employment come July and no longer will they have to work as van drivers.

Johnson and Morley arrived at Salford mid-season two years ago, bringing most of Ramsbottom United's team with them. Neville was stung by criticism following the sacking on New Year's Day 2015 of the previous manager, Phil Power, when Salford stood second in the Evo-Stik North First Division table. Power, born in Salford, gave an interview where he branded Neville and the other owners as 'hypocritical' because his removal was handled by chairman Karen Baird and none of them had the courtesy to call him. When Phil Neville had lost his job as assistant to David Moyes at Manchester United, his brother supported him by saying that Moyes deserved more time to get it right. Accordingly, Power pointed out that he had only worked for the Nevilles for six months.

'Though it was the right decision, I wasn't comfortable with it at all. None of us were,' Gary says. 'I think two to two and a half years is the minimum a coach should get. The problem with Phil was, he wasn't our appointment. People will say we could have made the change at the start of the season but that wouldn't have been fair on him. Ultimately, ownership is defined by the appointments you make and Phil was with Salford before us.'

The episode sharpened Neville's appreciation of why perception might be key to Salford's progress. It means he is willing to satisfy the requests of the club's original members ahead of anyone else. Neville is pointing across the pitch again.

'See Bill over there, he's been doing the same thing for nearly twenty-five years for nothing. Now, we've given him a full-time job as stadium manager. I'm proud that, one, because he still wants to do it with us and, two, we can pay him. He's the best person to do it because he cares about this club in a way that I don't. Twenty-five years' service, purely for the love of it, means I'll never be able to compete with him.

'Each one of the original members are still here, doing the same job. Four or five of them will be full-time and the rest will get paid for their roles. Our groundsman, George, is seventy-two. When I first met him he asked for five hundred pounds to reseed the pitch. Last year we spent nearly six grand, relaying the thing completely. We insisted from day one that we'd listen to what people need and help them out the best we can. The owners don't do anything from an operational point of view. Instead, we meet every Friday morning from seven until eleven to discuss administration: the structure, the values, the academy, the community projects. It has worked well. We've not interfered in what the members do. Salford is their club more than ours.'

Since Moor Lane was given planning permission, Neville says he has met the residents that live close to the ground face-to-face once a month.

'You get some complaining about the development and I find it difficult to understand, really. You live next to a football ground and always have! When you live near a football ground unfortunately there's a chance some cars will be parked on the roads on a Saturday afternoon. But I think most residents are starting to understand that development can benefit them as well. They'll be able to use the ground for meetings, events, coffee and tea – whatever they want.'

Once the lounges are built, Neville would like to interview ten start-up businesses from Greater Manchester and give them free office addresses. 'Football, you win or lose at the end of the day. I enjoy watching the games here. But the bits I really enjoy doing around the club are the long-term projects that impact upon people's life in a positive way. People are always looking for a catch and there is no catch. We're not sacking fourteen committee members; we're actually giving them jobs. For our original thirty-five season-ticket holders, we've frozen our prices at fifty pounds for ten years. We're not looking to stitch people up. What's in it for us? We want people to come with us.

'It's life nowadays, people are pissed off with everything,' Neville adds. 'You invest into a local club: you're an idiot. You don't invest into a local club: you're not putting anything back. There's no in-between. Everyone's always looking at you and they're thinking, "What do you want out of this?" It's a really cynical world and some people are so determined to be proven right, they won't give you a chance. Social media means everyone is living in an argument now.'

'Unless something changes dramatically Salford is likely to remain the main competitor with Wakefield for recognition as the largest city without a League side,' wrote Gary James in 2008 when his epic Manchester: A Football History was first published.

One hundred and one years earlier, Salford United had applied for League status but did not earn a single vote, with Oldham Athletic earning entry instead. James speculates that Manchester United – already a Division One club – were planning to move to the Trafford area and had identified the Salford population as their own. With more power, they were able to sway opinions when it came to the ballot. Salford's failure affected performance and by 1910 – with new residents at Old Trafford – Salford United disbanded and Manchester United became regarded by many Salfordians as the city's team.

Though Salford City were formed in 1940, it had since been a club struggling for interest – even identity – as the powerhouse of Manchester United grew into a global force just around the corner. When Neville changed the colour of Salford's kit from orange shirt and black shorts to red and white – the colours of United – suspicion immediately fell. He reasons he was able to take the decision because Salford had played in three different colours over the previous 25 years and that after blue and white versions were ditched, it only became orange because there was no money available and Blackpool were forthcoming with spare kit. 'This happened twelve years ago and so you can't really say we've meddled with the identity,' he says.

By crossing the Irwell, the 'river the colour of lead' immortalised by Shelagh Delaney in A Taste of Honey and Morrissey in The Smiths' 'This Night Has Opened My Eyes', you can walk from Manchester to Salford in just five minutes. Salford has its own cathedral, university and charter. As local writer Paul Gent put it, the two cities are 'like Siamese twins, joined at the chest and sharing several vital organs; but one is permanently aggrieved at the strength and health of the other'.

Stuart Maconie wrote in 2006 that Salford and Manchester are, indeed, 'still mucky kids at heart but having been mithered by Mam and had their faces wiped with spittle on some big civic hankie, they've scrubbed up dead smart'.

He was referring then to Manchester's economic emergence from Thatcherism, aided by the Commonwealth Games held there in 2002, as well as the regeneration of Salford Quays where more than 10,000 people were employed – many at the Lowry Centre, named after local artist L.S. Lowry, which was described as 'not quite Salford's Guggenheim' upon its opening in 2000 by the New Statesman. 'It is ultimately too small and too well behaved.'

By the time the BBC announced it would be moving its operations to Salford in 2009, the world was in the midst of an economic crisis, one fundamentally caused by American banks lending too much money, albeit one blamed from inside British politics on the government by the opposition; it became an easy stick for the Conservatives to beat Labour with, simply because it happened on their watch.

The austerity that followed under the Tory/Lib Dem coalition led to rising unemployment and falling house prices, and when austerity happens, it is places like Salford that are affected the most. Though Salford and Manchester are very different, they are linked by politics and while Manchester is undeniably Labour, so is Salford.

It was a reflection of the mood that after I'd met Neville and after he'd driven into Manchester for further discussions about the controversial St Michael's project, it was revealed that the Kersal area of Salford had turned Conservative for the first time in a quarter of a century following a 21 per cent swing in a by-election.

In simple terms perhaps the result really shows just how so many voters don't know who to believe any more; so when Neville, a wealthy ex-footballer, commits himself with so much vigour towards a new venture he is often greeted by scepticism – even when it means employment for lots of people. Neville is from a Labour family in Bury and he is comfortable enough in himself to admit that, while creating jobs, he is also involved at Salford because experiences will lead to a personal development.

'Aligning sport, business and administration is probably where I want to be in the future, it's where I'm moving towards,' he says. 'I'm forty-two years of age now and I'd like to think that when I get to fifty, I'd be known as a successful businessman and an experienced football administrator because I don't think you can achieve the second part without the first. When I finished playing that was always my long-term aim. The idea of mastering a new trade excited me, learning how to deal with staff, budgets and finance: making key decisions.

'Here, I never go and watch a training session. I'm not interested in knowing who has trained well and who has trained badly; how many sprints they've done, how far they've run. That side of football bores me. I'm more interested in structure, building blocks like an academy here. I want to build the best academy that anyone could build. I want to make sure that we have a number of those players coming through into our first team. I want our season-ticket holders to have access to mental-health help. Historically, football clubs were the heart of the community. The reality is, many aren't any more. We've got to try and deliver something that really is.'

Neville tried at football management and, listening to him, it doesn't seem like he wants to have another go. In December 2015 he was appointed at Valencia – the club owned by Peter Lim, the Singaporean who also owns half of Salford City. Despite being sacked by his business partner less than four months later, Neville is adamant the decision did not affect their relationship, largely because he can admit it was the correct thing to do, with Valencia only six points above the relegation zone. Vital lessons, he says, were learned.

'That's the bit I need to get better at, the decision-making – definitely. Valencia was a huge experience for me, where I made mistakes in not making correct decisions: seeing something and not following it through. You need to have courage in your convictions and learn to ignore the doubts that creep in because otherwise, you're in a world of confusion. One part of you tells you to trust your gut and the other part tells you to let it breathe a little bit. It means you're always in that situation where you're asking yourself, "When's the right time?"'

He can't help thinking about Sir Alex Ferguson: how he'd have dealt with the problems posed by Valencia, arguably the most idiosyncratic club in Spain.

'Sir Alex never passed wisdom on, it was just a case of observing him and seeing how a man at the top of his game operated,' Neville says. 'Above everything, he taught me work ethic. Every morning he'd be in Carrington at half-six whether or not we'd had a game the night before. He was relentless, completely obsessed with work. A lot of his team talks were around work. But he also made big decisions and was fearless when making them. He was able to make the type of calls that would make people go, "Wow, that's harsh." And yet, he was still someone who commanded loyalty. He was at United for twenty-five years and in that time he had the same secretary, the same receptionist and the same kitman. I think that's the approach you need to have. That's what I'd like here at Salford.'

Neville visited Wimbledon, AFC Fylde, FC United of Manchester, Morecambe and Fleetwood Town, speaking to chairmen and chief executives about what needed to be done to get Moor Lane in shape. He learned from the mistakes of others and crucially, he believes, decided to rebuild the ground in one hit because the ambition is there to move up the leagues and doing it stage by stage has cost other clubs more money than it should have done. Andy Pilley, Fleetwood's chairman, had told Neville that he should appreciate the first few years of involvement at the lowest levels like he did, 'when you don't have so much boardroom crap to deal with', appreciating that professionalism brings an inevitable seriousness.

For the time being, Salford are the cheapest match ticket in the top six English leagues and the cheapest season ticket as well. Neville wants to keep prices at £7 for adults and £3 for children and OAPs while clubs in their league charge more than double in both age categories. It is the members presenting the economic reality to Neville at the moment, suggesting that prices should rise to £10 and £5, and though Neville is considering the option he realises that he will be the one at the receiving end when criticism comes – even if they then elect to proceed with a proposed prize freeze for the next three years.

Neville says that in the first two years of his involvement at Salford, the club more or less broke even because of an FA Cup run to the second round and the income raised from a documentary series featured on the BBC, where one of the most significant lines about the realities of ownership was delivered by Paul Scholes: 'We've bought a football club and we can't fucking talk about football.' Sacking Power taught them a vital lesson. Though Neville says he speaks twice a day to chairman Karen Baird, contact with players and managers is restricted.

'The managers have a great relationship with Karen but with me they don't,' he admits. 'I've not spoken to them face to face for six months. We've exchanged texts on issues completely unrelated to football but I stopped texting them after matches ages ago. I stay away from them. Very quickly, I found out that a "well done" one week, when you don't send it the next it's harmful. Management really is tough. You've got all these voices. You've got the fans, the media, the players – you don't need the added confusion of a Neville, a Scholes or a Giggs saying, "I thought you should have done this today with your team selection." When that happens, your head as a manager is all over the place, your brain is a spaghetti bolognese. Having been there as a coach, you don't want confusion. You want clean thoughts and the best thoughts are usually your own because it's your reputation on the line, nobody else's.

'On a match day, we walk through the gate at a quarter to three and stand over there in the corner of the ground. As soon as the final whistle has gone, I go home. I don't go over to the players and say, "Well done, lads." That would be unhealthy. We see that as the chairman's job, she builds the relationships – giving them a bollocking when they need one, or even a shoulder to cry on.'

The only time Salford's owners contact players is when they are trying to sign a new one.

'It only happens occasionally,' Neville says. 'It's not us saying to the manager, "We want that player for you." It's us presenting Salford City as a place to come and play your football.' It was around this time twelve months ago, Neville had a conversation with Josh Hine, a Chorley striker Salford ended up signing in order to help with their promotion push. Neville has studied patterns in non-league football and he sees clubs that are mid-table in January cutting their budget to save costs for the rest of the season because they won't go up and have enough distance between themselves and the bottom not to go down. 'If you can go up, you'll throw a little bit more at it. If you're risking going down, the same happens. By the end of the season, the only clubs still actively signing players are usually the top six and the bottom six. They get their funds through a local benefactor – one of the board: "There you go, there's a few grand to get that striker we need." February and March is a good time to pick a couple of decent players up because clubs want to save on the wage bill.'

When it comes to committing money towards signings, Neville says Scholes pushes the hardest if he feels a new player will give the team an advantage, while his own first question to Baird is always the same: 'Does it fit in the budget?' Like at Fylde, dealing with the expectations of potential recruits is challenging.

'The perception of what we're doing here is potentially damaging rather than the reality,' Neville says. 'We have a budget and we stick to it. You're now seeing agents at a level of football where they didn't used to be. I know we've shifted the wages up just by being here and that helps nobody. I'd be happy to produce our wage bill for the last three seasons tomorrow. I think everyone would be shocked.'

He tells the story of three players Salford lost the previous summer to another club. Before leaving, each player presented him with a copy of the contract they were being offered. 'I couldn't believe it – no chance, no chance could they be getting paid that!' When Salford tried to sign players from Halifax and Stockport County, the demands were, as Neville puts it, 'immoral'.

'They thought we were paying players more than a grand a week. Our top-paid player is on £650 a week and that's high – don't get me wrong.' Most players at Salford are paid between £300 and £500. 'Our wage budget this year is lower than at least four clubs in the Conference North,' he insists. 'But everyone believes we're paying a lot more because a story appeared in the Mail which claimed that Danny Webber [the former Man United youth striker who forged a successful lower-league career] was on £800 a week when the truth is, he was on half of that.'

The conversation leads back to the very beginning. Non-league football is changing, like it or not. I ask him what he'd say if it was suggested investment like his at Salford is going against the ethics of what non-league is supposed to be about. His response is swift.

'In two seasons here, we've had two promotions, we're building a 5,000-capacity stadium and the community will benefit from what's happened at a time when there is very little public or private investment in football; so I would say this is all positive. Somebody else will argue that we've ruined non-league, it's all about celebrity, they've changed the kit, the residents are unhappy. There are ten arguments on either side. For every person that mentions we're employing forty to fifty full-time staff next year and call it "job creation", others will always argue, "that's not non-league is it?"'

He returns to a point he's keen to press home. The only responsibility the original members don't deal with any more is the playing budget.

'They still do the programme notes, they still do the club shop, they still do the food hut, they still do the bar, they still do the turnstiles, and the key for me is, they still like it,' he says. 'A measurement of failure for this club isn't related to performance on the field, whether we miss out on promotion or get relegated. A measurement of failure would be losing any of the original members. I'm not being disrespectful to the managers or the players but they come and go. They are nowhere near as important as any one of those committee members or any of the original fans. I know if we lose them, we are dead. People will think we've come in here and steamrollered through it. That cannot happen. If it does, we have failed. And if this fails – if the fans don't like the redevelopment of the ground – then there's nobody else to blame other than us because we've designed it. We are designing a football club in our name. You can't pin the blame on anyone else when it goes wrong. This is us. We can't blame the managers if we lose a game because we're the ones who made the appointments. Karen recommended them, we sat down with Jonno and Bernard before they got the job. We could have said, "No." There's no one else to blame here and I like being in that position. People say it's control. Maybe it is. But with control also comes risk. I can't blame anyone else if this turns to shit. It is what this is. It's me, it's Phil, it's Butty, it's Scholesy, it's Giggsy.'

And with that, Neville drove off to deal with St Michael's.

20

SLEEPING NEXT TO A GIANT

IT WAS SHORTLY BEFORE MIDNIGHT WHEN, AMID THE CELEBRATIONS in the hours after Manchester City had snatched the Premier League title from Manchester United on the final day of the season to secure their first championship in 44 years, a balaclava-wearing gunman entered the Cotton Tree pub and fired seven shots that killed one man – a rival in a long-running feud – and injured three others.

The date was 13 May 2012. The gunman was Dale Cregan. The Cotton Tree pub was in Droylsden, two miles away from the Etihad Stadium if you travel east on Manchester Road. Cregan fled to Thailand, the country where he had previously lost his left eye in a fight, and was arrested as he got off the plane at Manchester Airport when he returned in June. Tragically, police had to release him on bail while they continued gathering evidence and two months later, after blowing the body of the deceased rival's father to pieces using a grenade, he murdered two policewomen after luring them to a location in Mottram.

The red-brick Victorian building that was once the Cotton Tree still stands but its door is bolted now, its moss-covered windows steel-shuttered, its sign removed. Over the crossroads and continuing on Market Street, a couple of hundred yards past the scruffy takeaway joints, the shopping arcades with discount stores and then a car wash promising cheap deals, is the home of Droylsden AFC – the

Butcher's Arms, a ground that earned its name because it replaced an abattoir.

'I don't see this as a bad area at all,' says Droylsden's owner, chairman and manager, Dave Pace, who responds just as emphatically when I ask him whether you've got to be tough to survive in this part of Manchester's eastern margins. 'Tough?' he asks. 'I wouldn't know what separates people that are tough and people that aren't. I'd say a lot of people here are survivors. You don't see many walking down the street with their heads bowed down. You've got to get on with life, roll yer sleeves up.'

In 2016, almost half of Manchester's neighbourhoods were in the 'most deprived' 10 per cent in the country, according to the Office for National Statistics. The top seven in Manchester's list of the most deprived zones were all former manufacturing and working-class neighbourhoods in the east, around the Etihad Stadium: Bradford, Miles Platting and Newton Heath, Harpurhey, Gorton South, Charlestown, Ardwick and Gorton North.

Pace was born close to Droylsden, in Openshaw; another exhausted area, which formed the grimy engine room of Victorian Manchester, the world's first industrial city. The first machine-woven towel in the world, indeed – the terry towel – was produced by W.M. Christy and Sons Ltd of Fairfield Mills in Droylsden. Robertson's Jam, meanwhile, was a significant employer for more than 150 years before closing in 2008.

Having led a slow decline from the 1920s onwards, Manchester's industrial death was confirmed in the 1980s by a Conservative government that turned Britain into a consumer society, with Manchester – and Liverpool – suffering the worst because it had furthest to fall. Considering no reliable work has since replaced the hard, grubby industry on which the city – like much of the north – was built, is it any wonder that at some point criminality appears and a villain like Cregan turns up at the door, dragging the reputation of a once-decent place like Droylsden even further down? Howard Donald from Take That might be from Droylsden but perhaps it was Noel Gallagher, who grew up not far away in Burnage, who was able to reflect the local mood best when the malaise set in during the 1980s, asking, 'Is it worth the aggravation; to find yourself a job when there's nothing worth working for?'

Pace admits he was once 'a bit of a lad myself', but having gone to play football in America and Greece, he returned to Manchester holding more focus than before, first getting involved at Droylsden because his firm, Alpha Windows, was going well and he wanted to please his father, William, a Droylsden supporter who stood quietly on the old one-step open terrace at the Butcher's Arms.

'Me, I'm a grafter,' Pace says proudly. 'I've never had money, really – never been given any on a plate. Most of the money I earn through the windows has been put into Droylsden. If we had £100 to spend on a player, I'd give him £110 to make sure he stays and find a way to make that tenner up. It means we've always been a bit short.

'People say to me, "You could be sitting in the sun in Barbados or somewhere fancy like that with everything [you've] given to Droylsden." But I've never been able to walk away. The stand here is called the William Pace stand. That means a lot to me. Family is the most important thing you have.'

Pace's involvement at Droylsden began in 1994 when Manchester City were playing at Maine Road in Moss Side, south Manchester. When, in 2003, City moved to their current site, a stadium built originally for the Commonwealth Games, it resulted in Droylsden becoming the non-league club situated closest to a Premier League ground in the north-west of England. Between 2003 and 2007, Droylsden enjoyed unprecedented success, with the 2004/05 season culminating in four new cups added to the trophy cabinet and qualification for the embryonic Conference North. Two years later Droylsden were promoted to the Conference National; within a month, Thaksin Shinawatra, the former prime minister of Thailand, became the first foreign owner of Manchester City.

'When Shinawatra showed up at City, City's trophy cabinet was pretty bare,' Pace remembers. 'I took a call off someone at City asking if they could borrow our four cups. They thought it was a good idea because we were the nearest club to 'em and even though I'm a United fan, I thought – OK, fair enough, maybe they'll help us out in the future. The roles are reversed now. I've written to them. They never got back to us, which is a bit sad. Obviously they have different owners now. But I'm not even sure whether the current regime at City knows we're here just a couple of miles down the road.'

Attendances at the Butcher's Arms had shot up, sometimes hitting the thousand mark the year before Droylsden became a Conference team. Pace believes Droylsden had 'pinched a few fans from City' in that time. But when Shinawatra came in, an interest in what City might achieve took them away again. Though Droylsden finished bottom of the Conference National, they threatened a return in each of the subsequent three seasons – campaigns which included high-profile runs in the FA Cup – but by then, City had been taken over for a second time, with Sheikh Mansour and Abu Dhabi making City the richest club in world football. Droylsden had become good at precisely the wrong moment.

'There's no doubt City coming to this part of Manchester has been terrible for us,' Pace believes. 'Before Shinawatra, they were knocking all sorts of deals out for kids because they were desperate to fill the stadium. You could go and watch Droylsden for a tenner or City for only a fiver more. There's no way we could compete with them.

'City were struggling when Shinawatra came in and we were doing well. We were on the way up and City were on the way down,' he continues. 'Attendances down the road weren't too hot and some people were starting to turn towards us because we were earning promotions. Overnight it seemed to change when Abu Dhabi came in. There was a feel-good factor about City again. Suddenly, Droylsden wasn't as attractive as it was maybe becoming for what might seem a relatively small number of people on the outside, but it was a significant number to us.'

The Manchester morning is unusually sunny when I meet Pace, though you wouldn't know it if you were sat all day inside a back room of the clubhouse at the Butcher's Arms, because Pace has curtains drawn to keep the heat in and the lights turned off to save money on an electricity bill he could do without. Droylsden's season in the Conference National competing with city clubs like Exeter and Oxford United seems long ago because they have returned to the level where Pace started at the beginning of his involvement following three relegations in five seasons. He says the standard in the Northern Premier League First Division is 'crap' but Droylsden are there because he could not pay players a wage for almost two years after he was landed with a VAT bill of around £250,000 that he decided to try and fight in court. Pace then had to decide whether to place the club into administration, wipe out a large portion of that debt and start again five divisions down, or to soldier on and attempt to pay it all back. 'It was administration or the hard way – I chose the hard way,' Pace recalls.

Droylsden were subsequently relegated from the Conference North and the Northern Premier League using Sunday league footballers and a collection of players studying at nearby universities and colleges. Pace describes the period as being 'battered on and off the field'.

'I would have resigned as manager but I had no money whatsoever so I didn't think it was fair giving someone the manager's job without having a carrot to work with,' he says. 'We were begging, stealing and borrowing off everyone. Everything was going wrong. One Saturday I got a call at 1.20 p.m. telling me one of our lads couldn't play because they'd been in a car crash. Earlier in the season another lad was arrested on the morning of a game. But I decided to stay with my number two, Aeon [Lattie] who is as loyal as anyone can be. Though we've more or less paid the debt off now, to say we've turned a corner would be wrong. We're always struggling for money.'

Pace had the option to remove Droylsden from the Northern Premier League and re-form again three divisions below in the North West Counties First Division. He decided to carry on and pay off the debt because he says he's a proud man and couldn't bear to consider what his father, William, might think if he was still alive.

'You carry on because you don't want to give in – to give others satisfaction. I could have gone bump and caved. But I have a trade myself and I also thought it was unfair to the plumber who's done £20,000 of work on the clubhouse but might only get a couple of quid because of my mistakes. In the end, I decided to pay back every penny. Would I do it again? I'm not sure.'

Pace is described by one former player as a 'wears his heart on his sleeve sort of bloke', and by another as 'not always the most diplomatic of people – he's very single-minded, what he says goes'. Having become owner and chairman in 1994, he appointed himself as manager in 1998 'because each of the eight managers I had in those four years were looking after themselves whereas I only look after the club'. Since then, every aspect of Droylsden's running has been under his sole control, or that of his brother Bryan who acts as secretary. 'I don't class myself as a chairman really, I am more a manager.'

Within non-league circles, Pace's prickliness has made him a character that divides opinion. When, in 2000, Droylsden won the Manchester Premier Cup, he was not in charge, instead allowing his wife Stella to sit in the dugout and preside over the victory that followed. A wider impression of him was formed in 2008 when his team faced Chesterfield in an epic second-round FA Cup tie which involved four games, two abandonments, ten goals scored, a Droylsden win and then an expulsion for fielding an ineligible player. With Droylsden 1–0 up at half-time in the first game, the referee decided to stop play due to fog; when the game was replayed, Chesterfield allowed Droylsden to equalise, according their manager Lee Richardson, because he 'wanted to avoid a riot', after Chesterfield's Jack Lester had accidentally scored past the Droylsden goalkeeper when he meant to return possession. Pace was so incensed that he reacted, according to the Daily Telegraph match report, by 'charging towards the home dugout and had to be restrained by stewards before getting involved in some aggressive exchanges with home supporters'.

With Chesterfield 2–0 ahead at the Butcher's Arms in the next replay, an electrical fault caused the floodlights to fail, a moment Richardson described as 'suspicious', and though Droylsden won 2–1 a week later in the fourth game, the scorer of the winner, Sean Newton, should not have played because he was suspended. The Chesterfield affair therefore proved not to be one of those occasions where a Football League club meets one from non-league and goodwill follows, with Pace's belligerent public persona coming under scrutiny. He remains adamant the victory over Chesterfield that would have given Droylsden a third-round tie at Ipswich Town, would also have meant a potential cash injection of anything up to £300,000, allowing the club to 'spend someone else's money for the first time'.

'What followed a few years later might have been avoidable,' Pace believes. Within two years, Droylsden had another shot at the FA Cup third round, taking Leyton Orient to a second-round replay. This time, interest was at a national level with ESPN and Radio Five Live covering the fixture. With Norwich City waiting in the next round, the money generated would have allowed Pace to strengthen an already talented squad to launch another crack at the Conference National. Droylsden took Leyton Orient to extra time. The final score was Leyton Orient 8, Droylsden 2.

The scene at the Butcher's Arms when Pace took over was grim. 'The club was struggling big time: terrible changing rooms, no floodlights – Gypsies nicked them, God knows how they did it,' Pace remembers. 'The situation was so bad, we put an advert in the paper asking for players. And then the clubhouse – which wasn't insured – got burned down. I was tempted to jack it in when that happened. I spoke to my dad about it. "You've never jacked anything in in your life," he told me. "Keep going."'

Pace built the ground in stages. A Portakabin was installed. The William Pace stand was constructed, with nearly 400 red seats. Then came the clubhouse, with a split bar between a function room and a small snooker hall. With Conference National football on the horizon Pace funded the covered terrace behind one of the goals. 'All of this cost money and it was only coming from one man's pocket,' he says. 'I'm pretty proud. You go to a lot of grounds and people are walking around with buckets to raise funds for the club. I don't do that here. It's more or less begging. When people go and watch a football match they don't want to be worrying about finance or the future do they? They want to escape it.'

In the Conference National, though, Droylsden became one of the sad cases, finishing bottom of the league and, by the end of a testing season, playing in front of home crowds of less than 200 against future Football League sides like Stevenage and Aldershot. It was the away games against city teams like Exeter that reminded Pace how far his club had travelled. 'They were Exeter City, after all, and they have an entire sports section of the local paper covering them. Us? We were Droylsden – a pub side. We're lucky if we get our score in the Manchester Evening News. You can walk in and out of Droylsden in thirty seconds. To play at that level was a massive achievement. I still feel with a little bit more cash we could have done something in that league.'

In 2018, Pace will have been in charge of Droylsden for twenty years and that makes him the longest-serving active manager in the north-west. He thinks he has signed thousands of players in his time and his current phone book has the names of hundreds of players that are currently active. On the morning I meet him, he has secured Ciaran Kilheeney on loan from Warrington Town for his third spell at the club, meaning the Mancunian centre-forward will not have to drive across the M62 motorway that connects Manchester and Liverpool. It is normal for Droylsden's players, however, to make the opposite journey. There have been occasions when Pace has named eleven Liverpudlians in his Droylsden team, much to the frustration of some supporters.

'Some of the fans didn't like it. "Why have we got so many?" they'd ask. "Because there's no one better!" I'd say back. You'd look around the Manchester leagues and the players weren't as good. A lad from Abbey Hey or somewhere – he wouldn't get in. I've always looked around Liverpool. I think the talent in Liverpool is better than in Manchester but there are more non-league clubs in Manchester than there are in Liverpool – clubs that can offer a decent wage as well. The Liverpool lads aren't afraid to travel.'

Pace's longevity at Droylsden means he is well placed to describe the changes in football at non-league level. He agrees with his friend at Southport, Liam Watson, that non-league is now infested with academy footballers – players who consider themselves professionals. For many, football remains their only source of income and it means that when another club offers slightly more money, they leave. Non-league is not the true alternative it is made out to be because it has not always been this way. Semi-professional footballers used to stick around in the same way amateurs would, because their mates were there and the income achieved from playing football was considered a bonus rather than a standard wage. Now, in non-league, it is not uncommon for a player to have three or four clubs in one season. Pace has dealt with players that have moved clubs nine times in less than three years.

'They're more money-orientated than they were,' he says of players. 'That comes down from the Premier League. They'll still do you a job but it's more difficult convincing them to stick around. You can't get good players out of the Sunday leagues like you used to be able to because instead of being fifteen teams in each division, there's about eight. It means there are less players to choose from. The players are less consistent as well. You've got to ram home to them all the time about what you expect. A lot of them have been playing academy football where the coaches are telling them what to do all of the time. The better players, they get it straight away: tell them once, they do it – no messing around.'

'In the 90s, you'd get a lot of players working their way up – lads out of Sunday league,' he continues. 'Now, a lot of them are taking a step down to play for clubs like Droylsden. Academy football affects the lives of so many players. I'm not sure whether they enjoy non-league as much. The standard isn't great either. Academies don't care how many they take in because they fear rival clubs will get them. I see a lot of players who've spent a year as a pro only to get released and they're not good enough to even play here.

'I've got a lad now, Luke Daly, who was at United all his life. He went to Burnley then Burnley let him go. He thought he was going to get picked up but no one called. So his old fella was on the phone, ringing round. I told the dad straight away, "You can't be ringing up for him – he needs to do it himself." It's a massive step turning from full-time to part-time. Mentally, unless you accept that you've had to take a few steps back to go forward, you'll fail again. After dreaming of playing for United or City and getting a whiff of it, playing for Droylsden and working on a building site for a living, it's a lot to take on board.'

Pace was trying to prevent Daly from joining Chorley after the Conference North club served seven days' notice on the midfielder's registration. Pace warned him that Chorley's style of football would not suit him – just like he'd warned Billy Cregg six months before only to see him join Altrincham and then fail 'because he spent most of his time watching the ball fly over his head'. Cregg left for Buxton and now he's back at Droylsden. 'He's wasted six months of his life trying to get a game for teams that don't suit him. He'd have been better staying where he is and letting the League scouts come. We're one of the few non-league clubs in the region that always tries to keep the ball on the deck rather than lump it forward like so many do.'

Pace plans to put more players on contract so clubs from higher leagues can't take them without paying a fee. 'I'm sick to death of working with them only to see this happening over and over again. If I had a pound for every time I've heard a player say, "I've got to look after my family," Droylsden would be thousands of pounds better off. They don't realise why it would be in their own interest to stick around in the medium to long term.'

Agents?

'Yes, I see plenty of them and they're a nightmare,' he says. 'They're offering players the chance to go here, there and everywhere on trial. I think if you're good enough, you should trust yourself to stay where you are, play well and let the scouts come and look at you. If you go on trial and a pro club signs you for nothing they'll stick you at the back of the queue because they don't have to justify your presence to the chairman. If they pay money for you, they'll have a good look at you. They'll have to justify the fee they've just paid. It's common sense but so many agents and players are chasing the money they don't think straight.'

One of Pace's ideas was to bring Argentinian players with Spanish passports to Droylsden. 'The agent representing them got greedy and asked for £50,000 up front. I said to him, "You're kidding, aren't you? You can make your money off the players when they're in the shop window. He didn't value the common sense of having his players in one place. Surely then they'd be more comfortable playing with each other and play better and, equally, the agent wouldn't have to travel here, there and everywhere across the country going to different clubs to take care of them. I've hit the crossbar a few times with ideas that might have worked.'

It is becoming harder for clubs like Droylsden and servants like Pace, not only because of the power of Manchester United and the growth and close proximity of Manchester City but also because of the emergence of moneyed or powerful non-league clubs like Salford City and FC United of Manchester, with dramatic falls like the one at Stockport County also impacting on the landscape.

Pace believes Droylsden's popularity has not been helped by media representation when the times have been good. When Droylsden drew Leyton Orient in the FA Cup second round of 2010, FC United of Manchester went to Brighton & Hove Albion. The Manchester Evening News proceeded to print a double-page spread previewing FC United's tie, which included a large colour photograph of the celebrations following their first-round win. At the bottom of the article a single sentence told readers that Droylsden were also still involved in the competition. As cursory as that seemed, it was more than the lengths ITV's

Granada Reports went to later that evening when a glorious five-minute story on FC United was screened and no mention whatsoever was made of Manchester's other remaining representative.

'You might argue that more people are interested in FC United than us and that's fair enough,' Pace says. 'But if Droylsden is a smaller club and we have achieved the same thing as FC United, doesn't that make our story more remarkable and therefore worth writing about?

'We're playing clubs now we haven't played for twenty years,' he adds. 'In that time we've been to the Conference and back while many others have stayed pretty much where they are. Salford are only achieving now what we did ten years ago but because they've got famous owners, they get a lot more publicity.'

Pace still dreams of managing in the Football League – 'to do an Accrington' – but for that to happen, he would have to first earn three promotions back to the Conference National and that would mean achieving the same feat twice.

'People tell me it's unlikely, but City bounced back from two relegations, didn't they? Look at them now.'

21

FALLOWFIELD, HULME, MOSS SIDE

OVER ON MERSEYBANK PLAYING FIELDS IN DIDSBURY, THE HEAVY doors of the changing rooms clank open and the musk of damp leather lingers. The concrete is cold. There are three rows of wooden benches and pegs above them with yellow shirts, blue shorts, blue socks and different-coloured boots scattered across the floor.

For Fletcher Moss Rangers there is a feeling that the circus has moved on and nothing has changed. In 2016, when Marcus Rashford scored the goals for Manchester United which led to his England selection as an eighteen-year-old, there was a desire to find out more about where he'd come from.

Dave Horrocks is the chairman, treasurer and development officer at Fletcher Moss. His mobile phone did not stop ringing for weeks. There were full interviews with three national newspapers and interest from news organisations in Norway and Qatar. United had picked Rashford up from Fletcher Moss when he was seven. They had also taken Cameron Borthwick-Jackson, Tyler Blackett, Jesse Lingard, Ravel Morrison, Zeki Fryers, Danny Welbeck and Cameron Stewart. Before that, there was Wes Brown and his brother Reece, as well as Danny Webber. The stories of 82 professional footballers involve Fletcher Moss at the beginning.

Fletcher Moss is to south Manchester what Senrab is to the east end of

London, or Wallsend Boys Club to Newcastle: a football club where many future professionals experienced the sensation of stud sinking into turf in a competitive environment for the first time. Unlike Senrab, which in 2014 was shortlisted for local team of the year in the Pride of Sport Awards, and unlike Wallsend Boys, a club which in 2008 was bestowed with the Freedom of North Tyneside in recognition of what the deputy mayor called their 'factory line of talent' – an award that helped when the Football Foundation was deciding where to send £850,000 worth of grants three years later – Fletcher Moss has received little support from anyone over the years.

'I don't think it's right we say, "You owe Fletcher Moss Rangers this or that." Nobody owes anybody anything, that's complete rubbish,' Horrocks says. 'The players that have been with us – they don't, because they could have gone round the corner to another team. We've had some absolutely phenomenal publicity off the back of the Wes Browns, the Ravel Morrisons and the Rashfords doing so well. It's encouraged more talented lads to come our way. It's only Tuesday and I've had seven emails about kids wanting to join.'

Horrocks is as Mancunian as they come and he admits to being conscious about not being perceived as whingey when he delivers his next comments. Ron Jamieson, the secretary of Fletcher Moss, was left feeling stung by one newspaper after he was quoted suggesting that Manchester United should pay his club £2million after selling Danny Welbeck to Arsenal for seven times that amount. A column was then published in the Daily Mail under the headline, 'Don't make Marcus Rashford the first £2million six-year-old,' with an argument against the idea seemingly based around the principle that Rashford had only spent two seasons with Fletcher Moss and more years at United. It was a classic case of an explosive line becoming the focus of the discussion when the context behind its delivery was more important.

Horrocks says that all Fletcher Moss really need is enough money that ensures their future. He isn't demanding state-of-the-art facilities. He just doesn't want bad facilities – facilities so bad, it leads to the closure of the club.

'The facilities available to Fletcher Moss haven't been improved since the club started in 1986,' Horrocks says. 'Think about all the money that has found its way into football since then. Not a penny has found its way down to us. There are times when you think about throwing your hand in.

'A club like ours has about £5,000 in the bank at the very best of times,' he reveals. 'If we had a facility to be proud of, it would act as a magnet for even more kids and keep them out of trouble. It would also allow us to improve our coaching, improve the kids that don't get recruited earlier and make the English game better from the very bottom. You're only as strong as your most vulnerable point, aren't you?

'Marcus, I believe, almost had his car written off. It wasn't his fault, someone rear-ended him. He was in his black Mercedes 450SL coupé. How much is that – £80,000? Don't get me wrong, best of luck to the kid – I don't begrudge him a penny. But when it's all up there and nothing is down here, either from the club, the player, the agent or sponsors, it's wrong – badly wrong – because clubs weaker than ours will die. The only player recently that has done anything for us is Jesse Lingard. He bought one of our under-10s teams a set of waterproof jackets for £600.'

It is a dreary Manchester morning when I meet Horrocks. He has the records to prove the number of scouts that watch Fletcher Moss games because he makes them sign the club's register before they pass through the gates that lead on to the fields. It is quiet now, with only the faint sound of the River Mersey draining westwards just behind the changing rooms, and the M60 ring road humming beyond the nearest housing estate. Two days earlier it had been different. He shows me the signatures and the names of the professional clubs present on the most recent Sunday morning. 'Look, Manchester City, Huddersfield, Blackburn, Man United, Huddersfield again, Stoke, Liverpool, Bury and Everton.'

I ask him whether life would be simpler if Fletcher Moss became an official feeder club to United or City. You can understand why there is a reluctance. 'Any contract written up would have to be weighed on our side rather than theirs,' he responds. 'When you're dealing with Premier League clubs, the matter of fairness for a club like ours is very difficult to achieve. We value our independence and having an independent junior club hasn't been a bad thing for United or City.'

At the moment, United, City, Liverpool and the rest know that Fletcher Moss are running soccer schools for children as young as three. The Premier League clubs are now looking in the lowest age category for players. Horrocks tells a potentially dark story about a toddler where he was approached to join Manchester City by someone purporting to be a scout in Merseybank's car park. After a parent complained, Horrocks was straight on to City and, though it transpired he was affiliated to the club, it was explained to him that the scout was, instead, a spotter – someone who works for the scouts and earns a fee when contracts are signed.

Horrocks only speaks positively of the parents that take their kids to Fletcher Moss. In an era of angry parents prowling the touchline, he says the majority of those he encounters appreciate the club's history in developing players and pushing them in the right direction. They know as well he has a season ticket at Old Trafford, insisting that does not matter when they ask him for advice on which professional club their child should sign for. He compares the process to looking at the record of a school.

'You look at the academic history: see what sort of qualifications the kids come out with. You look at the standard of the teachers. It's the same with football clubs. You look at Liverpool and their record over the last thirty years has been only second to United. You look at City: when was the last time they had an academy player come through? Micah Richards doesn't count because they signed him from Oldham. It's the same for Daniel Sturridge, who came from Coventry.

'City have got less heritage than United or Liverpool in bringing through players. Fair play to them, that's something they're trying to change. It's an impressive amount of money they've pumped into the Beswick area. I was invited there after I complained about the incident with the spotter. My God, it's impressive. But there's no feel; no history – no ghosts. If you do the same at the Cliff, and I know this sounds a bit soppy – but I can feel the ghosts: Duncan Edwards kicking a ball around, Dennis Viollet or George Best pushing a wheelbarrow. That place has got history. City will probably have it in fifteen years' time. But it won't happen overnight for them.'

When Fletcher Moss celebrated thirty years of existence in 2016, it was established that more than 5,000 young footballers had served the club, with another 400 or so signed up in the present. Horrocks is in his sixties now and has retired as a heating engineer. He got involved in junior football when he was forty because his thirteen-year-old son played for a team and they needed a manager. It wasn't always this way; the professional clubs trying every trick to convince parents they have the best interests of the kids at heart when they don't always.

'The Premier League is a business. It's not about football, really,' he says. 'When you see how the money was divided up to get Paul Pogba back to Man United, you realise that. Players are commodities. It sends the wrong impressions to parents. Every time they get told, "We're going to make your son the main man in this team." It rarely happens.'

When one Premier League club signed Fletcher Moss's under-8s goalkeeper, Horrocks says they offered his mum £9,000 a year in expenses. 'The mum is a single parent who doesn't work, so what is she supposed to do?' Horrocks wonders. He tells another story, where one club persuaded the parents of a ten-year-old from Newcastle to relocate. They bought the family a house and as part of the contract enrolled him into a private school that charges £20,000 a term. The agreement stipulated that he stayed in the school until he was sixteen, whether he was still at the club by then or not.

'You can understand why the parents make their decisions. Morally it stinks but aside from the money, when they promise education at a private school your kid is more than likely going to come out with some qualifications. These offers – let's have it right – you can't turn down because you are guaranteed to come out of a private school with at least a few GCSEs and therefore something to fall back on if the football doesn't work out.'

Many players at Fletcher Moss are, indeed, second-timers. Horrocks says he has come across children as young as eight who are demoralised by rejection, their love of the game harmed by sport becoming too serious too soon.

'Liverpool used to have a couple of dozen development centres around the north-west, though I think that number has decreased after the club decided to streamline their academy at every level – a good decision in my opinion,' he says. 'You were talking between twelve and fourteen players at three different age groups, sixes, sevens and eights. That's a lot of kids in the system, as many as a thousand. At the end of the season Liverpool would sign only twenty players from each age group – so sixty in total out of the thousand they've seen. Think about that. It means a lot of disappointment and sadness before kids are ready to handle it. It's how they are let go that will determine whether they stay in the game or fall out. At the moment the Football Association does not have an idea of the numbers that exit the game prematurely because there is no central registration system. What does that say about the priorities of the authorities?'

Horrocks thinks he knows the answer to his own question. Earlier that day, he'd received an email from the Manchester County FA outlining plans for a new facility at the Hough End playing fields, a couple of miles away. 'They call it a football hub,' Horrocks says, disdainfully. 'It means it's going to be in direct competition to anything we want to do here in terms of funding. It's a kick in the crutch. I think it means the funding for us will be nonexistent.'

He believes two more facilities will appear in Manchester, one in the north and another centrally. 'The FA will think they are developing football when, really, they'll be private, commercially driven entities. They'll end up pricing the facility out of people's grasp.'

What makes it even more challenging for Fletcher Moss is its location in Didsbury, which in political and social terms is considered an affluent area, meaning there are limited subsidies available for sporting initiatives. Of the 2,600 kids on the club's soccer school register, Horrocks says only 1 or 2 per cent come from Didsbury, with everyone else travelling from deprived inner-city suburbs like Fallowfield, Hulme and Moss Side for a better chance at making it, even though many families struggle to afford the costs, which explains why many will listen when financial inducements are offered from the professional clubs.

There are coaches within Manchester that run soccer schools as commercial enterprises. They know that Fletcher Moss is a multicultural success, with 52 per cent of the players classed as non-white. Horrocks has had requests to borrow 'four or five black kids' for photo shoots. 'A couple of Asian kids would be great as well . . .'

'I say no straight away,' Horrocks tells me. 'Aside from it being misleading and immoral, how could I say to the parents, "Come down for a photo shoot because your son is black?" They have enough on their plates without being sidetracked by stuff like that.'

Without the efforts and financial contributions of the parents, Fletcher Moss would not exist. The council charges the club £6,000 a year to lease Merseybank while it costs around £10,000 to make sure seventeen teams are insured for the year. The greatest challenge is for the mums and dads of the seven-year-olds because there are three seasons in a year and it costs £500 to enter the league each season. It means that seven players – or the families of seven players – have to come up with £70 every twelve weeks before paying out for anything else like subs, new shin pads, boots or travel. 'You can only go to the well so many times,' Horrocks recognises. 'On every team we make sure that the coach has a facility for a hardship case. One parent at the moment has three kids at the club in different teams. Twenty pounds per kid every month is a lot of money. We've asked her to pay a tenner each for the first two and the third one can play for free.'

At Merseybank, the bleak windows of the changing rooms are protected by railings, and barbed wire makes it more challenging to reach the flat Stramit roof. It looks like the sort of venue for grim punishments. You would not think a packed trophy cabinet is to be found inside, along with a wall of team photographs that include future Premier League players.

The club are trying to secure the changing rooms at Fletcher Moss Rangers as an asset through Manchester City Council. Horrocks says the building serves a purpose but is not fit for purpose considering the arrangement, with one central chamber, then showers and toilets in adjoining rooms. It means parents are not allowed to use the facilities at all when kids are around because, as he puts it, 'it's just not appropriate'. There is even a concern within Fletcher Moss that Manchester City Council might decide to offload the responsibility of the building, 'because they know it's a white elephant'.

'There's a chance we could get shafted,' Horrocks explains. 'We have no idea how the building was constructed. We also fear it's possible there might be a large amount of asbestos in the place. It's OK at the moment because it's encapsulated. But what would happen if the building was to be demolished or refurbished?'

Horrocks would like to flatten the changing room, replace it, and improve the standard of the pitches, which in winter become boggy because of its position, being on the banks of the River Mersey as it spills out of Manchester. 'It's not too much to ask for,' he says. 'Some kids are reluctant to leave their gear in the changing room because they think the locks don't work; they don't have a shower because the water's cold; the games get called off regularly because the council don't maintain the pitches properly. If the pitches were given to community groups like ours, they'd get looked after. The council love us being here at the moment because we do their work for them, but to get toilet rolls, we still need to ring up and ask for them to be supplied.

'We lease this place on a season-by-season arrangement. While we're here there's no vandalism. One or two residents don't like us being here, though, because of the cars and the crowds on a Sunday morning. But they need to be careful what they wish for because if we go, the space will be empty and where that's happened in other areas of Manchester, you've soon found Travellers moving in with their caravans.'

There is an ambition for Fletcher Moss Rangers to become a sports club rather than merely a football team, with representation in netball, basketball, handball, dodgeball and badminton. Didsbury has an ageing population and if the facilities were there, Horrocks says Fletcher Moss would run Zumba clubs for the elderly as well.

'Maybe there's too much money being made for football to care about helping out other sports,' Horrocks wonders. 'Someone with a bit of vision would realise that the football clubs in Spain and Germany are helped in terms of branding and financial stability by being a sports club.

'What drives me mad now is the hoops that a junior football club has to jump through to remain a football club,' he continues. 'Before a child can even kick a ball, they have to be coached by someone who has had a DBS check. They need the minimum of a level-one coaching certificate. Myself, every other coach and any parent who wants to get involved has to pay for it out of their own pocket. A level-one course is £150 a time. Level two is £350. Level three comes in at around £1,400. Pro licence? £4,000. Before moving up a level you also have to complete a number of courses, which means taking time off work and more hours over the weekend. Some of the courses you have to pay for. A lot of people can't afford all of this either.'

It was at one of those courses, labelled "Football for All", where Horrocks met Sir Trevor Brooking. Brooking was a keynote speaker and the face of the Football Association at the event.

'Sir Trevor was walking past, so I approached him,' Horrocks remembers. 'I said, "Sir Trevor, can I buttonhole you for a moment?" I asked him about his definition of grassroots football. "Yeah, it's the academies and the school of excellences – that's grassroots football."

'Stunned, I was. Stunned.

'To me, grassroots football is the dad who is kicking the ball around with his lad in the back garden. His wife is having a go at him for ruining the grass so he takes his lad to the nearest park. He's dodging around dog shit, burnt-out cars and broken bottles. The lad sees a couple of his mates playing and they start a team. They enter one of the local leagues.

'I outlined this to him. "That's grassroots football, Sir Trevor." And then I asked him, "Do you think the kids at academies just appear by magic?"

'Honestly, his eyes glazed over and then he walked away. I felt like shouting to him, "What's the weather like on your planet?"'

22

MANCHESTER, MELBOURNE, NEW YORK

MAURICE WATKINS WAS REGARDED AS THE BEST FOOTBALL LAWYER in the business. For 28 years he served Manchester United, seeing it all, having a hand in much. His first job had been to deal with Tommy Docherty's controversial dismissal after the manager's affair with the wife of United's physiotherapist Laurie Brown emerged. Watkins later made it on to the board and had an important role in Sir Alex Ferguson's appointment. A key advisor when the club became a plc – the decision which ultimately sent it into the clutches of Malcolm Glazer thirteen years later – Watkins's mark appeared on the contracts of almost every player United signed. Few were more important than Eric Cantona. If a single footballer helped create modern United as we see it today, it was Cantona. The Frenchman, though, would have gone to jail had it not been for the intervention of Watkins in the weeks after the forward kung-fu kicked a Crystal Palace supporter at Selhurst Park in 1995 for telling him to 'fuck off back to France'. Jurists later described it as 'the most famous common-assault case in the history of the English legal system'.

Watkins managed to get Cantona's two-week prison sentence reduced to community service. When Watkins decided there should be a press conference, Cantona agreed but only if he could speak. Just before it was about to begin, Cantona went to Watkins's hotel room with a piece of paper and he started to write. Cantona asked Watkins two questions: in English, what is the name of the big boat which catches fish, and what is the name of the big sea bird. 'Trawler and seagull,' Watkins replied. In front of the assembled media downstairs a few minutes later, the immortal lines appeared to flow from Cantona's soul. 'When seagulls follow the trawler it is because they think sardines will be thrown into the sea.' Cantona stood up, left the room. Watkins smiled a little awkwardly.

'I found Eric a good client, we got on very well,' Watkins says, wondering where the time has gone because it has been 22 years since the incident. 'He didn't miss meetings. Right from the word go he did not try and justify his actions. His explanation was clear. The decision by Manchester United to ban Eric for such a long period of time was unprecedented and it was a surprise when the FA decided to add more time. Perhaps that was something clubs looked at afterwards: "What if we do what we think is right and then get clobbered further for it?"

'Eric's case was unique,' Watkins concludes. 'You'll never get another one like that, where his name dominated headlines in the media for so long. I remember Eric going on holiday to the French West Indies where there was another incident – this time with a reporter. The fact of the matter was, the reporter had breached Eric's privacy and the French are very strict in law about that. Whereas here it was portrayed as Eric being the villain again, over in the French West Indies it was the reporter being arrested.

'The importance of Eric in Manchester United history is enormous,' Watkins says. 'Not only was he a very talented individual, the young players saw the way he trained and followed him. Considering Alex had so many young players around the team at that time, they gravitated towards this mysterious character, a brilliant hard-working footballer.'

Watkins is in his 70s but he still works six days a week, balancing his time between responsibilities as chairman of Barnsley Football Club, various other sporting boards and his role as a senior partner at law firm Brabners in Manchester city centre. I met him at his office just around the corner from the famous Albert Square (which will change in appearance if Gary Neville has his way) because he was as close as anyone to the events that changed Manchester United forever. To explain the landscape of north-west football, to explain the economic domination of the Premier League, to explain the obsession with youth recruitment and what it can mean for a club when they get it right, is, indeed, to explain Manchester United's financial capitalisation of their on-field success in the 1990s.

Watkins qualified as a solicitor in 1966 after completing a law degree at University College London. He confesses to having spent more time playing amateur football in the 1960s for his team, Old Mancunians, than standing on the Stretford End watching Bobby Charlton, Denis Law and George Best. He was a supporter of Manchester United rather than a fan, 'and there's an important distinction', he says. 'I was always able to switch off after a bad result and push on the next day.'

Watkins's career and involvement at United did not happen by design.

'I was working with a firm called James Chapman and Co. who were Manchester United's solicitors,' he recalls. 'I first got involved with the club when the senior partner Bill Royle died very suddenly. He had a meeting scheduled the following day with Manchester United. Somebody came around to my house with a file. "Sad news about Bill . . . but the meeting at Old Trafford tomorrow will go ahead and you're delegated to go and deal with it." This was in 1976. The first main job that I had was in relation to the termination of Tommy Docherty's contract. I went to Louis Edwards's house in Alderley Edge and Tommy was already there. I walked in, gave advice on the matter, waited in the kitchen for them to make a decision and a short while later the decision had been made for Tommy to go. I then helped with the draft of a press release which told the world that he'd gone. It was a surreal day because after meeting Louis and Tommy, I went to another job in Wilmslow. Driving home a few hours later my press release was read out across BBC radio. It was my introduction into just how newsworthy Manchester United actually was.'

Watkins admits there was little other work to do in those days because the club largely ran itself. There were few commercial contracts to advise upon and fewer signings because players did not move around as much. When in 1979 there was a rights issue after owner and chairman Louis Edwards tried to increase the shareholding body, it required Watkins's involvement. Edwards had started his working life as a family butcher in Salford.

'The rights issue was opposed, not by a shareholder, but by a supporter who did not think this was the right thing for the club to do,' Watkins recalls. 'He issued proceedings against each director for an injunction to stop the rights issue. It required a lot of detailed work done under considerable time pressures.

Louis had delegated his son, Martin, to deal with it and this was when I first worked with Martin closely. The club won the case but it really showed me that supporters have a view on everything, which is healthy because balancing expectations is part of the challenge. Because supporters often have an unrealistic view on what can or cannot be done, it takes strong leadership and persuasive arguments rather than ones that lead to alienation.'

When Louis Edwards died suddenly, Martin Edwards, aged 35, was the youngest board member at Old Trafford. He was determined to succeed his father and in 1980 his appointment to the position represented a broader trend where old-style chairmen were being phased out by a new entrepreneurial breed.

His first big decision was to sack Dave Sexton as manager. And yet, it is a reflection of United's status within English football that by the time they found a replacement, he was fourth choice. Edwards wanted Southampton's Lawrie McMenemy, but McMenemy's wife did not want to live in Manchester. Ipswich Town's Bobby Robson was then approached but Robson believed Ipswich were in a stronger position than United. Ron Saunders, meanwhile, turned Edwards down flat – refusing to even enter a discussion. Edwards spoke of a 'bleak period' where United did not have the money to compete at the highest level. Inconceivably, United were struggling to find a manager – a solution was only found when journalist John Maddock phoned Edwards and suggested that Ron Atkinson was willing to talk.

Though there were good days under Atkinson, who won the FA Cup twice, United always fell away at crucial times during league campaigns. In 1986, it was decided Atkinson should be removed. The name of the board member who first suggested Aberdeen's Alex Ferguson as a replacement changes depending on who you listen to.

'The Manchester United board was very small; Martin, myself, Mike Edelson and Bobby Charlton,' Watkins explains. 'There was a discussion about making a managerial change and each person was given the opportunity to speak about who they'd want to bring in. I've always claimed it was my idea first about Alex, though I'm sure the others might suggest otherwise. I'd had contact with him in 1984 when we signed Gordon Strachan from Aberdeen. It was a complicated transfer because it transpired that Gordon had signed more than one contract and Cologne had reached a prior deal for him to go there. As a result of Manchester United's interest, Gordon wanted to come to Old Trafford instead of Cologne. Reliant on that agreement, Ray Wilkins was being sold to AC Milan. It was my job to untangle the law between UEFA, FIFA, Cologne and Aberdeen. At a meeting in Paris we finally resolved it as part of a tripartitie agreement.

'Throughout the process, Alex had been involved and though his interest belonged to Aberdeen and making sure they received what was owed to them, his application had impressed me. His track record with Aberdeen was clear to each board member, though. We all felt that he had a considerable interest in youth development and that ultimately he was the right person to take the club forward because of this. In the years before his appointment, more money was being spent on players than ever before following the first million-pound transaction for Trevor Francis between Birmingham City and Nottingham Forest in 1979. Remembering that Manchester United had won the European Cup for the first time in 1968 using many youth-team players, we felt as though the past should be a reference point for the future.'

It took Ferguson seven seasons to deliver the first of what would be thirteen league titles. By the end of the 1980s there had been questions about his suitability as manager. Gates at Old Trafford had dropped alarmingly and Martin Edwards was concerned about the level of finance that would be needed to make United great again. He was willing to sell the club for £20million and on at least two separate occasions in the 80s negotiations with other parties began. After Robert Maxwell was deemed too publicity-hungry to broker an agreement in 1984, Michael Knighton got closer, and so confident was he of completing the deal, he appeared on Old Trafford's pitch on the opening day of the 1989/90 season in a full replica United kit, juggling the ball before striking a shot into an empty net. Knighton, of course, later went on to own Carlisle United, but he did not get United for a combination of reasons, partly because he did not appreciate the size of the divide between the boardroom and the terraces at the time but mainly because he did not have the money and was relying on two business colleagues who he quickly fell out with after the Old Trafford pitch stunt.

'I know Martin was very much concerned about the amount of money it would take to make Manchester United successful again,' Watkins says. 'He wasn't an incredibly wealthy man. The ground needed developing and so did the team. He was looking for someone who might be able to take that burden off him. There was no Premier League and no sizeable television contracts and so, if you wanted to advance your football club, cash injections had to come from the major shareholder, i.e. Martin.

'I wasn't at the meeting where he and Michael [Knighton] sat down and discussed figures but Michael persuaded him to sell his stake for £10million or so, which I thought was a bit of a steal. When Michael pulled away from the table,

Martin decided to float the club on the Stock Exchange and this enabled Martin to raise funds not only to clear significant debt but also rebuild the Stretford End. Of course, once you become a plc and your shares are listed you are always open at some stage to a takeover because if a buyer bought a certain amount of shares he could force the sale of any remaining ones. And that's what happened.'

Following the Hillsborough disaster and the Taylor Report that insisted upon all-seater stadiums being built in England's top flight, the construction of the Stretford End was paid for by higher ticket prices and in 1992, outraged United fans formed a group called HOSTAGE (Holders of Season Tickets Against Gross Exploitation). The loss of the terraced stand was bemoaned as an example of the movement away from football's working-class roots. Despite United's on-pitch development, many fans were unhappy with the direction United were heading off it. In 1995, IMUSA (the Independent Manchester United Supporters' Association) was formed but Edwards was not prepared to entertain them, feeling that no matter how much he tried to please it would never be enough. Edwards reasoned that United already had supporters on the board anyway, with Les Olive and Mike Edelson. Watkins was another.

IMUSA were unhappy with the increasing commercialism of the club. In 1992, Edwards appointed Edward Freedman, who had led a merchandising revolution at Tottenham Hotspur, a club with a much bigger turnover than United in 1991 and his arrival coincided with the increased revenues from Sky Television and their deal to cover Premier League football. While the majority of clubs used the new revenues to improve their squads, United invested in Old Trafford itself, the stadium becoming bigger and bigger while manager Alex Ferguson turned instead to cheaper – and more talented – options from United's youth system.

Ferguson's team pushed into the Premier League era as the competition's dominant force. The creation of the Premier League had been rather like Brexit. The Football League had run the English top flight for 104 seasons but in 1992, the top clubs in the country wanted structural change.

'The debate stemmed from a simple question: who is going to be in charge of our lives as football clubs?' Watkins remembers. 'Philip Carter [Everton] and David Dein [Arsenal] were effectively booted out of their positions as chairman and vice chairman of the Football League and many of the clubs agreed that the tail was wagging the dog: no matter what we wanted to do, we'd find ourselves outvoted. It contributed towards a wider feeling about destiny and being in control of what was happening. Of course, how do you do that? It's not so easy.

The Football League had changed its articles which meant it required two years' notice if you wanted to leave. That presented its own problems, particularly in sport. We found out, though, that the Football League hadn't gone to the FA to get the article changed as they should have done. This resulted in a High Court case which the Football League lost. In the meantime, a founder members' agreement was signed between the clubs that were going to break away. Though there had been lots of meetings to get to this point, the terms of the new constitution were agreed within a day and that in the main related to the way television money would be distributed and shared.'

Watkins refers to the founder members' agreement as 'a declaration of independence'. The genius was its simplicity, particularly relating to the issue of money earned from domestic television rights: 50 per cent would be shared among all participating clubs, 25 per cent shared based on TV appearances, with the remaining quarter covering final league position.

'At that time overseas rights were not very lucrative so that income was lumped in with revenue like sponsorship and shared equally. Some clubs are claiming that this should change because overseas TV income has risen considerably and certain clubs have higher profiles in certain areas of the world and this has driven the interest, so they should have more of the profit. But the founder members' agreement is set in stone and it contributes towards why the Premier League is competitive. This is the basis of why the league was set up. Healthy competition is ultimately healthy for the clubs with the greatest financial weight, because otherwise the league might become very boring and predictable and without clubs there is no League.'

Capitalism, though, had eaten so far into football that when Malcolm Glazer, the billionaire owner of Tampa Bay Buccaneers, decided to buy United in 2004, it should have felt very predictable. In 1999 the government had blocked Rupert Murdoch and BSkyB's £623million bid to take over from Martin Edwards following a six-month investigation by the Monopolies and Mergers Commission. Stephen Byers, Labour's Trade and Industry Secretary, announced that it would be anti-competitive, against the public interest, and would damage the quality of British football.

Though a famous banner appeared at Old Trafford warning Glazer, 'Manchester United Is Not For Sale', the opposite had long been the reality. The sad irony is it had been the willingness of fans to buy shares in 1991 which helped the club become a plc in the first place. United's shares were listed on the stock market and therefore offered for sale every single day. All a buyer needed to do was ring a stockbroker and buy enough to force a purchase. And so, while flotation helped Manchester United rise into what it became, it also made it vulnerable. 'Becoming a plc meant we were always in play, that's a good way of putting it,' Watkins concludes.

*

Bruno Fornaroli was born in Salto, the remote border town in Uruguay where the land meets Argentina. Fornaroli was twelve years old when he travelled across the country by bus for a trial with Nacional, one of the two biggest football clubs in Montevideo. On the bus sitting in front of him that day was another twelve-year-old who'd been home visiting relatives, having already moved to Montevideo from Salto. Luis Suárez would become one of the world's great centre-forwards but back then, Fornaroli would be chosen ahead of him in Nacional's youth teams. Coaches believed that Suárez's impact was felt more when he was introduced as a substitute.

While Suárez followed a path to Groningen, to Ajax, to Liverpool and to Barcelona, and while Edinson Cavani went to Palermo, to Napoli and Paris St Germain, unless you are Uruguayan or unless you watch Australian A League football you probably haven't heard of Fornaroli, even though within the City Football Group – the central services facility created by Manchester City's Abu Dhabi owners – he is regarded as one of the company's best signings.

Like Suárez, Fornaroli moved to Europe early but flopped at Sampdoria in Italy then Panathinaikos in Greece, clubs he did not score a single goal for. He was 27 and back in his homeland with Danubio and not doing particularly well when a scouting report was delivered to Manchester, urging further investigation into the striker. Despite the lack of goals, other data backed the theory up and a decision was taken by the City Football Group to buy the forward, not for Manchester City but for Melbourne City.

Across the next two seasons Fornaroli scored 48 goals, proceeding to win all of the A League's individual awards. His story reflects not only the effectiveness of the City Football Group's scouting networks across the globe but also just how a project which began with Manchester City has widened to the point where decisions taken in Manchester impact on the future of football clubs not only in Melbourne but New York and Yokohama – other places where the City Football Group now have a footprint. If the history of Manchester United explains where football has been in the north-west, City's present surely details where it is going.

While Manchester United emerged from the 1990s having changed largely through the decisions of Sir Alex Ferguson but also Martin Edwards, Bobby Charlton and, indeed, Maurice Watkins, the City Football Group are pushing into the future having bought five football clubs across five of the six continents, having signed deals with five other clubs to become training and scouting partners, having built an academy in one of the continents where they do not own a professional club, and having made ties with clubs in Spain and Holland where young players go to earn work permits or gain experience in a first-team environment. It is fair to say that Manchester City, a club that was competing in the third tier of English football when Manchester United were treble winners, are not just Manchester City any more.

Manchester City's owners believe their investment has not just changed a football club's image but the community that exists immediately around it as well, with social living standards improving in the areas nearest the Etihad Stadium in east Manchester, areas like Ardwick, Ancoats and Miles Platting – albeit areas earmarked for regeneration as part of the Commonwealth Games legacy, long before they arrived. There remains a frustration that it is regularly assessed how much City have spent, rather than how much they have grown or given back.

Upon purchasing the club from Thaksin Shinawatra, the former Prime Minister of Thailand, in 2008 City became the richest club in the world overnight. Abu Dhabi were not afraid of telling everyone they wanted to be successful; since then, the club has been accused of everything from financial doping to distorting the value of players in the transfer market and thus weakening the chances of fair competition. City deemed it necessary to spend £200million a season in order to take the club from lower mid-table in the Premier League and into the Champions League, a competition which gave not only huge revenues from prize money but also an increased global profile, meaning new fans and illustrious sponsors.

While critics like Juventus president Andrea Agnelli have attacked City for creating a 'false economy' in their accounts (City have been able to broker deals like a record £400million with Etihad to become their stadium sponsor, despite the airline being owned by the Abu Dhabi government and both having links to Sheikh Mansour, a member of the Abu Dhabi royal family), City consider their financial position to be an undisputed success. The club's losses may have stood at £200million when their revenues were only at £80million but now, because of the high investment, the revenues have stretched to around the £400million mark and the club is closer to self-sufficiency than it has been since Abu Dhabi arrived. It is even believed inside City that the club's growth will be studied in the business schools of the future: how a football club can accrue so much debt so quickly and post a profit soon after.

This prompted Mansour to think about how City's growth could accelerate further and, indeed, whether the model could be achieved elsewhere, albeit without the scale of £200million losses. Places with potential were identified. Melbourne came first in Australia, where football is now played by more people than cricket, and in 2015 Melbourne City was born – with Bruno Fornaroli being sent there. New York was identified next, a sports-mad city which did not have a modern soccer rivalry. Though New York Cosmos had returned to the scene after its emergence as the most glamorous football club in the NASL during the late 1970s, Cosmos have not managed to rejoin the MLS, leaving New York Red Bull as the state's only representative in the top division. Gates as big as 40,000 have been achieved since New York City arrived on the scene. It had cost $80million for City just to enter a franchise in the MLS in 2015. In 2017, when new clubs from Minnesota and Atlanta made the same decision, it cost each club $120million to participate – the figures reflect the growth of the competition. The next big decision for New York City, who have gone bigger than Fornaroli with their recruitment, signing Andrea Pirlo, Frank Lampard and David Villa – players with 319 caps for Italy, England and Spain between them – will be where to move next. Though there is a ground-share agreement with the New York Yankees, the baseball stadium is not fit for purpose and discussions about a new site have taken place. It has been recognised that New York Red Bulls are based in New Jersey, that they sometimes struggle to get crowds and, therefore, New York City are desperate to find a location in one of the five boroughs of New York, though that has proven challenging because of land prices.

Decisions about New York City's future are not just made in New York. They are made in Abu Dhabi and they are made in Manchester. Step inside Manchester City's sprawling Etihad Campus, and the reception area is decorated like a boutique fashion house with the badges of four clubs on the wall and the names of the cities they represent: Manchester, Melbourne, New York and Yokohama. There, in big letters, are the words: "Beautiful football/Football citizenship/a Global approach", and this is a reminder that you are in the landing station for the City Football Group.

The ambition from Abu Dhabi when they arrived in 2008 had been to create something that was unique – the best in class. There were subsequent visits to different facilities across the world determining what would work at City and what would not. The former training ground at Carrington had been like a Tardis, apparently small in appearance but vast and more complex when inside. It was possible to walk for five minutes without seeing anyone. A decision was taken that the Etihad Campus had to be big while feeling smaller, so the design was important – deciding which communities within the club needed to connect with each other. Having been to Tottenham Hotspur's new L-shaped training ground in Enfield, it was recognised that the hydrotherapy pool was too far away from the first-team changing area, which meant it wasn't being utilised in the most efficient way. City's first-team dressing room is circular in shape and different doors now lead to the gym, the players' lounge, the pitches, the medical area and finally, of course, the hydrotherapy pool. City had recruited Brian Marwood, a former Sheffield Wednesday and Arsenal winger, from Nike to oversee the £200million change which transformed a previously neglected brownfield site into 'one of the best sporting facilities in the world', as City describe it, which also included sixteen pitches, its own 7,000-seater reserve stadium, an accommodation block and a sixth-form college to serve the local community. Marwood, a decent man, was determined to create a culture like the one he had seen at Nike, where staff took pride in their place of work and did not see it as a stepping stone to a better future elsewhere but rather a place where they'd stay forever because they were treated well and liked it. It is here, beyond the dotcom-style chill-out zones for workers with salad bars and water coolers, that the biggest decisions are made about City's global strategy, where Ferran Soriano, the group's chief executive officer, outlines his plans for the clubs in Manchester, Melbourne, New York and Yokohama.

The depth of management inside the City Football Group is unparalleled. Each club has an appointed chief operating officer who runs the business and a football director who takes on football-related responsibilities. At Manchester City Omar Berrada and Txiki Begiristain fill these roles, both of whom worked with Soriano at Barcelona. Meanwhile in New York there is Jon Patricof and Claudio Reyna – Reyna being a former Manchester City midfielder. In Melbourne there is Scott Munn and Michael Petrillo.

Underpinning this structure, you then have the shared services of the City Football Group, which is a global resource that provides help to each club with everything from scouting and recruitment to analytics and innovation. The central-service figures act like auditors. The clubs operate with autonomy but there are regular checks that each one is maintaining a level of compliance with the methodology set in Manchester; that the decisions taken are collaborative and that everyone is benefiting.

The arrangement is geared towards helping Manchester City as well. When a player suffers a complicated hamstring injury in Melbourne, the idea is that research is shared so if the same thing happens to a City player in Manchester, recovery times can theoretically be improved. If opponents try new free kicks or corners in America, a package of video content can be sought and then utilised by Pep Guardiola, Manchester City's manager. Manchester, New York, Melbourne and Yokohama share coaches, physios, doctors, scouts – even press officers. Patrick Vieira coached Manchester City's Elite Development Squad for three years before earning a secondment to New York City to develop his management skills at a senior level in the MLS. When Manchester City bought Yangel Herrera, a Venezuelan midfielder in the mould of Vieira, it was decided there was no better place for him to learn his trade than New York. The fact that the City Football Group's tentacles stretch so far makes it easier to attract young players particularly, because recruitment staff can make the case that if life does not work out for them in Manchester, they might later find their level in other appealing cities.

It is perhaps Manchester City's youth recruitment strategy that has led to the fiercest criticism, especially after it was revealed that the Football Association had issued the club with a fine for making illegal approaches for players and banned them from signing ten-to eighteen-year-olds contracted at other Premier League clubs for two years.

Despite Liverpool's interest, City had been able to sign, for example, Steven Gerrard's cousin Bobby Duncan, who became the first player at any international level for England to score a hat-trick against Brazil for the under-16 team in November 2016. City were able to sweep up the best talent across the north-west because of their financial clout, which included the offer of inducements like private education. City executives say this decision was taken after Michael Johnson decided to retire before his 24th birthday. Johnson had been expected to emerge as the next Colin Bell, a former midfielder who now has a stand named after him. Yet Johnson's Premier League career amounted to just 45 games. This prompted City to ask questions of themselves: how could they help with their responsibilities, their parentage of players? Despite his abilities and the confidence other people had in him, as a professional, Johnson could not find peace in his mind. As a club, City found a conclusion in private education. If a player's time could be divided between City and higher-achieving schools then there would be more chance of the end product being prepared for what followed. It also meant that if a player did not make it as a footballer, improved academic results would mean he would have a future elsewhere – at a time when so many other drop-outs have nothing else left to turn to.

It had been a delicate operation preserving City's identity while progressing at the same time. Before it was taken over by Shinawatra, City's academy had produced local players capable of playing in a struggling Premier League team but the challenge is now much harder because they have to potentially be better than what they have competing in the Champions League. The financial rewards of the Champions League mean it can't be considered a stage for players to learn on the job, risking City's new-found status among the European elite, and so the chances of making it to the first team are harder than they've ever been, even though the depth of young talent available to City is greater than it was before.

There is a feeling that the combination of high finance and limited opportunity is leading to the football equivalent of a brain drain. The data from the City Football Group's shared services department says that in the last decade of Champions League competition, of the players involved at every club that has reached the quarter-finals, 83.5 per cent were playing senior minutes at the age of eighteen.

Manchester City's solution has been to forge a partnership with NAC Breda in Holland. During the 2016/17 campaign five youngsters – three Manchester-born – experienced senior football for the first time in the Dutch second division.

There is an appetite, though, to bring a lower-league English football club under the City Football Group umbrella. Potentially, a club like Oldham Athletic could use the training facilities at the Etihad Campus because there is more than enough space. Oldham could also benefit from shared central service information. Financially, any arrangement would surely bring some stability for a club like Oldham after years of insecurity. In return, City would have a level of control: being able to see their players in an environment every day on site, while playing for Oldham and gaining English Football League experience. Where would that leave Oldham, though? Would their interests ever be served first again? Manchester, Melbourne, New York, Yokohama, indeed, and Oldham doesn't seem to fit any sort of fair narrative at all.

Early in 1998, Dennis Tueart, a director at Manchester City, received a call from Raymond Donn, a friend of the ousted former chairman Peter Swales.

Donn, like Maurice Watkins over at Manchester United, was a solicitor and his influence would grow, eventually becoming vice president of the team he supported. Though it never came close to happening, Donn had told Tueart that his connections with Juventus in Italy could turn City into one of their feeder clubs.

Six years before Manchester City had been the fifth-best team in the country under Peter Reid. Now in the third tier and having been being beaten by Stockport County, Bury and Oldham, City were struggling to be the fifth-best team in the Manchester area.

'Raymond's proposition wasn't an attractive one to me anyway because City were much bigger than a feeder club and even though we were struggling, every decision should not be made with finance in mind,' says Tueart, whose overhead kick against his boyhood team Newcastle United won the League Cup in 1976 – City's last trophy before Abu Dhabi came along and helped them to the FA Cup in 2011.

I wanted to meet Tueart, a spirited character, because he connected the past with the present: he'd been a successful player, a successful businessman and a successful director; a combination that so few footballers manage to achieve. There are notes, files and ledgers on matters of all kinds stored in the drawers of his office in Cheshire and one of them relates to the donations made into the players' pool when he reached the FA Cup final with Sunderland in 1973, beating Leeds United 1–0.

Because of the team's success, the workers of Sunderland were happy and that meant absenteeism was at an all-time low and production at an all-time high. And so, among the contributions from the local companies like Joblings who made Pyrex pots and pans, there was a £1,850 total donation from Sunderland's ship-builders. 'It was the corporate way of the companies thanking us,' Tueart says proudly. 'A salary or a bonus meant we had to pay tax. Through donations, the players kept everything. The players and the fans weren't different people back then. We didn't earn very much money at all, really.'

Tueart's view of the game began to change five years later when he made the bold decision to leave Manchester City for New York Cosmos, making him the first England international to join a North American Soccer League club on a full-time contract. He speaks about this experience as though it were an awakening: 'It allowed me to see into the future,' he says. 'The Cosmos were owned by Warner Communications, a multimillion-dollar organisation. In England the football clubs were owned by the local entrepreneur. The Warner

Building was in Rockefeller Plaza, Manhattan, and the Cosmos offices were on the nineteenth floor. As the elevator doors opened there was a life-size picture of Pelé and Franz Beckenbauer on one side. On the other side there was Carlos Alberto and Dennis Tueart.'

'We lived on the thirty-sixth floor of the Galaxy Tower building on the banks of the Hudson on the New Jersey side overlooking Manhattan,' he recalls. 'Remember that plane that landed on the river? It would have glided past my bedroom window. Every morning I would look across at that glorious skyline. It was an exciting time. Before Frank Lampard went over there to play a few years ago I bumped into him. He was a member of my gym at Hale Country Club. I said, "Frank, you'll love New York – unbelievable place for successful sports franchises."'

Tueart began to appreciate how closely business and sport were linked, how fitting in to a dressing room that featured thirteen nationalities was a foretaste of the mercenary culture that pervades today's Premier League, along with staggered kick-off times that are more convenient with television rather than fans, and private club jets and brand-flogging tours to exotic places.

'The Cosmos were forty years ahead of the game,' he insists. 'Warner Brothers promoted the tours. For pre-season, we went to Bermuda, the Bahamas, across the Caribbean, South America. We'd go to Europe, Asia and Australasia. The foreign players were considered non-resident aliens and it meant we could only stay in the country for six months a year. The rest of the calendar was filled with exhibition matches around the world, promoting US soccer. It was Hollywood on the road. The friendlies were worth $50,000 a game to the club – far more lucrative than domestic matches. We played Argentina a few months after they won the World Cup in 1978. We were treated like royalty wherever we went. None of the English clubs were doing this at the time.'

Ultimately, both the Cosmos and the NASL would disband.

'It was the right place, the right strategy but the wrong time,' Tueart says. 'The Cosmos were throwing money at the foreign players but the other clubs couldn't match it. I was on £500 a week in England and £1,500 a week over there. Football – or soccer – was brand new to a lot of cities and they were ready to get excited but there was a poor product in front of them and the NASL could not get a regular TV contract. ABC tried one year but the ratings were so poor, it only lasted a year. They'd go once or twice but they wouldn't go again. American crowds are demanding. The competitiveness needs to be there for the competition to flourish. You can't have an inverted pyramid where the top sides are strong but the bottom sides are made of mush. That's why the Premier League is so popular. You rarely get an easy game.'

Tueart's successful running of a video and conference production company as well as his passion for Manchester City led him back to Maine Road in the mid-1990s.

'The set-up was a shambles,' he admits. 'If you're talking about structure and reporting lines, we didn't have any. In my first board meeting it came to any other business. I said, "Yeah, we need to appoint a PR officer because I get the impression anybody can ring a number at this club and whoever picks up the phone will give them the inside track." Our fans were getting misleading information – confusing information. "We need to think as a club and make sure there is one direct line of communication rather than someone's daft opinion." At all football clubs, you'll always get some daft opinions.

'There were decent people in the organisation but few were aspirational,' he continues. 'They were happy to run a corner shop. Manchester City, with due respect, was a bit bigger than a corner shop. I'd been at the club as a player and seen how big it could be. Fifty thousand people were attending games at Maine Road. But when you have the people running the show being happy to come in at nine and go home at five, you know they are unwilling to have their limits pushed and ultimately this impacts upon the club. One of our directors used to say, "Our best salesman is the fax machine." He thought that anything with Manchester City's crest on would sell. It shows you there was a limited amount of vision. Admittedly, we had other issues to prioritise first. The team we inherited from the previous regime was in poor shape.'

Tueart quickly realised that his position as a director was one that could lose him friends. He had played with Joe Royle at City and was significant in Royle's recruitment as manager. Royle would help City return to the Premier League but then struggled to adjust when the transfer market became global, 'blue collar' British players being phased out in favour of individuals like George Weah and Paulo Wanchope.

'Joe was excellent at getting the most out of a lesser quality of player,' Tueart says. 'But when you have a former World Footballer of the Year and a precocious Costa Rican, the task is slightly different. He fell out with Paulo in a big way. We decided to support him even though he was struggling in the Premier League and we could have sacked him for the things that happened but we didn't. He struggled thereon in. Joe couldn't manage the change of the new demands of the Premier League. He had thirteen great years at Oldham and then did exactly for us what we hoped for. He got the club to the level we wanted to be at but couldn't keep us there because there was a different dynamic of players. Eventually, a decision needed to be made and Joe had to go. As a director, you can only offer strong, convincing opinion. With the managers I worked with, I'd like to challenge them. Debate is healthy. If they came back to me with a strong opinion of their own, proving they'd analysed situations, I'd back them if we could afford it. It's the directors' duty to ask difficult questions. Unfortunately, Joe no longer had convincing answers. I still regard Joe as my friend but I don't think I'm his.'

With struggles on the pitch and rivals Manchester United sprinting away from them financially, perhaps the most important decision taken at City was the one to move from Maine Road in the south of the city to what was then called the City of Manchester Stadium in the east.

'We had to dig down and add an extra tier of seats, losing the running track, even though the authorities didn't want that to happen,' Tueart remembers. 'It was the best decision we ever made. David Bernstein [the chairman] dug his heels in and said, "We'll not move there unless it's a football-dedicated stadium." The deal with the city council was for any gates over 34,000 – the capacity of Maine Road – we'd pay rent. It was on a sliding scale so for the last 5,000, the council received a bigger portion of the revenue. The value of Maine Road was then ploughed back into the new ground. I was on the stadium design sub-committee and the two things I was after were a good pitch for our players and because of my conference experience great function rooms, so we could generate revenue on non-match days. The stadium simply had to make money for us.'

Abu Dhabi would see the potential of the new surroundings. Before that takeover, though, Thaksin Shinawatra bought Manchester City, having failed to purchase Liverpool eighteen months earlier. Tueart and chairman David Bernstein had changed the way they dealt with agents over their transfer dealings, mainly because everything previously had gone through Jerome Anderson. Now, Anderson was advising Shinawatra and suddenly, Tueart's presence as a director was no longer required, which did not surprise him.

Tueart, who still works hard at his conference business at 67, continues to hold strong views about the game.

'I'm disappointed they're not regulated more,' he says of agents. 'There are a lot of barrow boys. The players – kids – they don't have a clue. There are decent agents but there are too many of the other kind, the ones who take advantage of the players and take an unfair percentage of the profit that doesn't reflect what they actually do.

'At football clubs, you also have more grey suits. Rather than looking after the business, they are looking after their own fiefdoms.

'Many foreign owners see Premier League football as a money pit and I am a bit concerned the foreign owners might change the constitution of the Premier League,' he says. 'They see the upside of the game: the excitement and the profile it offers. It's exciting for egos when their names and pictures appear on the back pages of newspapers as headlines. Business practices that made them successful in the first place get forgotten. You can waste ten million pounds as easy as you can waste ten pounds.'

Tueart believes football, however, is nowhere near reaching its financial ceiling. He thinks back to his time in New York.

'My old club Sunderland received just under a hundred million pounds for finishing bottom and Real Madrid received less for winning the Champions League,' he says. 'When you think about the domestic revenues generated by Premier League clubs being less than the NFL and when you think the Super Bowl audience was 170 million people across the US and Canada, you think about what the Premier League could do considering the NFL has North America and the Premier League has a global market. The potential is frightening.'

SEASON'S END

ON THE PENULTIMATE WEEKEND OF THE 2016/17 PREMIER LEAGUE season, Pep Guardiola was asked about the amount of money he would spend in the transfer market over the summer, what it might mean for the young players at Manchester City's academy and their chances of progressing into his first team. Guardiola, the Catalan hired with the intention of winning the Champions League, had finished his first year in English football without a trophy. He was shaking his head, intercepting the question before it had even finished. 'The problem we have with the second team is that they don't compete,' he said. 'The gap between the second team and the first team is so big. They play between each other in the small ages with no spectators. The quality is there.' Guardiola explained that the reserves in Spain and Germany, the European countries that over the last decade have offered the most debuts to teenagers, play against other professional sides, sometimes in front of 40,000 people. 'They are playing against guys who are twenty-eight, twenty-nine and thirty years old. That is the best way to learn. Here, they don't compete.' When Guardiola spent £75million on players from Portugal and Brazil within two weeks of the season finishing, it was a reminder that even though he and City wanted the structure of English football to change, though money can buy you influence and respect, it cannot buy you everything.

Across the city the season ended with the news that Manchester United's debt under the Glazer family had risen to £464million – around £150million more than any other club in Europe. A Footballing Landscape report commissioned by UEFA revealed that while debt levels across the continent had decreased each season for the past five years – something UEFA puts down to its Financial Fair Play regulations – United's had grown by 25 per cent in 2016 alone. One of United's new contracts had been for Jesse Lingard, the old Fletcher Moss player. Having played only seventy games for United, Lingard's four-year deal was worth £100,000 a week. Meanwhile, the changing rooms over at the Merseybank Playing Fields continued smelling of damp.

Slightly to the north, Salford City's Moor Lane ground – thanks to the direction of Gary Neville – was renovated and met grading standards and though Salford would not earn promotion having suffered disappointment in the Conference North play-offs, their drive towards professionalism continued with nine new signings from clubs in higher leagues announced by 1 June. Droylsden, meanwhile, had signed nobody by that date.

Things were looking up for Bolton Wanderers, who won automatic promotion back to the Championship in spite of low attendances, and while Oldham Athletic ensured they would remain a League One club for the twentieth year in a row, relegation to English football's bottom tier was only avoided in the final weeks of the campaign and Simon Corney, the club's owner, was still desperate to sell.

Stockport were improving steadily under Jim Gannon, who was right about Danny Lloyd, his top scorer whose efforts were recognised with a move to League One Peterborough. Over in Winsford, 1874 Northwich decided to appoint Ian Street's assistant as their new manager in the interests of continuity, while Witton Albion, who lost to them having fielded a reserve team on that cold Thursday night ahead of vital league fixtures, saw their campaign end in promotion despite a points deduction for fielding an ineligible player. As for Northwich Victoria, they headed into the summer not knowing what league they would compete in during the 2017/18 season due to uncertainty about which stadium they would play at, with a further demotion a distinct possibility.

Towards Merseyside, there were mixed outcomes. Tranmere did not return to the Football League but Jeremy Corbyn, the Labour leader, made an impromptu stage appearance at the Wirral Live concert held at Prenton Park, much to the delight of Tranmere Rovers and Mark Palios, with Prenton Park suddenly appearing a relevant venue. Corbyn was a week away from losing an election where he would end up somehow seeming to be more a more popular figure than the actual winner, the forlorn Conservative Theresa May.

Home Bargains made it past Ferrybridge Progressive, winning 2–1, but their run in the FA Sunday Cup ended in the next round. Frustratingly for Jimmy Vaughan, the semi-final was going well until Peter Mason, the young midfielder, was sent off for serious foul play and, with the extra man advantage, the north east's Hardwick Social went through instead.

City of Liverpool and Litherland REMYCA would meet again in the North West Counties League first division play-off final and, this time, Paul Manning's team would prevail. Among the near 1,300 crowd in May were dozens of small groups of young lads enjoying themselves together in a way they perhaps might not be able to at Anfield.

While Jürgen Klopp's Liverpool finished the season by qualifying for the Champions League and, in turn, returned to Europe just at a time when the rest of the country was thinking about how Britain might leave it in a very different sense, Joe Anderson, the Everton-supporting mayor of the city, was willing to relinquish his position to become Labour's candidate in Walton, the area that Everton will leave when their new stadium is built. Anderson was determined to take the fight to the Conservatives in Parliament, to try and make people understand the damage being done through austerity measures. Anderson, though, was overlooked by Labour's National Executive Committee, a decision which prompted him to conclude that Labour is 'not always a meritocracy'.

Up the coast, Southport were in turmoil. Relegation from the Conference National was followed by Charlie Clapham's decision to sell after 37 years in charge and the new owners, two local businessmen, were treated with suspicion. Portchat had got its wish but – suddenly and mysteriously – the Internet forum was closed down. By then, Liam Watson had already been made redundant by email.

After an Omar Beckles goal sent Accrington Stanley into the fourth round of the FA Cup where they would lose to Middlesbrough, it was revealed that Mino Raiola, Paul Pogba's agent, had trousered more than £40million from the deal that took the French midfielder back to Manchester United. Andy Holt, the Accrington owner, attacked the Premier League for its 'largesse', accusing it of 'destroying the game' and pointing out that his club's annual budget was twenty times smaller than the fee paid to Raiola. The Premier League responded to Holt's accusations in a passive/aggressive and altogether arrogant manner, asking whether he wanted the organisation to withdraw its funding to lower-league clubs. The following month, Mike Garlick, the chairman of neighbours Burnley, announced that the club would spend to 'new levels' to ensure it remained in the top flight, after Sean Dyche secured safety with three fixtures to go.

Preston North End did not reach the play-offs but Fleetwood did, only to lose to Bradford City. AFC Fylde went up, winning the Conference North title at a canter as expected, and somehow Jim Bentley kept Morecambe in the Football League before it was announced that his players had not been paid again, leading towards a summer of uncertainty. Though Barrow's narrow defeat to Rochdale at Holker Street in the FA Cup was watched by 4,414, only 956 turned up the following Tuesday when struggling Southport were the opponents; figures that will remind Paul Casson of how much work he still has to do to convince his townspeople of the club's worth.

Finally, Carlisle played Exeter City three times in the month of May, winning their final league game of the season in Devon before drawing the first leg of the play-off semi-final at Brunton Park 3–3. Carlisle's players must have believed the tie was heading to extra time in the return having equalised in the ninetieth minute, but Exeter would head to Wembley at Carlisle's expense after scoring a winner in the fifth minute of injury time. With a 350-mile journey home to contend with on a Thursday night, it would be understandable if Carlisle's supporters concluded they were cursed after all.

ACKNOWLEDGEMENTS

THIS IS MY FIFTH BOOK, OR SIXTH IF YOU COUNT SOMEONE ELSE'S autobiography, but there are always people to thank – several who have featured on this page before, others new to the process.

Firstly, I hope you agree that Alex Baillie's excellent photography adds a layer of feeling to this project that perhaps hasn't been present in my previous efforts.

From deCoubertin, James Corbett has always been very encouraging and understanding of flexible needs. Leslie Priestley's patience and diligence in design and layout has been noted; Ian Allen's editorial skills, invaluable. Jack Gordon Brown and Megan Pollard too, for their organisation and enthusiasm.

I am fortunate to count Ian Herbert, formerly of the Independent and now of the Daily Mail as a friend as well as a working colleague. Ian is someone who always gives the right advice, someone who cares deeply about journalistic standards. In my opinion, he is the outstanding sportswriter of these times.

It has taken more than 50 interviews to complete On the Brink, though not all feature in the final edit. To Andy Hall, Jon Colman, William Watt, Darren Bentley, Matt McCann, Jack Gaughan, William Hughes, Emma Norris, Simon Heggie and, indeed the great Jamie Carragher; your assistance is appreciated.

ACKNOWLEDGEMENTS

I would like to thank my closest friends for their dependable backing but mostly for being a reliable source of amusement. I am talking about you, Mark (and his daughter, Matilda), Matt, Ian, Andy, Andrew, James, Billy, Paul and Paul.

I would also like to recognise the support of my family throughout six chaotic months of research, writing and deadlines. That means my dad, Peter, who is far handier than me at DIY, and most of all my wife, Rosalind – who inspires me every day with her intelligence, compassion and kindness.

BIBLIOGRAPHY

BOOKS

Banks, Tommy, **Ah', Tellin' Thee** (*Paragon*, 2012)
Bose, Mihir, **Manchester DisUnited** (*Aurum, 2007*)
Conn, David, **Richer Than God** (*Cuercus, 2013*)
Ferguson, Alex, **My Autobiography** (*Hodder, 2014*)
Glass, Jimmy, **One Hit Wonder** (*History Press, 2004*)
Hughes, Emlyn, **Crazy Horse** (*Futura, 1981*)
Keoghan, Jim, **Highs, Lows and Bakayokos** (*Pitch, 2016*)
Maconie, Stuart, **Pies and Prejudice** (*Ebury, 2008*)
Mitten, Andy, **Glory Glory!** (*Vision, 2009*)
Pearson, Harry, **The Far Corner** (*Abacus, 1995*)
Prestage, Michael, **Bolton Wanderers, Heroes of Winter** (*Breedon, 2000*)
Tueart, Dennis, **My Football Journey** (*Vision, 2009*)
Walker, Michael, **Up There** (*deCoubertin, 2014*)

continued overleaf

NEWSPAPERS AND MAGAZINES

Independent
The Guardian
The Observer
The Times
The Telegraph
Manchester Evening News
Lancashire Telegraph
Liverpool Echo
News & Star
North West Evening Mail
Westmorland Gazette
Blackpool Gazette
New Statesman
When Saturday Comes
FourFourTwo

DECOUBERTIN BOOKS

Touching Distance
Martin Hardy

The Manager
Ron Atkinson

Up There
Michael Walker

The Unbelievables
David Bevan

Love Affairs & Marriage
Howard Kendall

When Friday Comes
James Montague

61 Minutes in Munich
Howard Gayle

The Acid Test
Clyde Best

The Binman Chronicles
Neville Southall

www.decoubertin.co.uk

deCoubertin
BOOKS

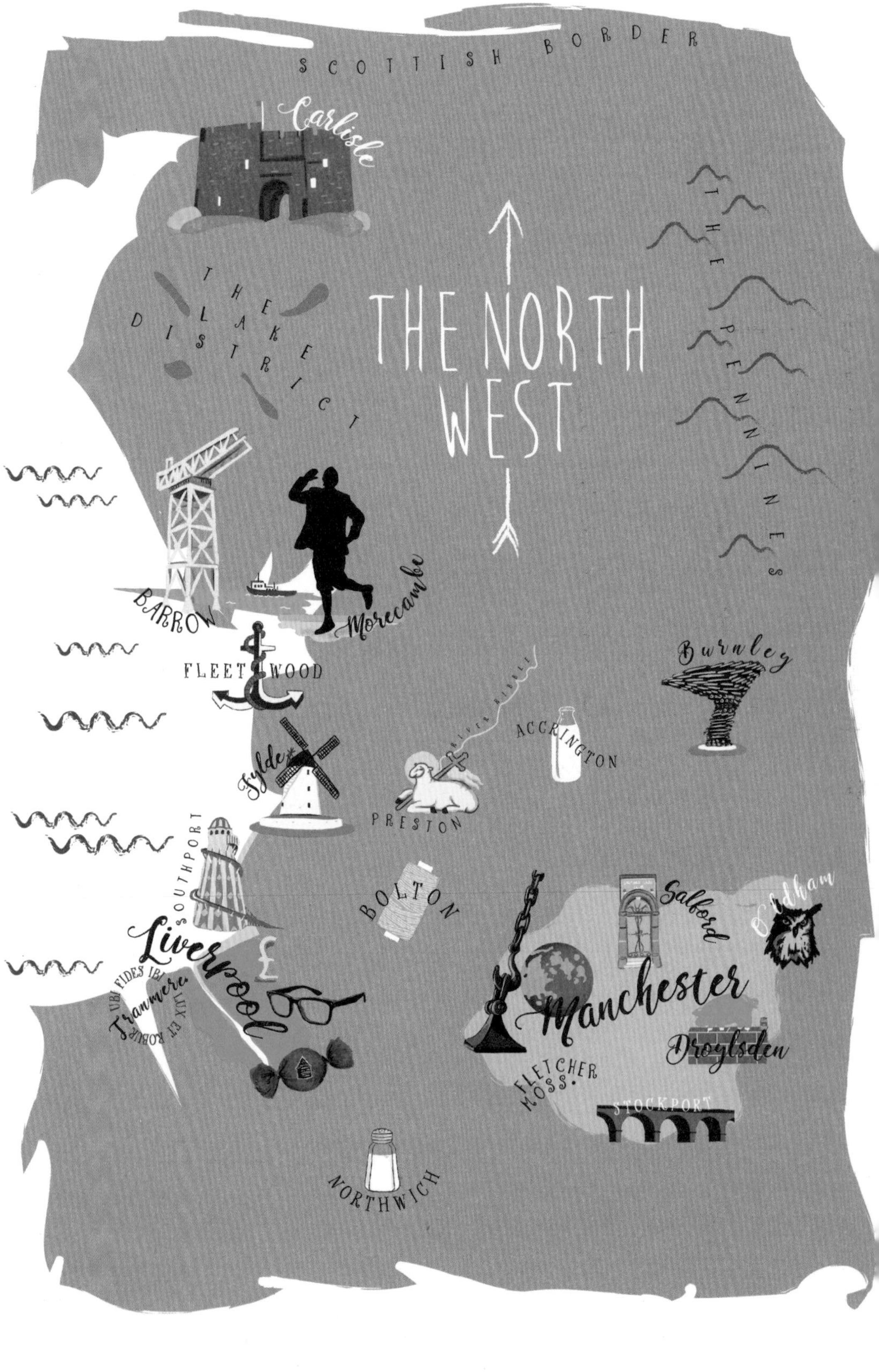
SCOTTISH BORDER
Carlisle
THE LAKE DISTRICT
THE NORTH WEST
THE PENNINES
BARROW
Morecambe
FLEETWOOD
Burnley
RIVER RIBBLE
ACCRINGTON
Fylde
PRESTON
SOUTHPORT
BOLTON
Salford
Oldham
Liverpool
UBI FIDES IBI LUX ET ROBUR
Tranmere
Manchester
Droylsden
FLETCHER MOSS.
STOCKPORT
NORTHWICH